Frederic William Farrar

The Bible

Its meaning and supremacy

Frederic William Farrar

The Bible
Its meaning and supremacy

ISBN/EAN: 9783337172220

Printed in Europe, USA, Canada, Australia, Japan

Cover: Foto ©Lupo / pixelio.de

More available books at **www.hansebooks.com**

THE BIBLE

ITS MEANING AND SUPREMACY

BY

F. W. FARRAR, D.D., F.R.S.

DEAN OF CANTERBURY

Γίνεσθε τραπεζῖται δόκιμοι—*Traditional saying of Christ*

'And why, even of yourselves, judge ye not what is right?'
LUKE xii. 57

'Prove all things; hold fast that which is good'—1 THESS. v. 21

'He that is spiritual judgeth (or 'examineth'—ἀνακρίνει) all things; and he himself is judged of no man'—1 COR. ii. 15

'We serve in newness of the spirit, and not in oldness of the letter'
ROM. vii. 6

NEW YORK
LONGMANS, GREEN, AND CO.
LONDON AND BOMBAY
1897

GENERAL MOTTOES

'Will ye speak unrighteously for God, and talk deceitfully for Him?'—Job xiii. 7.

'Not walking in craftiness, nor handling the word of God deceitfully; but by the manifestation of the truth commending ourselves to every man's conscience in the sight of God.'—2 Cor. iv. 2.

'Melius est ut scandalum oriatur quam ut veritas supprimatur.'
S. Greg. Homil. 7 in Ezek.

'O superbi Cristian, miseri, lassi,
  Che, della vista della mente infermi,
  Fidanza avete ne' ritrosi passi,
Non v' accorgete voi, che noi siam vermi
  Nati a formar l' angelica farfalla,
  Che vola alla giustizia senza schermi?
Di che l' animo vostro in alto galla?
  Voi siete quasi entomata in difetto,
  Si come verme, in cui formazion falla.'
Dante, Purgat. x. 121–129.

'Idola fori omnium molestissima sunt; quæ ex fœdere verborum et nominum se insinuarunt in intellectum.

'Idola theatri innata non sunt sed ex fabulis theoriarum et perversis legibus demonstrationum plane indita et recepta.'
Bacon, Nov. Org. i. lix. lx.

'Being persuaded of nothing more than this, that, whether it be in matter of speculation or of practising, no untruth can possibly avail the patron and defender long, and that things most truly are likewise most behovefully spoken.'—Hooker.

v

'His words I did use to gather for my food and for antidotes against my faintings.'—BUNYAN.

'The older error is, it is the worse,
Continuation may provoke a curse:
If the Dark Age obscured our fathers' sight,
Must their sons shut their eyes against the Light?'

BISHOP KEN, Edmund.

Μεγάλη ἡ ἀλήθεια καὶ ὑπερισχύει.—1 ESDRAS iv. 41.

'Omni studio legendæ nobis Scripturæ sunt . . . ut probati trapezitæ sciamus quis nummus probus sit, quis adulter.'

JER. Comm. in Ephes. l. iii. 5 (Vall. vii. 637).

'If Truth do anywhere manifest itself, seek not to smother it with glosing delusions, acknowledge the greatness thereof, and think it your best victory when the same doth prevail over you.'

HOOKER, Eccl. Pol. Pref. ix. 2.

'If it is certain that the writings of the Old Testament offer to us many grave difficulties which we are, at present, unable to overcome; it is no less certain that they offer a revelation of a purpose and a presence of God which bears in itself the stamp of truth. The difficulties lie in points of criticism; the revelation is given in the facts of a people's life.'

BISHOP WESTCOTT, The Revelation of the Father, p. 159.

CONTENTS

INTRODUCTION

PAGE

Thoughts of men in the present day necessitate a plain and truthful as well as reverent expression of opinion. Duty of ex-
ercising the reason. Views of Butler; Locke; Whichcote;
the 'Westminster Confession.' Attacks which are beside
the mark. Importance of removing stumbling-blocks from
the path of religion. The greater part of this book consists
of proofs of the grandeur and supremacy of the Bible. The
benefits which resulted from the plain speaking of 'Eternal
Hope.' Assailants of the Bible often misstate the doctrine
of Christians on the subject of Inspiration. Difficulties of
'working men.' *Opinions* are not *doctrines*. Current and
all but universal religious opinions may form no part of the
Christian Creed. Illustrations: (i) from views of the Atonement; (ii) from views of 'the Double Procession' of the
Holy Spirit; (iii) from the supposed duty of intolerance and
persecution. Simplicity of the essential elements of the
Christian Faith. The urgent necessity for insisting on 'the
simplicity which is in Christ Jesus.' Progress in the apprehension of truth. The things which cannot be shaken and
remain. My object is to strengthen the cause of Christianity
by separating it from untenable propositions. Truth may
be assailed, but will ultimately triumph. 1. The views here
stated are those of the Church of England. 2. I am estab-
lishing, not attacking, the true authority of Holy Scripture.
Peril of mistaken estimates, as stated by Hooker and Chillingworth. True and false claims 1

CHAPTER I

WHAT THE BIBLE IS, AND IS NOT

CHAPTER II

THE BIBLE REPRESENTS THE REMAINS OF A WIDER LITERATURE

CHAPTER VIII

'PLENARY INSPIRATION'

CHAPTER XV

FURTHER MISINTERPRETATION OF THE BIBLE

CHAPTER XVI

THE WRESTING OF TEXTS

CHAPTER XVII

SCRIPTURE DIFFICULTIES

CONTENTS

CHAPTER XVIII

SUPREMACY OF THE BIBLE

CHAPTER XIX

THE BIBLE AND INDIVIDUAL SOULS.

CHAPTER XX

THE BIBLE THE CHIEF SOURCE OF HUMAN CONSOLATION

CHAPTER XXI

SPECIAL CONSOLATIONS OF SCRIPTURE

THE BIBLE

ITS MEANING · AND SUPREMACY

INTRODUCTION

'Ea quæ aperta continet, quasi amicus familiaris, sine fuco ad cor loquitur indoctorum atque doctorum.'—AUG. *Ep.* iii. *ad Volus.*

'Some too have not integrity and regard enough to truth, to attend to evidence which keeps the mind in doubt, perhaps perplexity, and which is much of a different sort from what they expected.'—Bishop BUTLER, *Analogy*, II. vii.

'We are bound never to countenance any erroneous opinion, however seemingly beneficial in its results.'—Archbishop WHATELY on *Bacon's Essays*, p. 11.

A CLERGYMAN who is constantly required to address numbers of his countrymen is bound, as far as he can, to ascertain their actual thoughts, and to offer them something less stereotyped and more real than the current conventionalities. He must not live in a fool's paradise. If he wishes to help serious men to meet their religious difficulties, he cannot succeed either by the ostrich policy of ignoring those difficulties, or by sliding over them with 'airy and fastidious levity,' or by trying to overwhelm them with vituperative phrases. He can adopt no policy more fatal than the assumption of a disdainful infallibility which denounces as 'wicked,' 'blasphemous,' or 'dangerous' every conviction which diverges from his own form of orthodoxy; nor must he assume that everything which he chooses, however ignorantly, to assert with sufficient dogmatism ought to be accepted with humble acquiescence. This was not the policy of the early Christian apologists. They acted like men, and spoke to men. They looked their opponents full in the face. They relied upon solid arguments, not on authoritative anathemas. Instead of meeting the taunts of pagan critics, and the arguments of pagan philosophers, by a conspiracy of silence or threats of eternal damnation, they confronted and grappled with them. Christianity was represented to the heathen in many false lights by Greek scoffers, by Eastern heretics, by Roman satirists. It was the task of such men as Justin Martyr, Clement of Alexandria, and Origen to prove to the world that, in its true aspect, their holy faith was not open to the objections accumulated against it. They relied upon calm reasoning for the diffusion of truth; not upon rude denunciations, nor upon the torture and persecution to which in later ages Rome so universally resorted. They repudiated all violence as hateful to God. The earnest reasoner can never injure the cause of religion; the inquisitor and the ruthless dogmatist have been its ruin and its curse.

In recent years much has been written under the assumption that Christianity no longer deserves the dignity of a refutation; or that, at any rate, the bases on which it rests have been seriously undermined. The writings of freethinkers are widely disseminated among the working classes. The Church of Christ has lost its hold on multitudes of men in our great cities. Those of the clergy who are working in the crowded centres of English life can hardly be unaware of the extent to which scepticism exists among our artisans. Many of them have been persuaded to believe that the Church is a hostile and organised hypocrisy. There are some, in all classes, who take refuge from doubt in the abnegation of inquiry and the blind acceptance of an unintelligent traditionalism. To quote the phrase of Cardinal Newman, they treat their reason as though it were a dangerous wild beast to be beaten back with a bar of iron. There are others to whom such a resource would be impossible and dishonest. No religious system will be permanent which relies mainly on the emotional and the ceremonial and is not based on the convictions of the intellect. The human reason is no seducing enemy, but a heaven-sent guide. 'The spirit of man is the lamp of the Lord.'[1] Reason, as Bishop Butler so truly said, is the only faculty wherewith we can judge of anything, even of revelation itself.[2] Locke wisely warns us that to attempt any subordination or sacrifice of reason to revelation is to put out the light of both: for revelation *can* only come to us through the reason, and one voice from heaven cannot utter oracles which are in direct contradiction to another. A wise English divine, Benjamin Whichcote, in his 'Aphorisms,' says: 'The sense of the Church is not a rule but a thing ruled. The Church is bound unto reason and Scripture and governed by them as much as any individual person.'[3] 'God alone is the Lord of the conscience,' says the 'Westminster Confession (ch. xx.), 'and hath left it free from the doctrines and commandments of men which are in anything contrary to this word, or beside it in matters of faith and worship; so that to believe such doctrines, or to obey such commandments out of conscience is to betray the true liberty of conscience; and the requiring of an implicit faith, and an

---

[1] Prov. xx. 27; comp. Rom. i. 19–21, 32; ii. 14, 15.
[2] *Analogy*, II. iii. § 3.　　　[3] Aphorism 921.

absolute blind obedience, is to destroy liberty of conscience and reason also.'

He therefore who helps to disencumber Christianity from dubious or false accretions is rendering to it a service which may be more urgently necessary than if he composed a book of evidences. I have frequently observed that the objections urged against Christianity are aimed at dogmas which are no part of the Christian faith, or are in no wise essential to its integrity. It is my humble hope that I shall be strengthening the cause of the Church, if I can succeed in showing that pure religion and undefiled before God even our Father is entirely separable from tenets by which many have supposed it to be hopelessly overweighted. The most effectual defender is often the man who succeeds in putting truths in their right perspective, and saves them from being confounded with illusory semblances and untenable traditions. But I would draw attention to the fact that this book is mainly positive, not negative. The larger part of it is occupied with proofs drawn from literature, history, and experience of what the Bible *is*—its eternal validity, its unquestionable supremacy, its inestimable preciousness. These indications of its grandeur and authority are not casuistical, nor do they consist of bald assertions. They furnish a *demonstration* of the unparalleled blessings which the possession of the Bible has in past ages conferred upon the human race. They show, from testimony which none can dispute, that its free study has uplifted nation after nation into grandeur; that it has saved some of the sweetest and loftiest of human souls from despair and death; that its inspiration has kindled the purest fires of genius, and nerved the sons of men to acts of the most heroic valour and the most blessed self-sacrifice. If in any part of the book I seem to take away a false exaltation of the prerogative of the Bible, it is only that I may more firmly re-establish its genuine supereminence. Nor must it be supposed that the statement of our beliefs can only be of use to the unlearned. Conversations with men of science and writers of the highest fame have long proved to me how many of the objections entertained against the Catholic faith are based on travesties of its real tenets. There are many scientific and literary men to whom current misconceptions create a far more insuperable obstacle to the acceptance of the faith than the true doctrines with which those misconceptions are confused. What fortifies such men in an attitude of antagonism is often an identification of Christianity with opinions wherewith it has no real connection. One of those opinions is that which maintains the supposed inerrancy and supernatural infallibility of every book, sentence, and word of the Holy Bible. Such a belief, if it were really *de fide*, would constitute a difficulty as colossal as it is needless to tens of thousands of earnest men. Let it at least be known what we do and what we do not hold; what we are and what we are not prepared to maintain and to defend. Ἐν δὲ φάει καὶ ὅλεσσον ('Slay us, so it be but in the light'), prayed the old Homeric hero. It is only imposture which *shrinks* from light.

I have already been permitted to attempt a similar service to the cause of faith, and, by God's blessing, not without a large success, attested by a widespread modification of opinions once all but universal. What a poet has called 'obscene threats of a bodily hell,' when stated, as they used to be in common manuals and by men like Jonathan Edwards, in their crudest and coarsest form, were sufficient to crush many tender souls under a burden of intolerable agony, and to drive many into fierce revolt against a sys-

tem which represented our Father in Heaven as a relent-
less Avenger.

'Such a belief,' said Archer Butler, 'if realised, would
scorch and wither up the powers of man.' 'Compared
with this doctrine,' said John Stuart Mill, 'every other
objection to Christianity sinks into insignificance.' In
spite of the anathemas which burst upon me after the pub-
lication of my sermons on 'Eternal Hope,' I have been
amply rewarded by the gratitude which for years has been
expressed by men of all ranks, of all ages, and of every
country where the English language is spoken; by the
testimony of men of science from whose faith a main
stumbling-block has been removed; by the assurances
both of men who had previously been alienated but have
now been led back to holy lives, and of many of the be-
reaved whose innocent faithfulness had been insufficient
to remove the agonising doubts forced upon them by the
traditions of men. The whole literature of disproof and
denunciation poured forth against me has sunk into
oblivion; and Dr. Pusey, in a book which professed to be
an answer to my own, conceded absolutely the only three
points of controversy upon which I had insisted as vital.
He frankly admitted that it is *not* 'of faith' to hold either
that hell is a place of material torments; or that endless
agony will be the doom of the vast majority of mankind;
or that every form of future retribution is necessarily endless. Another eminent divine, the greatest, in my opinion,
of all the theologians of this generation, thinking that I
should quail under the fury of 'religious' animosity, spon-
taneously came to tell me that he had himself been teaching
for more than twenty years exactly the same conclusions.
Both these high authorities admitted that 'views' which
were then almost universally taught, or at any rate had

rarely, if ever, been publicly repudiated, since my friend and teacher Professor Maurice had been deprived of his fellowship at King's College for impugning them—were *not* Catholic doctrines at all, but human opinions largely founded, in times of ignorance, on mistaken inferences from the misinterpretation of Eastern metaphors. Widely current as such dogmas had become, there is scarcely any age of Christianity in which they have not been more or less distinctly repudiated by some saints, fathers, and teachers of the Church. Calvinists may, if they will, still assert that God, by a decree which their leader himself characterised as 'horrible,' condemns the vast mass of mankind to 'writhe for ever in sulphurous flames;' and may doom even unbaptised infants 'a span long' to crawl on the floor of hell. Such opinions concern themselves only. They may assert them at their pleasure and at their peril, but every Christian is at perfect liberty to regard them as 'idols of the theatre,' created by the pride of system, the ignorance of exegesis, the obstinacy of opinion, and the terrors of guilt. No Christian is called upon to defend them when he hears them branded as cruel or unjust by the natural horror and indignation of mankind.

But it seems to me that another service is now no less imperatively required.

No one can take up a book or newspaper which contains the arguments of sceptics, without seeing that nine-tenths of their case is made up of attacks upon the Bible. They seem to think that if they hold up to ridicule this or that narrative, almost invariably of the Old Testament, they have demonstrated the futility of the Christian religion. I would fain take this quiver out of their hands, and show how its broken arrows, so far from piercing the shield of Christianity, do but tinkle harmlessly upon its rim. As regards the true faith such assaults are irrelevant. They are aimed at theories which are not required in the Church of England, and have never been held by some of the greatest Christian teachers. What such assailants demolish so entirely to their own satisfaction is not Christianity, but a mummy elaborately painted in its semblance, or a scarecrow which they, or others, have set up in its guise.

I should rejoice with all my heart if the views of Scripture set forth in the following pages proved to intelligent readers that such attacks need in no way trouble the faith of a Christian. I have been sometimes asked to speak about the Bible to mass-meetings of working men in London, Birmingham, and other cities, and after the address the subject has been thrown open to free discussion. I have always said that I would give a frank answer to every objection which might be raised, if I had an answer to give; and that if I were unable to meet the objection I should say so like an honest man. The attacks made were a singular revelation of modes of thought with which the clergy rarely come in contact. To many of my hearers there seemed to be no medium between the doctrine of 'verbal dictation' on the one hand, and the opinion that the Bible contains a mass of immorality and imposture on the other. Only one or two of the speakers have ever adopted an absolutely hostile tone, but there was scarcely one argument which did not cease to be valid when it was shown that no doctrine about Biblical inerrancy has ever formed any necessary part of the faith of Christendom.

When men who have drifted from Christianity do not accord their full confidence to a speaker they are apt to fancy that he is playing fast and loose with them; that he is denying or accepting just what may happen to suit the exigencies of the immediate controversy. They say, 'If *you* do not hold these views, every other clergyman does.' In this they are mistaken; but their mistake is excusable because there has often been so little courage among the clergy to speak out boldly what multitudes of them really think. When my sermons on 'Eternal Hope' were preached, a leading London clergyman said to me, 'You have only spoken out what many of us have long really held.' I have learnt by experience that it costs something to speak out, but the man who maintains an interested or pusillanimous reticence is not a faithful servant. If he is influenced, either by the fear of injuring his own interests, or by shrinking from the odious attacks of party hatred— if he stoops to use language in one sense which he knows will be understood in another—he is untrue to the example of Christ and His Apostles. He is trying to serve God and mammon. He is treating the verities of religion as though they were only meant to be vested in effeminate euphuisms. Some may be influenced by another motive. They are unwilling, they say, 'to disturb the faith' of any. As if to remove error were to disturb faith! As if a faith built on error ought to be left for ever undisturbed! As if the twilight of ignorance were better than the revealing day! St. Gregory the Great truly said that, 'If a scandal be caused by the utterance of truth, better the creation of the scandal than the suppression of the truth.' God is a God of truth. He who thinks to serve God by the offering of falsehoods, or of half-truths, is as if he offered swine's flesh upon the altar. The City of God will have no stability if instead of being founded on jasper and adamant it is simply piled upon loosely shifting sands. Christians must make their choice between freely admitting that there is a human, and therefore a fallible, element in some of the sixty-six books which we call the Bible; or the adoption of 'reconciliations' which may be 'accepted with ignominious rapture,' but which are so transparently casuistical as to shock the faith of men who are unprejudiced. 'I know no more encouraging proof,' said Maurice, 'that the God of truth is still among us, much as we are offending Him with our lives, than that the faith of scientific men in the Bible has not wholly perished, when they see how small ours is, and by what tricks we are sustaining it.'[1] 'Those who hold the traditional view have not been free from fault,' says Canon Girdlestone. 'We have been afraid of allowing textual corruption, late editorial work, the use of ordinary materials, and human ways of putting things. We have confused inspiration with omniscience, and have forgotten that the treasure of sacred truths is committed to earthen vessels. We have minimised inconsistencies and refused to face difficulties. We have imported modern science into ancient books, and have sought to shut up those questions about age and authorship which God in His providence has left open.'[2] But those who are misled into the supposition that they must believe every word of the Bible to be supernaturally sacred and divinely infallible, may be helped by two considerations which will serve to show that even if many still hold such a view it is not binding upon any Christian.

1. For the Catholic faith means the faith of the Catholic, the Universal Church, as expressed in the creeds of the Church.

Opinions may be held by all the members of any one branch of the Christian Church; but if they are rejected by other acknowledged branches of the Church they are not an *essential* part of Christian faith.

---

[1] Maurice, *The Bible and Science*, p. 37.
[2] Girdlestone, *Foundation of the Bible*, p. 196.

For instance, the Roman Church believes in the efficacy of prayers to the Virgin and the Saints; the Christians of the first three centuries held no such belief; the creeds do not require it; the Reformed Churches regard it as entirely baseless. Therefore it is no part of the Catholic faith. To attack or to disprove it is not to attack a truth of Christianity, but only to disprove *an opinion held among some Christians*.

2. Again, an opinion may be current among Christians for hundreds of years; it may be held by the vast majority of teachers and believers in any particular age; it may have been held by their predecessors for many ages; yet if it has been repudiated by recognised branches of the Church, and has never found a place in the Catholic formularies, it remains an opinion; it is not an essential part of the Christian faith.

i. For instance: all Christians alike believe in the Atonement, and the forgiveness of sins. Particular *theories* of the Atonement, and of the *manner* in which sins are forgiven, have been prevalent in every age, and have sometimes united the suffrages of most Christians. Yet if they have never been formally sanctioned they are opinions only, not matters of faith. Thus, in early days, some leading Fathers and teachers seized upon the metaphor of *ransom*, used in Scripture to express the results of forgiveness to guilty man. Needlessly pressing the metaphor into spheres to which it was not intended to apply, and which transcend the ken of man's reason, they asked *to whom* was the ransom paid? They decided, most erroneously and unwarrantably, that it was paid to the devil.[1] That opinion prevailed in the Church all but universally for a thousand years, from the days of St. Irenæus to the

[1] Irenæus based his error on Heb. ii. 14.

days of St. Anselm. St. Anselm, in his book 'Cur Deus
Homo?' decisively rejected it,[1] and though it had been
held so long and so all but universally, yet, being an
opinion only and not a doctrine of the faith, it rapidly
crumbled into dust; it now finds not one defender; and the
faith of Christians was left exactly where it was.

ii. I may add an instance still more crucial. The sole
important difference between the Western (or Latin) and
the Eastern (or Greek) Church as regards the creeds is in
the single word '*Filioque*'—'proceeding from the Father
and the Son.' This last expression, '*Filioque*,' was added
to the Nicene Creed at the Provincial Council of Toledo,
in Spain, A.D. 589, and afterwards at a Council of Charlemagne's Bishops at Frankfort in 794. Charlemagne wished
the Pope Leo III. to insert the word '*Filioque*,' and the Pope
refused. The word, however—apparently without any
formal authorisation—crept into the Nicene Creed, in spite
of the vehement protests of the Eastern Church. That
Church insisted that when the Council of Constantinople
(A.D. 381) had added to the Nicene Creed 'proceeding from
the Father,' and that addition had been accepted by the
Council of Ephesus (A.D. 431), a decree was passed, under
an anathema, that no one should ever make any further
addition to the Creed. It has been supposed by some that
the whole dispute depends on the difference of meaning
between the *Greek* word for 'proceeding' (ἐκπορευόμενον)
and the *Latin* word (*procedens*). The Greek Church does
not deny that in the *sense of the Latin word* the Spirit pro-
ceeds from the Son, but it does not admit the addition to

---

[1] St. Anselm rightly argued that the devil could have no rights
over man, and 'quamvis homo juste a diabolo torqueretur, ipse tamen
illum injuste torquebat.' *Cur Deus Homo?* i. 7; Oxenham, *On the
Atonement*, p. 114.

the Creed. 'Yet,' says Bishop Pearson, 'they acknowledged under another Scriptural expression the same thing which the Latins understand by procession, though they stuck more closely to the phrase and language of the Scripture; and therefore when they said "He proceedeth from the Father" they also added "He received of the Son."[1] Afterwards, however, divers of the Greeks expressly denied the procession from the Son.'[2]

iii. Once more. The notion that intolerance is a duty, and that it is not only right but imperative to persecute, torture, and burn those whom the dominant Church of the day may regard as heretics, prevailed for centuries. It was acted upon in age after age to the suppression of God's truth and the unspeakable danger of the faith in the name of which such horrors and crimes have been perpetrated. This belief is still avowed by the Romish Church; yet it involves nothing less than a crime against the Spirit and the Gospel of Christ. It was abhorrent to primitive Christianity, and in spite of its thousand years of dominance it is rightly repudiated by all the Reformed Churches of the present day.

Opinions therefore may be held by Christians, even by the majority of Christians, and by all or nearly all of their accredited teachers in any particular age, and for successive ages, and yet may be disputable opinions; may even be opinions which, when rightly apprehended in the broadening and revealing light, are seen to be erroneous and even hateful. But such opinions form no part of Christianity. The defence of Christianity is unconcerned with

1 τοῦ Υἱοῦ λαμβάνον. Epiphan. *Hær.* lxix.
2 Pearson, *On the Creed*, Art. viii.; Waterland, *Hist. of Athan. Creed*, Works, iv. 133; Bishop Harold Browne, *Thirty-nine Articles*, 114–117.

them. We may repudiate them, while yet we hold fast to the great primitive creeds of Christendom, and believe with all our hearts that Jesus is the Christ the Son of God, the Saviour of the World, and that the Gospel is a direct revelation from the God of all consolation to the suffering and sinful family of man.

It should then be clear that Christianity, as set forth in her universal creeds, may be one thing; and Christianity, as identified with the opinion of even the majority of Christians about a multitude of subjects at any given time, may be quite another.

God's education of us never ceases. The fundamental truths of Christianity are unaltered and unalterable; but the points of view from which they are regarded, and the thousands of minor propositions which have often been attached to them, are altering, and have altered from age to age. They need to be constantly re-examined and re-vised. For we believe that Christ is *with* us, not absent from us. He is living, not dead. The inspiration of His Spirit is a continuous influence, an ever-brightening sun-beam, not an exhausted spasm of energy, or a flash of vanished light. It is a beam in the darkness which must broaden and brighten more and more into the bound-less day.

One of the most urgent duties of good men in the present day is the simplification of religion into its primitive and essential elements; its purification from centuries of alien influx; its disseverance from elements which owed their origin, not to the teaching of its Divine Founder, but to Pagan or Jewish survivals, to Eastern mysticism, and to Manichean error. It has suffered unspeakably from the ambitions, inventions, and usurpations of men; and most of all from the confusions, corruptions, and ignorance which during the Dark Ages, and under the sway of the mediæval Papacy, invaded the God-given liberty of Christians; quenched, or tried to quench, the light which came from heaven; subjected free human souls to the cruel, degraded, and effeminating bondage of ignorant teachers; and utterly marred the truth and beautiful simplicity of the primeval Gospel.

An unprogressive Christianity will be of necessity a stagnant and corrupt Christianity. 'He hath promised, saying, Yet once more will I make to tremble not the earth only, but also the heaven. And this word, *Yet once more*, signifieth the removing of those things that are shaken, as of things that have been made, that those things which are not shaken may remain.' Opinions about Christianity, and systems and churches which have built upon such opinions their superstructures of wood, hay, and stubble, may again and yet again be shaken to the dust; but true Christianity cannot be shaken, for it is an eternal thing.

Let Christians then beware of the inveterate obstinacy, the passionate prejudices, and, above all, the furious and blood-stained idolatry of false traditions, which render impossible the acceptance of new truths. Those new truths, which cause the general opinions of Christians on many subjects to differ widely from age to age, are nothing less than a continuous revelation. Truth is not a stagnant pool, but an ever-streaming fountain; the river is eternal, but its waves are perpetually changing, and being constantly purified and renewed. 'Even within the Church,' says one of our most eminent writers, 'the fulness of truth was only slowly recognised; and the earliest heresy was simply the perverse and obstinate retention of that which had once been the common belief, after that a wider view had been sanctioned by a Divine authority.'

In the following pages I wish to show that the true attitude of Christians towards the Bible is not that which, by many antagonists of the Christian faith, it is assumed to be. It is no part of the Christian faith to maintain that every word of the Bible was dictated supernaturally, or is equally valuable, or free from all error, or on the loftiest levels of morality as finally revealed. There are myriads of faithful Christians who would at once declare their inability to accept any such doctrine. To them Christianity is entirely unburdened by the numberless difficulties of all kinds—psychological, chronological, historical, scientific, religious, and moral—which would be necessarily involved in the defence of such an hypothesis. I shall make the defence of Christianity infinitely more simple and more secure if I show that such views form no part of the faith. I do not deny that such a doctrine of inspiration has often been popularly expressed in the loose, inaccurate rhetoric of Fathers and teachers; and often by men who show, in more serious passages, that it does *not* represent their true and accurate conviction. But no such view has ever formed any part of the Catholic creeds of Christendom.

In order, then, to support the faith of all who are now shaken by assaults on the Bible, I wish to illustrate what the Bible is, what the Bible is not. That my statements will be attacked can make no difference in my duty; that many readers, and especially those who have been left by their teachers in an ignorance which takes itself for knowledge, will at first disagree with much that I say, is certain. I hold it to be no less certain that the opinions here maintained will become those of the whole Christian world; and I hold this because they are in accordance with a general drift of evidence which is daily acquiring more and more the volume and majesty of an ocean tide.

> For while the tired waves, vainly breaking,
>   Seem here no painful inch to gain,
> Far back, through creeks and inlets making,
>   Comes silent, flooding in, the main:
> And not by eastern windows only,
>   When daylight comes, comes in the light;
> In front the sun climbs slow, how slowly,—
>   But westward, look, the land is bright![1]

I need only add two remarks.

First, I do not deviate in the smallest particular from the definite teaching of the Church of England,[2] or of the Catholic Church in general, on the subject here handled. I repudiate no single proposition respecting Scripture on which real Christian doctrine ever insisted.

[1] A. H. Clough.

[2] Our Christian liberty on this question was legally vindicated by Dr. Lushington and Lord Westbury in the 'Essays and Reviews Case,' 1862–63. 'In the first hearing of the case, before the Court of Arches, Dr. Lushington said: "Provided that the Articles and Formularies are not contravened, the law lays down no limits of construction, no rule of interpretation, of the Scriptures."'

At the final trial, on appeal before the Privy Council, Lord Westbury pronounced the freedom of the English people and clergy yet more emphatically. He said: 'We are confined . . . to the question whether in them [the Articles] the Church has affirmed that any part of the Book of Scripture was written under the inspiration of the Holy Spirit, and is the Word of God.

'Certainly this doctrine is not involved in the statements of the 6th Article, that Holy Scripture contains all things necessary to salvation. But inasmuch as it does so from the revelations of the Holy Spirit, the Bible may be denominated "holy" and be said to be "the Word of God," "God's Word written," or "Holy Writ;" terms which cannot be affirmed to be distinctly predicated of every statement and representation contained in every part of the Old and New Testaments.

'The framers of the Articles have not used the word "inspiration" as applied to the Holy Scriptures, nor have they laid down anything

2

I shall not state one single view which is untenable by
Christian men in any great division either of the Eastern
or the Western Church. For every assertion which I make
I can produce the authority of divines of unimpeachable
soundness, whose right to be regarded as orthodox has
never been challenged, and some of whom are among the
acknowledged Fathers and canonised Saints of the Church
of God.

Secondly, I may be liable to the careless and ignorant
taunt that I have been 'attacking the Bible.' The guilt
of such a falsehood must rest on those who make it. St.
Paul, in answer to the charge that he had been nullifying
the Law of Moses, replied, 'Do we then make void the Law
through faith? Nay, we establish the Law.' The spirit
of that reply is applicable to all that I shall here say of the

as to the nature, extent, or limits of that operation of the Holy
Spirit.'

In a letter to the *Times* quoting these judgments, Mr. Fitzroy adds:
'It may be worth stating, in illustration of this, that at the Westminster Assembly of 1643 it actually was proposed to make such use
of the word "inspiration" and to lay down something "as to the
nature, extent, or limits of the operation of the Holy Spirit." It was
there suggested to add the enumeration of the books of the New
Testament to those of the Old, and to conclude with these words:
"All which books, as they are commonly received, we do receive,
and acknowledge them to be by the inspiration of God, and in that
regard to be of most certain credit and highest authority." The
rejection of this amendment shows that even at that date English Churchmen did not feel justified in closing their own or their
children's ears to the voice of God in nature and in human reason.'

I may also refer to Sir J. F. Stephen's speech in the Court of
Arches, in which there is a catena of evidence on this subject; to
Paley's *Evidences,* vol. iii. ch. iii.; Alford, *Greek New Testament,* i.
19; Maurice, *The Bible and Science,* p. 172; and to multitudes of high
authorities which will be quoted in the following pages.

Bible.[1]   I have attacked nothing which is tenable, least of all the Bible, which year by year grows to me more inestimably precious, and which on the contrary I best defend by saving it from the wounds wherewith it has been wounded in the house of its friends.   The Bible furnished the main training of my youth; it is the chief blessing and most indefeasible consolation of my advancing age.   I have devoted to its elucidation the labour of the best years of my life.   At my ordination I vowed that I would be 'diligent in reading of the Holy Scripture, and of such studies as help to the knowledge of the same;' and that vow to the best of my ability I have endeavoured to fulfil.   But there is a style of defence which is more perilous and less faithful than the worst attack.   It was the object of Rabbis and Pharisees to maintain, to expand, to deify the Mosaic Law; 'to construct,' as they phrased it, 'a hedge about the Law.'[2]   They treated our Lord as One who 'attacked' their law.[3]   How did He Himself view what they regarded

---

[1] 'Critical investigations concern really not the fact of revelation, but its mode, or form, or course; upon faith and practice they have no bearing whatever.'—Prof. Driver, *Cont. Rev.* Feb. 1896.

[2] *Pirke Aboth*, I. i., 'Make a fence for the Law;' iii. 20, Aqiba said: 'Tradition is a fence to the Torah;' 'Make a *mishmereth* to my *mishmereth*,' Lev. xviii. 30; see Taylor, *Sayings of the Jewish Fathers*, pp. 25, 68.

[3] The Rabbis said that the Law had existed 974 generations before the world was created, *Shabbath*, f. 88. 2; *Aboth d' Rabbi Nathan*, 31. 'On account of the Law the whole of the world was created,' *Tse-enah Ure-enah* (Hershon, *Talm. Miscellany*, p. 316).   For specimens of the exaltation of the Torah by the Jews see Weber, *Syst. d. altsynag. Paläst. Theol.* 1–60; Wildeboer, *The Origin of the Old Testament Canon* (E.T.), pp. 94–98.   They called the Law 'the jewel of jewels;' 'Whoever asserts that Moses wrote so much as one verse out of his own knowledge is a contemner of the Word of God,' *Sanhedrin*, f. 99. *a*.

as His 'attack' of it?   He said, 'Think not that I am come to destroy the Law or the Prophets.   I am not come to destroy but to fulfil.'   What did He think of their defence of it?   After exposing the futility and falsehood of their 'traditions of the elders,' He indignantly quoted the denunciation of Isaiah: 'In vain do they worship me, teaching for doctrines the commandments of men.'   Resorting —as priests and Pharisees have so constantly done—to the syllogism of violence, they crucified the Lord of Glory.

Similarly they cursed, persecuted, slandered, and tried to murder St. Paul, on the plea that he taught men to ignore the Divine sanctity of the Levitic ordinances.   But St. Paul's answer was that he was commissioned to cut away from the Law its alien accretions and its dead or perishing rudiments, that he might perpetuate its eternal holiness and justice.   'The Gospel itself,' said the holy and learned Neander, 'rests on an immovable rock, while human systems of theology are everywhere undergoing a purifying process.'

I place, then, in the forefront of this book the declaration of my most solemn reverence and love for the Holy Scriptures, and of my heartfelt acceptance of every message of God contained therein.   It is *because* I thus deeply reverence the Bible, and *because* I thus absolutely accept the Word of God which it contains, that I refuse to be guilty of the blasphemy of confusing the words of men with the Word of God, or the inferences of ignorant teachers with the messages of God.   I say with the fervid Chillingworth, 'Take away this presumptuous imposing of the senses of men on the Word of God; of the special senses of men on the general words of God, and laying them on men's conscience together, under the equal penalty of death and damnation.   This deifying our own interpretations and tyrannous enforcing them upon others; this restraining of the Word of God from that latitude and generality, and the understanding of men from that liberty wherein Christ and the Apostles left them, is and hath been the only fountain of all the schisms in the Church, and that which makes them immortal; the common incendiary of Christendom which tears in pieces not the coat but the members of Christ, *ridente Turca nec dolente Judaeo.* Take away this persecuting, burning, cursing, damning of men for not subscribing to the words of men as the words of God; require of Christians only to believe Christ, and to call no man master but Him only.'[1]

I desire to base the claims of Scripture on true grounds, and not on false prerogatives supported by a specious and repellent casuistry.

In thus doing I follow the initiative of the greatest of our English divines; notably of one of the wisest of them all—Richard Hooker. After pointing out that there are concerning the sufficiency of Scripture two opinions, each extremely opposite to the other, and each repugnant to the truth—that of Rome, which teaches Scripture to be insufficient without tradition; and that of the Puritans, which held that no act of life and no triviality of Church order was lawful without direct Scripture authority—he concludes the second book of his 'Ecclesiastical Polity' with these words:

'Whatsoever is spoken of God, or things appertaining to God, otherwise than truth is, though it seem an honour, it is an injury. And as incredible praises given unto men do often abate and impair the credit of their deserved commendation, so we must likewise take great heed, lest, in attributing to Scripture more than it can have, the in-

---

[1] *Religion of Protestants,* ch. iv.

credibility of that do cause even those things which it hath most abundantly to be less reverently esteemed.'[1]

The underlying error which has led to so much pernicious misinterpretation of Scripture has been the violation of the laws of human language by the extension of general phrases to applications which they were never intended to include. The necessity of balance and correlation was freely recognised by some even of the early Christian writers as a principle of ordinary common sense,[2] but no one has set it forth more powerfully than S. T. Coleridge in his 'Confessions of an Enquiring Spirit':

'Add to all these, the strange—in all other writings unexampled—practice of bringing together into logical dependency detached sentences from books composed at the distance of centuries, nay sometimes a millennium from each other, under different dispensations, and for different objects. Accommodations, incidental allusions to popular notions, traditions, apologues—fancies and anachronisms—these, detached from their context and contrary to the intention of the sacred writers, first raised into independent theses, and then brought together to produce or sanction some new *credendum*. . . . By this strange mosaic, Scripture texts have been worked up into passable likenesses of Purgatory, Popery, the Inquisition, and other monstrous abuses.'

---

[1] 'The attempt to attach a name of special sanctity to all the contents of the Bible ends in the degradation of that name itself.' —Mackennal.

[2] See passages (quoted by Prof. Sanday, *Inspiration*, pp. 42, 43), such as Tert. *De exhort. cast.* 3. Jerome (*Prol. in Philem.*) quotes a remarkable passage of Origen, and (referring to such verses as 2 Tim. iv. 13; Gal. v. 12; Phil. i. 22, &c.) fully admits the principle that 'inspiration' admits of many degrees, and cannot be regarded as *unum tenorem Spiritus Sancti*.

To me, then, the Scriptures, not in every line and word of them, but in their total and final revelation, are and ever will be 'Holy Scriptures,' 'Sacred Writings,' 'Sacred Books,' 'the Divine Word,' 'the Divine Scriptures,' 'the Scriptures of God,' as they were called by Theophilus of Antioch, Clement of Alexandria, Origen, and Gaius; they are still and ever will be *Scriptura Divina, Divinum instrumentum, Divina litteratura*, as they were called by Tertullian; *Divini fontes, Divina magisteria, praecepta Divina, Sancta traditio*, as Cyprian styled them.[1]   They are still and ever will be as a whole the *Sancta et adorabilia Scripturarum verba* which they were to Lucius of Thebeste (A.D. 256). But *because* they are and ever will be thus to me, and because they themselves have taught me the indefeasible majesty of Truth, I should shudder to maintain for them the false claims which they never make for themselves as a whole, but which have been foisted upon them by ignorance and superstition to the immense diminution of their sacred authority, and to the deep injury of the Church and of mankind.[2]

---

[1] See the original passages referred to by Prof. Sanday, *Inspiration*, p. 29.

[2] The present Archbishop of Canterbury, in a letter to Archbishop Tait, says: 'What can be a grosser superstition than the cry of literal inspiration? But because that has a regular footing it is to be treated as a good man's mistake, while the courage to speak the truth about the first chapter of the Book of Genesis is a wanton piece of wickedness' (*Life of Archbishop Tait*, i. 292).

CHAPTER I

THE BIBLE IS NOT ONE HOMOGENEOUS BOOK, BUT
A GRADUALLY COLLECTED CANON.

'Primam esse historiæ legem ne quid falsi dicere audeat; deinde
ne quid veri non audeat.'—Cic. *De Nat.* iii. 15.

'God's orthodoxy is truth.'—KINGSLEY.

THROUGHOUT these chapters I would ask the reader to bear
in mind what is the belief of all Christians respecting the
Bible. There is not a Church, nor a branch of the Church,
which does not reverence Holy Scripture. All Churches
admit that therein God reveals Himself to man; that, as
a whole, the Bible stands unapproachable in human literature; that its final truths have a unique claim upon our
acceptance; that in it alone is revealed the doctrine of
man's salvation through Jesus Christ our Lord. There
are also many Christians who hold that every word of it
is supernaturally dictated and infallibly true. That opinion
is untenable. It has not been held always, nor everywhere,
nor by all; there is not the least merit involved in its acceptance; it is not helpful to the religious life of the
individual or of nations; it has, on the contrary, been
prolific of terrible disasters. The acceptance of it may be
due, not to faith, but to a faithless materialism and a petri-

fied tradition; the rejection of it is not a sign of unbelief, but a duty to truth, and to the God of Truth.

No student can historically understand the Bible until he is ready to lay aside all prior considerations, and examine it analytically, arriving by induction at a real knowledge as to its claims and character.

1. First of all, we must never lose sight of the fact that the Bible is not a single nor even a homogeneous book. The Bible is, strictly speaking, not a book but a library.[1] It is not a single book, but a collection of sixty-six books. To thirty-nine of these we give the collective title of the Old Testament, and to the remaining twenty-seven the title of the New Testament. They constitute, as Edmund Burke said, 'an infinite collection of the most varied and the most venerable literature.'

These books were commonly referred to as 'the writing' (Scripture) or 'the writings' (Scriptures),[2] to which names were frequently added the epithets 'sacred' or 'holy.' They were called 'sacred' because they dealt with the relations of God to man, and contained revelations of His will. They were called 'holy' because their ultimate end was to promote the cause of holiness. We trace in the Old Testament nothing which approaches to a conception of 'the Bible' as such; or even of the 'Law' as a recognised *document*, till the discovery of some volume—which many have conjectured to have been part of the Book of

---

[1] 'And the same things were related both in the public archives and in the records that concern Nehemiah: and *how he, founding a library*, gathered together the books about the kings and prophets, and the books of David, and letters of kings about sacred gifts.' 2 Macc. ii. 13. See p. 32, n. 2.

[2] So in Sanskrit the word for 'revelation' is *Sruti*, from *Sruta*, 'heard.' Max Müller, *Sacred Books of the East*, i. p. xiii.

Deuteronomy[1]—in the reign of Josiah (*circ.* B.C. 624). The High Priest Hilkiah found it in the Temple, and said to Shaphan the Scribe, 'I have found the Book of the Law in the House of the Lord.' 'Hilkiah the Priest hath "delivered me a book,"' said the cautious scribe. When the scribe read the book to Josiah, the king was astonished and horrified to find himself unacquainted with the most essential and elementary rules which Moses was there said to have ordained. So completely had they fallen into desuetude that the people knew nothing about them, and seem never to have heard of them. Neither the Passover nor the Sabbatical year had been kept, and there is not an allusion in the whole Old Testament—after the Pentateuch —not even in the Levitic ideal of Ezekiel, not even in Zech. v. or viii., not even in Nehem. viii.-x., nor until Ecclus. l. 1–5—to the Day of Atonement. There is no evidence that 'the Book of the Law' was co-extensive with the Pentateuch, nor is there any proof of the existence of a *collected* Pentateuch earlier than the days of Ezra (B.C. 444). 'The Bible and the reading of the Bible as an instrument of instruction,' says Dean Stanley, 'may be said to have begun on the sunrise of that day when Ezra unrolled the parchment scroll of the Law.'[2] From that era till the days of John the Baptist prophecy ceased. Scribes and Pharisees more and more substituted the dead letter for the living voice of God, and soon they elevated the dead letter upon an idol-pedestal, and paid to it a new and no less perilous idolatry.

The sacred writings were not referred to as 'the Book'

---

[1] As even some of the Fathers thought: Jer. *Adv. Jovin.* i. 5; Chrys. *Hom. in Matt.* p. 9.

[2] October, B.C. 444. Nehem. viii.-x. ; Deut. xxxi. 11. See Cornill, *Einleit. in d. A. T.* pp. 62–67; Kuenen, *Hexateuch,* § 15.

till a late epoch. The particular name 'Bible' dates from the fourth century. St. Jerome (d. 420) called the Scriptures 'a Divine Library.' St. Chrysostom called them 'the Books.' The neuter plural 'biblia' was mistaken in the Western Church, in the thirteenth century, for a feminine singular, and from it is derived our familiar name 'the Bible.'[1]

2. The multiform elements of which the Bible is composed will appear if we glance at the history of the Canon.

The Canon of the Old Testament—that is, the list of those books which were finally accepted by the Jewish Church as authoritative—was arrived at by slow and uncertain degrees. It had, however, been agreed upon in its general outline before the time of Christ. The books of the Old Testament which we now receive are in great measure the same as those which were regarded as canonical by Philo (A.D. 30)[2] and Josephus (A.D. 93).[3] Both

---

[1] See Bishop Westcott, *The Bible in the Church*, p. 5.

[2] In a treatise attributed to Philo, *On the Contemplative Life*, there is a general classification of Old Testament writings. The book is regarded as a forgery of the third century (Kuenen, *Rel. of Israel*, ii. 204), but Mr. F. Conybeare has urged strong reasons for holding it to be genuine. Philo quotes all the books of the Old Testament except Nehemiah, Ruth, Esther, Chronicles, Ezekiel, Lamentations, Daniel, Ecclesiastes, and Canticles. On the other hand he quotes from the Pentateuch ten times more frequently than from the other books, and seems to attach to it an immeasurably higher importance and authority. The Sadducees did the same. The Samaritans accepted no Scriptures except the Pentateuch.

[3] Josephus (*c. Ap.* i. 7, 9) says that his Canon consisted of twenty-two books (the number of letters in the Hebrew alphabet). It is not possible to assert with certainty how he arranged the books. He refers to all the books except Proverbs, Ecclesiastes, Canticles, and Job. On the other hand the Essenes extended the Canon, including many books which are not regarded as canonical. See Bishop Westcott, *The Bible in the Church*, pp. 25–30.

were competent witnesses; both (perhaps) were of priestly descent; one represented the cultivation of Alexandria, the other the traditions of Palestine. Analogous proof is furnished by the Jews of Babylon in a passage of the Talmud, which gives additional testimony to the late editing of many of the books.[1]

The writings which we call 'the Apocrypha' were not placed by the Jewish Church on the same footing as the rest; and although the New Testament has quotations from every book of the Old Testament except twelve, it has no direct quotation from, nor many *certain* references to, any book of the Apocrypha.[2] It recognises the classification of the Old Testament into three broad divisions —the Law, the Prophets, and Psalms.[3]

3. The Canon of the New Testament was formed in the same gradual and tentative manner, by the exercise of the enlightened reason. In the first two centuries many Gospels, Epistles, and Apocalypses were current, to some of

---

[1] In the Gemara *Baba Bathra*, 14. b. In 2 Esdr. xiv. 44 we read of ninety-four books, but seventy of these are reserved for 'the wise' (ver. 46). The Talmudic passages which bear on the Canon are collected by Wildeboer, p. 63.

[2] St. Jude, however, quotes the Book of Enoch (which is not in our Apocrypha), and there are traces in the Epistle of St. James of some use of the Book of Wisdom. Rom. i. 20–32, ix. 21; Eph. vi. 13–17; Heb. i. 3; 1 Pet. i. 6, 7; Jas. v. 6, are thought to be suggested by the Book of Wisdom; and 1 Cor. vi. 13, Jas. i. 6, 19, by Ecclesiasticus. Some suspect allusions to lost books in 2 Tim. iii. 8; Heb. xi. 37; Jude 9. In Heb. xi. 34, 35, 37 are references to 2 Macc. vi. 18, 7, 42. See, for an account of apocryphal Jewish literature, Schürer, *Hist. of the Jewish People*, Div. iii. 1–155. Wildeboer (p. 51) says 'that the New Testament writers quote from apocryphal books can only be denied by dogmatic prejudice.' But see also Bishop Westcott, *The Bible in the Church*, pp. 46–49.

[3] Luke xxiv. 44.

which St. Luke refers without formal reprobation, and some of these obtained in the Church a brief and limited acceptance. Other books, such as the Shepherd of Hermas and the Epistles of Clement and Barnabas, were so highly regarded that they too were quoted as sacred books, and read aloud in some Christian churches.[1] There were also certain books undoubtedly spurious which were quoted by early Christian writers as possessing 'inspired' authority, such as the prophecies of Hystaspes and the Sibyl.[2] None of these long held their ground, nor were they ever placed on exactly the same level as the books now regarded as canonical. Most of the New Testament books were universally received and were called 'Acknowledged Books' (*Homologoumena*). Seven of them, however—the Second Epistle of St. Peter, the Second and Third Epistles of St. John, the Epistle to the Hebrews, those of St. James and St. Jude, and the Revelation—were classed together as 'Disputed Books' (*Antilegomena*).[3] There was no final test of their canonicity except the verifying faculty of the Christian consciousness. In the Lutheran Church some of these disputed books, and especially the Revelation of

[1] Just as the Apocrypha is found, without any distinction between it and the canonical Old Testament, in the Septuagint, so in two of the oldest MSS. we find early Christian writings—the two Epistles of Clement added to the Alexandrian MS. (about A.D. 430), and the Epistle of Barnabas and the Shepherd of Hermas to the Sinaitic MS. (about A.D. 331).

[2] See Just. Mart. *Apol.* i. 20, 44; Clem. Alex. *Strom.* vi. 5, p. 761; Lact. *Instt. Div.* vii. 15, 18.

[3] Many of the books of the New Testament were but little known to the mass of Christians even in the fifth century. St. Chrysostom preached on the Acts of the Apostles because he tells us that many of the Christians at Constantinople were hardly aware of its existence (*Comm. in Act. Apost.* i. 1, *Opp.* ix. 1).

St. John, have never been admitted as more than Deutero-canonical; that is, they have been regarded as of inferior value and authority to the rest. Luther, relying on the promised guidance of the Spirit of God, 'sought for the Canon in the Canon;' and, though his judgments were not always sound, he shows true faith by the masculine inde-pendence with which he felt himself at liberty to speak of some books of the Bible as inferior to others in essential value.[1] He did not value the historic accuracy of the Books of Chronicles; he regarded Ecclesiastes as pseudony-mous, and rejects Esther from the Canon.

His prefaces to the various books, as originally printed, furnish a noble specimen of the attitude which approaches Scripture with reverence, and yet with the knowledge that the vivifying spirit of the Christian is quite as sacred as the printed letter of the book.[2] His test of the books of Scripture (*der rechte Prüfestein*) was whether they did or did not testify to Christ.

4. The formation then of the Canon alike of the Old

---

[1] It must, however, be admitted that he showed a defective dis-crimination in his rash language about the Epistle of St. James, which he metaphorically tossed aside as 'a right strawy Epistle' (*recht strohern*) which lacked all evangelical character. He also held the Apocalypse in small esteem, *Preface to New Testament;* Seventh Thesis against Eck; *De Captiv. Bab.;* Dorner, *Hist. of Prot. Theol.* (E.T.) i. 241–245; Luther's *Werke* (Walch), viii. 2138. 'If any one should press thee with phrases which speak of works and which thou canst not bring into concord with the others, thou oughtest to say, Since Christ is the treasure whereby I am bought, . . . I care not the slightest jot for all such phrases of Scripture. . . . At the same time it is impossible that the Scriptures should contradict themselves. . . . Hear thou well, thou art almost a bully with the Scriptures, which are nevertheless under Christ as a servant.'

[2] For an account of Luther's views of Scripture see my *History of Interpretation*, pp. 324–340; Köstlin, *Luthers Theologie*, ii. 258–285.

and New Testaments was a work which God left to the *ordinary* influences of the Holy Ghost. It was not due to any external inspired authority. No vision of the night, no voice from heaven declared the books of the New Testament to be the Word of God; nor did any Church council for some centuries certify their canonicity until it had been practically settled by the common methods of criticism. God has given man a lamp which is sufficient to enable him to discern truth from falsehood in all essential things. Having bestowed on man his Reason and his Conscience, He does not speak to him by voices in the air. God never reveals to man what He has enabled man to discern for himself.

i. The fixation of the Canon of the Old Testament was the work of Scribes and Rabbis who exercised their own judgment in accordance with the best insight which they possessed.[1]

There were long hesitations in the Jewish Church about admitting the 'Song of Songs' into the Canon. Some Rabbis looked on it as a mere love song, unworthy to be admitted as a sacred book. Others saw its purity and beauty, and partly by the help of the allegoric senses in which it was gradually interpreted, it overcame the feeling of opposition. Its acceptance was determined by the emphatic eulogy pronounced upon it by R. Aqiba (d. A.D. 135?), the most influential of the Rabbis—the St. Thomas

---

[1] The division of the Bible into Law, Prophets, and 'other books of our fathers' (Hagiographa) (Torah, Nebiim, Kethubim, known in the Massorah as *Tenak*, from the initial letters) is first found in the Preface to Ecclesiasticus about B.C. 132 or earlier (?). The Law was regarded as the most fully inspired ('mouth to mouth,' Num. xii. 8). The Prophets were said to be inspired by 'the Spirit of Prophecy;' and the Kethubim by the 'Holy Spirit,' *More Nebochim*, ii. 45. For details see Wildeboer, *Canon*, pp. 2-19; Ewald, *Gesch. d. V. Isr.* vii. 458.

Aquinas of Talmudic scholasticism. But the whole school of Shammai called it the 'Holy of Holies' of all Scripture (*Yaddayim*, iii.).[1]

Similarly many of the Jewish teachers objected to what appeared to be the gloom and scepticism of the Book of Ecclesiastes; but the practical piety of its conclusion secured its final admission (*Yaddayim*, ch. iii.; *Eduyoth*, v. 3).

Even the Book of Ezekiel was not admitted without hesitation, because some Rabbis looked upon various passages of it as contradicting the words of Moses (*Menachoth*, 45. 1; Ezek. iv. 14, xxxiv. 10, xliv. 31, xlv. 20, &c.). The explanation of the apparent discrepancies was due to Rabbi Chananyah ben Hezekiah (*Shabbath*, fr. 13. 2); but the beginning and end of Ezekiel could not be read till the age of thirty (Jer. *Ep. ad Paulin.* Epp. liii. 8).

It is commonly asserted that the Canon of the Old Testament was finally fixed by Ezra and the so-called Great Synagogue. The assertion only rests on a sentence in the 'Sayings of the Jewish Fathers,' a tract of the Mishna which was not reduced to writing till A.D. 200. It finds no support in Philo, in Josephus, the Greek translators,[2]

---

[1] Rabbi Judah decided that Canticles defiles the hands—*i.e.* is canonical—A.D. 120. It is clear that the allegoric interpretation began early; see 2 Esdr. i. 24 (Cant. ii. 14, vi. 9), vii. 26. Aqiba (*Sanhedrin*, 34, 1) argued from Ps. lxii. 11: 'One thing God spake, twofold is what I heard.' Edersheim, *Life of Jesus*, i. 35. See too Jer. on Eccl. xii. 13.

[2] It is true that in 2 Macc. ii. 13 there is a talk of a *library* of Nehemiah, but it occurs in a letter full of absurdities and devoid of all historic value. See König, *Einleitung*, 445. The Talmud speaks of Ezra and the men of the Great Synagogue 'writing' certain entire books, and Jerome goes so far as to say, 'Sive Mosen dicere volueris auctorem Pentateuchi, sive Ezram ejusdem instauratorem, non recuso,' *Ep. ad Helvid.* Cf. Clem. Alex. *Strom.* I. xxii.; Iren. iii. 25.

or the New Testament.[1] It is in direct opposition to the
fact (1) that the MSS. of the Greek translators (the Seventy,
B.C. 270 and onwards) make no distinction between apocryphal and other writings; and (2) that the Canon of the Old
Testament was still a subject of discussion after the Christian era. For the Old Testament Canon was not regarded
as settled before A.D. 70. In that year the Jews at Jamnia
(Jabneh) decided in favour of our present thirty-nine
books, which they called twenty-four: namely, (1) the five
books of the Law; (2) eight books of the Prophets—by
which they meant Joshua, Judges, Samuel, Kings, Isaiah,
Jeremiah, Ezekiel, and twelve minor prophets; (3) eleven
writings, called by the Jews Kethubim, and in Greek
Hagiographa—Ruth, Psalms, Proverbs, Job, Ecclesiastes,
Canticles, Lamentations, Daniel, Esther, Ezra, Nehemiah,
and Chronicles.[2] The gathering at Jamnia [3] was a tumul-

---

[1] Our Lord refers to the Law, the Prophets, and the Psalms (Luke
xxiv. 44), but this is not more definite than the reference of Ecclesiasticus (B.C. 120) to the Law, the Prophets, and other books trans-
mitted to the Fathers. Ecclesiastes, Proverbs, Canticles, Esther,
Ezra, Nehemiah are not quoted in the New Testament, and Ezekiel
and Chronicles are only referred to distantly. On the whole subject
see Cornill, *Grundriss*, § 48; Wildeboer, pp. 58–62. A Baraïtha of
the Babylonian Talmud (*Baba Bathra*, f. 14. *b*, 15. *a*) gives the views
of the Jews in Babylon.

[2] Just as the Prophets were divided into *Nebiim Rishonim* (or
'earlier'), viz.—Joshua, Judges, 1, 2 Samuel, 1, 2 Kings, and the
Nebiim Acharonim (or 'later'), so the Kethubim were divided into
Rishonim, and *Acharonim* which contain the latest books, Daniel,
Ezra, Nehemiah, Chronicles. The five *Megilloth* (rolls) are placed in
the middle, viz.—Canticles, Ruth, Lamentations, Ecclesiastes, Esther.

[3] At this meeting the celebrated 'eighteen rules' were adopted.
Another assembly was held at Jamnia about A.D. 101 under Rabban
Gamaliel II., in which Ecclesiastes was admitted (*Eduyoth*, v. 3;
Grätz, *Gesch. d. Juden*, iii. 355, 494–502; Wellhausen, *Einleit.* 550;
Derenbourg, p. 295).

3

tuous assemblage, and in the faction fights of the Rabbinic parties, blood was shed by their scholars. Hence the decision was regarded as irrevocable and sealed by blood. From this time forwards the Talmudists limited the books of the Scripture to twenty-four.[1]

ii. Exactly the same influences were at work in the formation of the Christian Canon.

One of the ablest of the Fathers, Dionysius of Alexandria, shared a widespread uncertainty about the Book of Revelation, and thought that it was written by a presbyter named John, and not by the Evangelist St. John. The Greek churches regarded it for the most part with little favour, and one early Christian writer went so far as to attribute it to the heretic Cerinthus.[2] To the imaginary John the Presbyter were also attributed the Second and Third Epistles of St. John.

The Epistle of Jude secured a tardy acknowledgment, but was long in peril of rejection because of its remarkable peculiarities, and its quotation from the strange and spurious prophecy of Enoch. 'The Epistle,' says St. Jerome, 'is rejected by most.' Of the Epistle of James, Jerome tells us, 'It is asserted to have been brought out by somebody else under his name;' and of the Second Epistle of Peter that most Christians denied it to be his.[3]

---

[1] *Talm. Babli.*, *Baba Bathra*, 14; Wildeboer, § ii. 2; and on the Synod, Grätz, *Gesch. d. Juden*, iii. 496; Robertson Smith, *The Old Testament and the Church.* On Jamnia, see Derenbourg, *Palestine*, 295; Cornill, *Grundriss*, pp. 281, 291; *Hamburger Encykl.* ii. *s.vv.* 'Synedrion,' 'Jabne.'

[2] Books were judged by the congruity of their contents with the general Christian conviction, and many objected to the Apocalypse because it was supposed to favour millenarian views.

[3] The Canon of the New Testament was first formally and officially settled by two provincial synods—that of Laodicea (A.D. 363), and

The Epistle to the Hebrews ran considerable risk of rejection from the Canon, partly because many perceived that it could not have been written by St. Paul; partly because of the intense and apparently exceptionless severity of some of its warnings; partly because the phrase 'to Him that made Him'[1] (τῷ ποιήσαντι αὐτόν) (Heb. iii. 2) was erroneously supposed to favour the Arian heresy which spoke of Christ as a created being. 'The custom of the Latins,' says St. Jerome, 'does not admit it among canonised scriptures.' Jude, 2 Peter, 2, 3 John, and Revelation were absent from the canon of the Syriac Church; and James and 2 Peter probably had no place in the early Latin translations current in North Africa.

If it be asked, then, on what authority we accept as canonical the sixty-six books of our Scriptures, many will reply, ' on the authority of the Church.' But this answer simply means, by the general consensus of Christians; for it can hardly be said that the whole Church, as such, has pronounced any opinion on the Canon. As regards the Old Testament the Christian Church accepted the conclusions of the Jewish Synod of Jamnia, and that synod simply reflected the critical and spiritual ability of Rabbis who were far from being unanimous, were bound in an impossible system, and were by no means free from error. The churchmen assembled at Laodicea[2] and Carthage exercised no independent judgment on their books, nor was their critical knowledge other than elementary. No œcumenical

that of two synods of Carthage (A.D. 397 and 419), the decrees of which were generally sanctioned by the Trullan Council, A.D. 692. See Bishop Westcott, *The Bible in the Church*, pp. 170, 188, 217.

[1] The phrase simply means, 'to Him that appointed Him;' compare 1 Sam. xii. 6, Mark iii. 14, Acts ii. 36.

[2] The Laodicean list is regarded as a gloss.

council has formally considered the question of the Canon,
but only two provincial synods. Even had they been
œcumenical we know from history, and are expressly
warned by our own Church, that general councils, 'forasmuch as they be an assembly of men whereof all be not
governed with the Spirit and Word of God, may err and
sometimes have erred, even in things pertaining unto
God.' St. Gregory of Nazianzus, one of the most learned,
profound, and eloquent of the Fathers, who himself pre-
sided at the second œcumenical council, was so far from
regarding councils as infallible that he had the lowest
opinion of their deliberations and said that he had never
seen a good result from any synod. Luther said, 'The
Church cannot give any more authority or power than it
has of itself. A council cannot make that to be of Scripture which is not by nature of Scripture.'[1] It follows
then that the decision as to what books are or are not to
be regarded as true Scripture, though we believe it to be
wise and right, depends on no infallible decision. It must
satisfy the scientific and critical as well as the spiritual
requirements of each age. When the Council of Trent, a
small assembly in which there were very few men of high
linguistic or critical attainments, declared on the authority
of Pope Eugenius IV. that six books of the Apocrypha
were to be 'received and venerated' with the same feeling
of devotion and reverence as all the books of the Old and
New Testaments, the Reformed Churches rightly ignored
their authority, and laid it down as a principle that 'any
man may reject books claiming to be Holy Scripture if he
do not feel the evidence of their contents.' The anathemas
of the Council of Trent are as complete a matter of indifference to the free conscience as those of the Synod of Jamnia.

---

[1] *Disputatio Eccii et Lutheri.* See Dorner, *Prot. Theol.* i. 94, 95.

The conclusion may be expressed in the archaic language of the Scotch Confession, 1560.

'As we believe and confese the Scriptures of God sufficient to instruct and make the man of God perfite, so do we affirme and avow the authority of the same to be of God and neither to depend on men nor angelis. We affirme therefore that sik as allege the Scripture to have no uther authoritie bot that quhilk it ben received from the Kirk to be blasphemous against God and injurious to the trew Kirk quhilk always heares and obeyes the voice of her awin spouse and Pastor; but takis not upon her to be maistres over the samin.'[1]

'The Bible,' says Bishop Westcott, 'is in its origin a slow growth of time, intimately connected with a long development of national life, bearing on its surface the impress of successive revelations, extended from time to time by the addition of new elements, accepted in its present form not by one act once for all, but gradually and, as far as can be traced by the help of existing records, according to natural laws of criticism exercised within definite limits.'[2]

---

[1] Art. xix. See Briggs's *Bible Studies*.

[2] *The Bible in the Church*, p. 2. The word for 'Scripture' ($\gamma\rho\alpha\phi\acute{\eta}$) is said to be first applied to the New Testament by Theophilus of Antioch (A.D. 180). The word 'canon' was not used of the New Testament for three centuries, but was confined to the Creed. To the early Christians, Christianity meant what Christ *was*, not what He said. It meant the eternal presence of the living Saviour, not the recorded words of a Christ who was exclusively preached and symbolised as dead (Westcott, *ib*. pp. 94, 110, &c.). The name 'Testament' applied to the books of the Bible is due to a mistake. It was also called *Instrumentum*, a record. Testament means 'a will.' St. Jerome, in his Latin translation of the Bible (the Vulgate), used the word *testamentum* to translate the Greek word *diatheke* in Heb. ix. 15–17; compare Gal. iii. 17. Tertullian preferred *instru-*

mentum (*Apol.* 17 *et passim*).   But *diathcke* does not normally mean
'a will' in the New Testament.   The Jews were not familiar with
the habit of 'making wills,' of which they only heard from the
Romans.   In the New Testament, with the exception of a passing
allusion in Heb. ix. 16 (the writer has explained his view of the passage in the edition of the Epistle in the *Cambridge Bible for Schools*,
p. 120), the word *diathcke* is always the equivalent of the Jewish
word *berith*, which means a 'covenant' (see Wildeboer, *Canon*, p. 6
(E.T.); Zahn, *Gesch. d. N. Kanons*, i. 105).   'Old Covenant,' as applied to the first thirty-nine books of the Bible, is in itself no more
than a gradual and, so to speak, accidental extension of the phrase,
'the Book of the Covenant,' which was originally applied to the Law
alone (2 Kings xxiii. 21).

CHAPTER II

THE BIBLE REPRESENTS THE REMAINS OF A MUCH WIDER LITERATURE.

'For the present it was intended revelation should be no more than a small light in the midst of a world, greatly overspread, notwithstanding it, with ignorance and darkness.'—BUTLER, *Analogy* II. vi. § 5.

THE marked separation of the Bible into the books of the Old and New Covenants is alone sufficient to show that the Bible cannot be regarded as a simple homogeneous book.   Both sections represent *the selected and fragmentary remains of an extensive literature,*[1] and those selections mainly fall into two great divisions separated from each other by the period of more than four and a half centuries which intervened between Malachi (B.C. 420) and the first book in the New Covenant, which is the earliest extant letter of St. Paul—the First Epistle to the Thessalonians, written about A.D. 53.

The Old Testament does not represent the whole literature of the Jews.[2] It contains quotations from and references to a number of other books—at least sixteen— which are now lost. Many such collections were quoted

---

[1] We have only one or two of Solomon's 1005 songs (1 Kings iv. 32).

[2] I need not here enter into the question as to how much of the Old Testament may be post-Exilic.

and utilised by the compilers and editors of the Pentateuch
and the Historic Books. Among these were 'The Acts of
Solomon,' 'The Chronicles of King David,' 'The Chronicles
of the Kings of Israel,' 'The Chronicles of the Kings of
Judah,' 'The Books of Nathan the Prophet, and of Gad
the Seer,' 'The Prophecy of Ahijah the Shilonite,' and 'The
Vision of Iddo the Seer.' Two were of special importance:
'The Book of the Wars of the Lord,' which is quoted in
Numbers; and 'The Book of Jasher,' or 'the Upright.'
The latter was, in part at any rate, a collection of poems
from which there are some remarkable and magnificent
quotations on the glory of the ideal Israel.

Many of the Old Testament books are anonymous; one
or two are certainly pseudonymous—that is, they are attributed by tradition to writers by whom they could not
have been composed.

Probably, too, our Sacred Books are even more fragmentary than at first sight they appear to be. Although
no final arrangement of the contents of the Pentateuch
has yet been found possible, few competent critics hesitate
to allow that it is a work of composite structure; that it has
been edited and re-edited several times; and that it contains
successive strata of legislation. Many critics—rightly or
wrongly—lean to the opinion that the Priestly code in the
Ceremonial sections of Exodus, Leviticus, and Numbers
may in its present form be no older than the days of Ezekiel,
or even of Ezra (B.C. 444); and the Book of Deuteronomy
than the days of Josiah (B.C. 621).[1] The Psalms are a

---

[1] The oldest nucleus is probably the Book of the Covenant (Ex.
xxi.–xxiii.), which some critics consider to be recast in the Deuteronomic code of Deut. xii.–xxvi. See Prof. Robertson Smith, *Prophets
of Israel*, pp. 109, 379; Reuss, *Gesch. d. Heil. Schrift*, § 294; Driver,
Introduction, pp. 9, 118–128. It is clear that throughout the later

collection of sacred poems in five separate books of very various antiquity, of which some may mount to an epoch earlier than David's, and some may belong to the later decadence of Hebrew poetry after the Exile. The Proverbs, again, as all admit, consist of four or five different collections, and the elements of song which were current among the Hebrews were often freely remodelled. Three at least of the books of the Prophets—Isaiah, Micah, and Zechariah—are now believed by many to represent the work of six or more different authors. Nothing is a more entire anachronism than the notion that such critical inquiries can be dashed to the ground by bald assertions or dogmatic ignorance. The revelation recorded in the Bible is a jewel which God has given us in a setting of human history, and it is only in connection with its historical surroundings that it can be truly judged.

The New Testament represents the extant portion of a Christian literature which was much more extensive in the earliest centuries.[1] St. Luke tells us that many Gospels were already in existence when he prepared his own. It

parts of history in the Books of Kings, the Levitic code was either unknown or disregarded; and that in the earlier parts the Deuteronomic law of the one altar was unknown to, or disregarded by, the Prophets.

[1] 'The Gospel to the Hebrews;' 'The Gospel to the Egyptians;' 'The Gospel of Peter;' 'The Travels of the Apostles,' by Leucius; 'The Preaching of Peter;' 'The Acts of Paul and Thekla;' 'The First and Second Epistles of Clement;' 'The Epistle of Barnabas;' the 'Shepherd' of Hermas; the 'Didache' or Teaching of the Apostles; 'The Two Ways;' 'The Apocalypse of Peter,' and other books, all possessed a sort of Scriptural authority in the early Church; and several of these works had a circulation and popularity considerably in excess of some of the books now included in the Canon. See Euseb. *H. E.* iii. 3, 24, 25; Westcott, *The Bible in the Church*, pp. 127–151; Sanday, *Inspiration*, p. 27.

is all but certain that St. Paul, and probable that the other
Apostles, must have written many letters which are no
longer preserved. (See 2 Thess. ii. 2, iii. 17; 1 Cor. v. 9;
2 Cor. x. 9–11.)

Some time elapsed before the books of the New Testament were placed on an equal level with those of the Old.
This is strikingly shown in the earliest writings of the
Christian Fathers. In the 'Teaching of the Twelve Apostles,' in Clement and Barnabas, there are quotations from
the Apostles and Evangelists, but they are not usually
adduced with formulæ which attribute to them the same
inspired authority as the quotations from the Old Testament.[1] Justin Martyr freely uses the Gospels under the
title of 'Memoirs;' but he does not name them, and he
seems to think it necessary to enforce them by the authority of Old Testament prophets.

Papias was Bishop of Hierapolis about A.D. 140. The
very simplicity of the man, combined with the fact of his
learning, makes him an unexceptionable witness. That
he hardly placed the New Testament on the same footing
as the Old appears from his remarks about the Gospels.
He speaks of them in tones less reverential than we should
now consider suitable. He seems to attach to them less
value—at any rate for his immediate object—than traditions which he had personally received. 'I did not consider,' he says, 'that the things from books were so
advantageous for my purpose, as things from the living
and abiding Voice.'[2]

And to this day our advancing knowledge of textual
criticism, together with the deepening study of many
sources of information which were once either unavailable

---

[1] But in Ep. Barn. iv. 14, ὡς γέγραπται seems to refer to Matt. xx. 16.

[2] Quoted in Euseb. *H. E.* iii. 39; Bishop Westcott, *u.s.* pp. 95–97.

or neglected, has necessitated the critical analysis even of those books which have been accepted as canonical. The fact that certain passages were to be found within the four corners of books regarded as 'inspired,' has not for a moment stood in the way of the rejection by our Revisers of such words or passages as did not meet the standard of modern critical requirements. In John viii. 1–11 the story of the Woman Taken in Adultery, exquisite and supremely valuable as it is, is now bracketed as of doubtful genuineness.[1] In Acts ix. 5, 6 we look in vain for 'Lord, what wilt thou have me to do?' and 'It is hard for thee to kick against the pricks.' The verse 'This kind goeth not out save by prayer and fasting' disappears altogether from Matt. xvii. 21. The word 'fasting,' interpolated in Mark ix. 29 and 1 Cor. vii. 5 by the ascetic tendency of the early Church, is unhesitatingly deleted in our Revised Version. The simple creed of the eunuch, and the demand for it by the Deacon Philip, disappear from Acts viii. 37. The last twelve verses of St. Mark are separated from the others by a gap, and the reader is warned of their uncertain authenticity. The famous verse about the three heavenly witnesses disappears without so much as a notice from 1 John v. 7.

The Bible is full of treasures new and old, but the golden keys of the treasure-house have been placed in the hands of men who have often misused them, and failed to ascertain rightly their original value and application.

If our traditional views respecting Scripture are liable to that modification which so many other Christian opinions undergo from age to age, this is no more than

---

[1] The margin in the R.V. adds: 'Most of the ancient authorities omit John vii. 53–viii. 11. Those which contain it vary very much from each other.'

we should expect from the entire method of God's economy.

'There is nothing so revolutionary,' said Dr. Arnold, 'because there is nothing so unnatural and convulsive, as the strain to keep things fixed, when all the world is, by the very law of its creation, in eternal progress; and the course of all the evils in the world may be traced to that natural but most deadly evil of human indolence and corruption that it is our duty to preserve and not to improve.'

'I am convinced,' said John Robinson in his farewell address to the Pilgrim Fathers before they sailed in the *Mayflower* from Delft harbour, 'I am convinced that the Lord hath yet more light and truth to break forth from His Holy Word.'

John Goodwin, in the preface to his 'Treatise on Justification,' argues that if America, so vast a portion of the world, remained unknown to all the rest of mankind for so many generations, 'well may it be conceived, not only that some, but many truths, yea, and those of maine concernment and importance, may be yet unborne.'

'Nor is it at all incredible,' says Bishop Butler, 'that a book which has been so long in the possession of mankind should contain many truths as yet undiscovered. . . . And possibly it might be intended that events as they come to pass should open and ascertain the meaning of several parts of Scripture' (*Analogy*, II. iii. 21).

Those who refuse to admit the facts about the books of Scripture which many learned and devout students have now accepted should beware lest haply they be fighting against God. This error has been committed all through the long centuries by those who, like Uzzah, thought that their aid was indispensable to prevent the Ark of God from falling. Men constantly fight on behalf of their own mistakes, limitations, prejudices, and traditions, because they forget that the ever-broadening light of human knowledge, which saves mankind from torpor, is light from heaven, and is a part of the Divine economy of revelation.[1] Their opposition is always unavailing. They constitute themselves the defenders of exploded errors, and waste their time in daubing tottering walls with untempered mortar. The majority of the controversialists who are so ready to hurl the names of 'infidel' and 'heretic' against men of a wider knowledge and a deeper love of truth than their own, are in many cases neither sufficiently learned, nor sufficiently able, nor sufficiently endowed with unbiassed openness of mind and passionate love for truth, to entitle them to any authority. Let me mention a single fact which should teach them a little more caution and charity in the judgment of views which they deem so 'dangerous.' They will hardly deny the debt which the English Church owes to the profound learning, indefatigable diligence, and often brilliant genius of the great theologians of Germany, of whom many have devoted their lives to the laborious and self-denying investigation of critical problems. If only one or two English and German scholars had accepted the main conclusions of the Higher Criticism, those who reject them might justify themselves by the authority of the remainder. But among scholars of note no one questions them. A German supporter of Biblical infallibility, Rohnert, Pastor in Waldenburg, writing on Inspiration in 1892, says, 'We only know of *one single theological Professor* in Germany who still believes in the inerrancy of Scripture,' and he a man very little, if at all known.[2]

---

[1] See strong warnings against this tendency in Matt. xv. 14, xxiii. 7, 8; Jas. iii. 1; 1 Tim. i. 6, 7; Heb. v. 12. Hermas says: 'Being ignorant, they wish to set up as teachers.' *Sim.* ix. 22.

[2] 'Wir kennen nur einen einzigen theol. Professor in Deutschland

Is any one so uncharitable as to believe that all these Christian students have combined in a conspiracy of scepticism? or can we fail to see that the number and eminence of the names show the enormous weight of the evidence which has compelled them, in the interests of truth and honesty, to abandon views which the revealing light of God has shown to be no longer tenable? Is this consensus of scholars—approved as it is by almost every eminent theologian in our English, Scotch, and American Universities—to be waved aside, as a matter of no moment, by any worshipper of humanly-invented dogma, however incompetent and however ignorant?

'Upon the very threshold,' says Mr. Gladstone in his 'Impregnable Rock of Holy Scripture,' 'I embrace, in what I think a substantial sense, one of the great canons of modern criticism, that the Scriptures are to be treated like any other book in the trial of their title.'

welcher noch an der Irrtumslosigkeit der h. Schrift festhält, das ist Herr Prof. D. Nösgen.' Rohnert, p. 2. He examines and tabulates the opinions of such men as Professors Von Hofmann, Luthardt, Frank, Zahn, Dieckhoff, Kübel, Zöckler, Grau, Cremer, Volck, Schmidt, and shows their general accordance in the conviction that complete infallibility is *not* an attribute of Scripture. To these may be added hosts of other names even more distinguished.

CHAPTER III

THE BIBLE COMBINES IMMENSE VARIETY WITH ESSENTIAL UNITY.

Heb. i. 1 : πολυμερῶς καὶ πολιτρόπως.

Ps. xlv. 9 : 'In vestitu deaurato, circumdata varietate.'

ἡ πολυποίκιλος σοφία του Θεου.—Eph. iii. 10.

> 'Slowly the Bible of the race is writ,
> And not on paper leaves nor leaves of stone,
> Each age, each kindred adds a verse to it,
> Texts of despair or hope, or joy or moan ;
> While swings the sea, while mists the mountains shroud,
> While thunder's surges burst on cliffs of cloud,
> Still at the Prophets' feet the nations sit.'—LOWELL.

FROM what we have already seen, it follows abundantly that the contents of the Bible are not all of the same value ; not all of the same importance.

In one sense this is a truism ; but when it is our object to clear away clouds of false hypothesis and erring tradition it is necessary to recall attention to the most obvious facts. And obvious as this truth is, the neglect of it has deluged with calamities both the Church and the world.

Let it not be overlooked that the view is not only sanctioned but expressly laid down by both our Lord and the

Apostles. Moses had permitted divorce. It might therefore have been argued, and *was* argued, that divorce was permissible under Divine sanction. Such was not our Lord's decision on that question. He treated the Mosaic concession as unprimitive and in itself undesirable. 'Moses for the hardness of your hearts suffered you to put away your wives, but in the beginning it was not so.' St. Paul, and St. Peter, and the author of the Epistle to the Hebrews, had thoroughly grasped the force of that lesson. The vision of St. Peter on the roof at Joppa emphasised in his mind the parable about what goeth into a man and what cometh out of him, in which Christ had reversed the law of Moses and made all meats clean. St. Peter and St. Paul did not hesitate to speak of the Levitical ordinances as 'a yoke that neither we nor our fathers were able to bear;' as 'the curse of the law;' as 'dead works;' as 'weak and beggarly rudiments.'[1] The writer to the Hebrews gradually carried on his convincing argument till at its climax he ventures openly to treat the law as the mere scaffoldage of religion, and to declare that its institutions had now become inherently weak and profitless;[2] that they were in fact mere 'carnal ordinances.'[3]

The preciousness of the Bible as a revelation of God through the minds of men is indefinitely increased by

---

[1] Acts xv. 10; Gal. iii. 13, iv. 3, 9; Heb. vi. 1.

[2] Heb. vii. 18. 'The way in which the New Testament writers use the Old Testament shows the complexity of the whole subject. Reverence and appeal to authority are everywhere manifest, but also a measure of freedom for which we are hardly prepared, and an evident desire to dwell on the substantial meaning rather than the form of the record, the spirit rather than the letter of the Word.'— Prof. Davison.

[3] For similar views in the Prophets see Jer. iii. 16, vii. 21, 22, xxxi. 31-33; Is. i. 11-17, &c.

these differences of standpoint. For truth is many-sided, and the total effect of Scriptural teaching is enhanced by its exquisite variety. The Bible is not, like the Qur'an, or the Zend-Avesta, or the Analects of Confucius, the work of a single intellect. It speaks to us in various languages, it speaks to us in many voices. It furnishes us with the wisdom and experience of widely different ages; it springs from the deep heart of humanity under the most opposite conditions of patriarchal simplicity or complex civilisation. The stream of revelation is swollen by multitudes of rills from different fountain-heads, in mountain ranges separated from each other as far as the east is from the west. God, as we are told in the singularly pregnant introduction to the Epistle to the Hebrews, spake in times past unto the fathers by the prophets 'fragmentarily and multifariously,' 'in many parts and many manners.' The wisdom enshrined in Scripture is, as St. Paul said to the Ephesians, a wisdom 'richly variegated.' For this reason the old writers delighted to compare the Church to 'the King's daughter' of the Psalmist who is 'all glorious within,' and who is 'brought unto the King in raiment of needlework, wrought about with divers colours'—*circum-amicta varietatibus:—*

> God's Spouse knows what will please her Lover best,
> And in a various-coloured Robe is drest.[1]

This variety of Scripture is one reason why it is of all books the most universal. Why is it that it has proved to be equally dear to men of all nations, of all times, of all conditions? Why does it come home alike to the profoundest philosopher and to the little negro child? Why is it to be found in the wigwam of the sub-Arctic Indian

[1] Bishop Ken.

and in the cabinet of emperors; in the knapsack of the rough soldier and on the bed of the dying maiden? Because its deepest truths came from stirrings of the Spirit in the common heart of mankind which is the same essentially amid all differences and under all disguises.

What other book or literature furnishes us with so many points of insight into the working of men's minds? Now a single Eastern emir is called out of an idolatrous world to preserve the knowledge of the one true God; now a great lawgiver delivers his moral code to a perverse multitude of slaves and fugitives from a granite crag in the wilderness; now seers and kings address a nation in the zenith of its prosperity or on the eve of its desolation; now priests or courtiers console its melancholy exile or inspirit its feeble resuscitation; now a little band of 'unlearned and ignorant men' record the life of its Divine yet rejected Messiah; now a converted Pharisee preaches that new Gospel with intense fire and wisdom; now a Galilean fisherman utters words of the deepest spirituality and clothes in mystic gorgeousness his heart-thrilling Apocalypse. Peoples and languages—Egypt, Palestine, Assyria, Babylonia, Persia, Greece, Rome—contribute their quotas to its wisdom.

As the three greatest nations of antiquity uttered their involuntary testimony to Christ in the title on His cross, so did they add the best results of their history, their language, and their organisation to the totality of His power. It is true in a deeper sense than Philo grasped that 'the servant of the Law is necessarily the best citizen of the World.'

Nor have we even now exhausted the diversity of the elements of which this revelation is composed. On one page we are reading the passionate pleadings of an afflicted

Chaldean noble; on another the rhythmic utterances of a great Mesopotamian sorcerer; on others the cynical confessions of a sated worldling, or the pathetic cry of a repentant king. Here we have exultant thanksgivings for some splendid deliverance; hard by we find the impassioned denunciation of some intolerable wrong. Within a few pages we find a stately poem, or a gorgeous vision, or a closely reasoned argument, or the decree of some Eastern autocrat, or the brief letter of an aged prisoner entreating forgiveness for an unprofitable slave. Such and so varied are its elements. 'Its light,' says Dr. Newman, 'is like the body of heaven in its clearness; its vastness like the bosom of the sea; its variety like scenes of nature!'[1]

Thus what we call the Bible was written by all sorts and conditions of men; by the poor as well as by the rich; by the lowly as well as by the exalted; by autocrats and peasants; by priests and prophets; by warriors and husbandmen; by poets and chroniclers; by passionate enthusiasts and calm reasoners; by unlearned provincials and Alexandrian theologians; by philosophers who attained from reasoning, and mystics who saw by intuition, and practical men who learnt by experience, the truths of God. Touched by one of these many fingers, our hearts cannot but respond. At the turning of a page we may listen to Solomon the magnificent, or Amos the herdsman; to Nebuchadrezzar the Babylonian conqueror, or Matthew the Galilean publican. If St. Paul be too difficult for us, we have the practical plainness of St. Peter; if St. John soars too high for us on the eagle wings of his mysticism, we can rejoice in the simple sweetness of St. Luke; if we find the Apocalypse too passionate and enigmatic, we can

---

[1] *Tracts for the Times*, No. 87.

rest in the homely counsels of St. James. The Scriptures have 'shallows which the lamb can ford,' as well as 'depths which the elephant must swim.' They have Poetry for the student; History for the statesman; Psalms for the temple; Proverbs for the mart. They have appeals, denunciations, arguments, stories of battle, songs of love. They have mountains and valleys, shadow and sunshine, calm and tempest, stormy waves and still waters, lilies of the green pasture and the shadow of a great rock in weary lands. 'Marvellous is the depth of Thy utterances,' exclaims St. Augustine. 'Its smiling surface allures the little ones; yet marvellous is its depth, my God, marvellous its depth! It is a shudder to gaze into it, the shudder of reverence and the thrill of love!'[1]

And yet the Scriptures have a glory far more consummate than all this, in that they contain the authentic record of the Incarnate Christ, the immediate revelation of the Son of God Himself.

By bearing in mind the rich diversity of Scripture we not only gain elements of the deepest interest, but we are proceeding on the right path for its due comprehension. We are in a better position for understanding the truth of God when we have studied the peculiarities of the language in which it is embodied, and know something of the individuality with which the expression of it is tinged. To the variety of sources from which the revelation comes are due both the inexhaustible interest of the Bible and its Divine universality. In this it is wholly unlike the sacred books of other religions. It has something for all nations.

---

[1] 'Mira profunditas eloquiorum tuorum, quorum ecce ante nos superficies blandiens parvulis; sed mira profunditas, Deus meus, mira profunditas! Horror est intendere in eam; horror honoris et tremor amoris.'—Aug. *Conf.* xii. 14.

In reading the Qur'an we can think only of Arabia; in reading Confucius only of China; in reading the Zend-Avesta only of Persia; in reading the Vedas only of Hindostan. But in the Bible we meet with all races, from Arabian troglodytes to Greek poets, from Galilean fishermen to Roman consuls. From Nineveh to Babylon, from Babylon to Damascus, from Damascus to Jerusalem, from Jerusalem to Tyre, and the isles of the Gentiles, and Athens, and Corinth, and Rome, we see the light of revelation ever streaming westwards through the pages of the Bible.

> The giant forms of empires on their way
> To ruin

fling their colossal shadows across its pages. The Bible is at once a sacred Iliad and a sacred Odyssey. Now its pages ring with the battles of the warrior, with their confused noise and garments rolled in blood;[1] now the sea is dashing in our faces as we traverse it in the ship of Jonah, or toss a night and day among its breakers with St. Paul. It has, indeed, deep speculations for the philosophic mind, but for the most part it is intensely concrete. There is in it no stifling system, no chilling gloom, no self-centred absorption, no frozen sea of abstractions. The sanctimonious formalism of the Pharisee, the selfish and unnatural asceticism of the Buddhist, the chill uncertainty of the Confucian, find no sanction here; nor are we placed at the mercy of the systematising refinements of the schoolman, and the cruel tyranny of priestcraft. The Bible shows us that religion may be as exquisite as music, as glowing as art, as rich as a gifted nature, as broad as a noble life. It is 'as universal as our race, as individual as ourselves.'

Hence, to the homilist and the preacher, dulness is an

---

[1] Is. ix. 5 (corrected in R.V.).

inexcusable fault, and one which should be most earnestly avoided. If the preacher is dull—dull to all his hearers— he cannot possibly rouse their consciences or touch their hearts. Dulness might be pardonable if we had no better text-book than the Qur'an or the Tripitaka; but it is hardly pardonable when our sacred Book is so intensely and widely humanitarian. Where the human, the concrete, and the individual element is introduced, hearers must find *something* to interest and instruct them; for the experience of one heart is more or less the experience of all hearts, and there is no one who does not sympathise with the multitude in the Roman theatre who rose to shout their delighted applause on hearing the line of the dramatist,

Homo sum; humani nihil a me alienum puto.

To the Buddhist the incidents, whether real or legendary, in the life of the Buddha Sakya Mouni furnish a theme of endless interest; the Chinese are never tired of even the dry and uneventful records of the biography of Kung-foo-tze; but the Bible furnishes us with thousands of thrilling incidents, and with human experiences under the most varied conditions. Not only so, but it comprises the writings of at least fifty different authors, who lived in the most widely separated spheres. The voice which speaks to us is now that of a Gentile sorcerer, now that of a suffering prisoner, now that of a conquering king. Lawgivers like Moses, autocrats like Solomon, warriors like Joshua, historians like Samuel, prophets like Isaiah, scribes like Ezra, poets like David, governors like Nehemiah, exiles like Daniel, peasants like Amos, fishermen like Peter and John, tax-gatherers like Matthew, rabbis like Paul, have all contributed to the sacred page. We may truly say that it is like the ash-tree, Ygdrasil, the great tree of Northern fable, whose leaves were the lives of men. It is for this very reason that nations, like birds of the air, shelter themselves under the shadow of it. It is a vine of God's planting,

> which outspread
> With growth of shadowing leaf and clusters rare,
> Reacheth to every corner under heaven,
> Deep-rooted in the living soil of truth ;
> So that men's hopes and fears take refuge in
> The fragrance of its complicated glooms
> And cool impleachèd twilights.

In both Testaments there is diversity; but whereas there are only nine authors for the twenty-seven books of the New Testament, and the great bulk of it is the work of two, on the other hand in the thirty-nine books of the Old Testament we enjoy the wisdom of a very much larger number of contributors.

We have seen the singular differences of station and circumstances among those to whom God sent His message of inspiration. But, further, by what divers *ways* also is their message delivered to us! It came sometimes in the facts of history, sometimes in isolated promises, sometimes by Urim, sometimes by dreams and voices and similitudes, sometimes by types and sacrifices, sometimes by prophets specially commissioned. It takes the form now of annals, now of philosophic meditation, now of a sermon, now of an idyl, now of a lyric song. Sometimes it expands, through chapter after chapter, the details of a single day in an individual life; sometimes it crushes into one single clause the sweeping summary of the records of twenty generations. At one time it will give the minutest incidents of one event in a single reign; at another it will heap the dust of oblivion over dynasties of a hundred kings. We may compare its course with that of a stream,

which sometimes dwindles into a rock-bound rivulet, and
sometimes broadens into a shoreless sea.   But it is a stream
whose fountains lie deep in the everlasting hills. Its sources
are hidden in the depths of a past eternity, and its issues
in the abysm of an illimitable future.   It begins with the
chaos of Genesis, 'vast and void;' it ends with a book
which has been called 'the majestic image of a high and
stately tragedy, shutting up and intermingling her solemn
scenes and acts with a sevenfold chorus of hallelujahs and
harping symphonies.'

Hence the Bible is inextricably mingled with all that is
greatest in human history, national literature, and individual life.   Its influence on literature has been invaluable
and supreme.   Dante and Milton are wholly based on the
words and truths of Scripture; Shakespeare is full of
them, and Wordsworth and Tennyson and Browning.
George Eliot and Victor Hugo borrowed from them their
best ideals; Carlyle, Newman, and Ruskin were saturated
with them from childhood. The laws of Alfred and
Charlemagne were inspired by them.   Judas Maccabæus
caught from them the fire of his patriotism; Gustavus
Adolphus pored over them before he charged at Lützen;
Cromwell was found absorbed in them on the eve of Nase-
by.   They have been on the lips of warriors and statesmen
and martyrs at the sublimest moments of their lives, and
so entirely have they decided the destinies of nations that
but for them the civilisation of Europe might still have
been as cruel as that of Egypt and as corrupt as that of
Rome.

Yet the *essential unity* of the writings is hardly less remarkable than their infinite variety, and in spite of its
manifold elements the Bible may be regarded, under certain limitations, as an organic whole.

It has the unity of the nationality from the bosom of which it mainly sprang. It has the unity of Monotheism. It has the unity which rises from the fact that it deals exclusively with religious ends, or with ends which were regarded as bearing upon religion. It has, lastly, the unity which rises from its being the history of the dealings of God with one chosen nation; with all other nations; with individual men; and with the whole race of mankind. It describes the gradual education of the Hebrews, of the heathen, and of many separate souls, in the knowledge of the Will of the Supreme. The deepest principle of spiritual life, which consists in the sense of man's communion with the living God, runs through all its diversities, and elevates even its rudimentary morality. Above all it finds its unifying element in Christ. This was pointed out by the Lord Himself. 'Ye search the Scriptures,' He said to the Jews, 'because ye think that in them ye have eternal life, and these are they which bear witness of Me.' 'If ye believed Moses,' He said, 'ye would believe Me, for he wrote of Me. But if ye believe not his writings, how shall ye believe My words?'[1] 'Your father Abraham,' He said, 'rejoiced to see My day; and he saw it and was glad.'[2]

In these words Christ seems to point out, as in one illuminating flash, that the centre of all that was best, greatest, and truest in the Old Dispensation was that hope of the Divine coming Deliverer, which was revealed to man after he had first lost the Eden of Innocence, and which shone like a pillar of fire on his horizon during his long wanderings through the wilderness of time. It was this hope which sustained Israel in many an hour of darkness and led him forward to the dawn of that great day

[1] John v. 39, 46, 47.   [2] John viii. 56.

when the Sun of Righteousness should rise upon the world
with healing on His wings.

The fact that, from the age of Origen onwards, allegory
and typology have been exaggerated to a most artificial
extent, and that many events and allusions and customs
have been made prophetic of Christ in which nothing of
prophecy was intended, must not blind us to the fact that
the Old Testament is full of Christ; for the very heart and
essence of the Old Dispensation, as its features are ex-
hibited in the writings of historians, lawgivers, and prophets, was the great and unquenchable Messianic hope.
In the Old Testament Christ is prefigured; in the New
Testament He is revealed.   In His teaching we see in all
their fulness those constant elements which all religion
strives more and more clearly to express—the holiness and
love of God, the dignity and brotherhood of man.   And
so He stands at the centre of all history as the fulfilment
of all the yearnings of the past, the justification of all the
hopes of the future.   'He lifted the gate of the centuries
off its hinges with His bleeding hand.'   Apart from Him
all the deepest elements of the Old Testament become unintelligible.   The Law is but the slave which leads us to
His school.[1]   He is the bruiser of the serpent's head in
Genesis, and the Lamb as it had been slain in the midst of
the throne in Revelation.   He is the Paschal Lamb of
Moses; the true star and sceptre of Balaam's vision; the

---

[1] This is rightly insisted on in our 7th Article, and will not be in
the least impugned by anything here brought forward. 'The Old
Testament,' we are there told, 'is not contrary to the New, for both
in the Old and New Testaments everlasting life is offered to mankind
by Christ.' As against heretics like Marcion and some of the ancient
Gnostics and modern fanatics, who treated the Old Testament as
coming from an evil or imperfect demon, the retention of this Article
was both necessary and instructive.

promised Son of David; Isaiah's rod of the stem of Jesse. The testimony to Him is the spirit of prophecy, and of Him bear all the prophets witness, as many as have spoken from Samuel and those that follow after. The due comprehension of this vast hope, and the power of unfolding it, will be one of the highest results which can reward the study of the preacher who desires to fulfil the duty of a wise scribe by drawing from his treasures things old as well as new.

CHAPTER IV

THE 'ALLEGORICAL METHOD' OF EXEGESIS UNTENABLE.

'Hæreticis mos est simplicia quæque torquere.'—TERT. *c. Her-mog.* xix.

'Eat in peace the bread of Scripture, without troubling thyself about the particles of sand which may have been mixed with it by the millstone. —BENGEL.

BUT while the Old Testament is not contrary to the New, since alike in the Old and New Testaments 'everlasting life is offered to mankind through Christ,' yet the Old Testament does not stand on the same level with the New. The treatment which attaches equal importance, equal value, equal validity to all the books of the Bible—the teaching which represents all their statements as equally authoritative, and which binds us to accept them without reference to the ages or circumstances in which they originated—is unnatural, dangerous, and false.

The Bible contains an ever-advancing revelation, and there can be no final rule for Christians which is not in accordance with the Gospel of Christ.

The great fact which the Jewish and Christian Churches failed for ages to understand was that God revealed Himself slowly and gradually. There were times of ignorance which God winked at in the Jewish as well as in the heathen world. In many of the books of the Old Testament the spiritual insight is limited, the moral standard as yet imperfect. Those who have undertaken to defend all the deeds committed by patriarchs, and sometimes narrated without disapproval—the wild actions of kings and patriots, even when invested with the sanction of priests and prophets—have done so by an allegorical method which may, indeed, within subordinate limits, be adopted for purposes of illustration, as it was by St. Paul, but which cannot be used to set aside plain history.

The very meaning of 'a *progressive* revelation' can only be that the earlier stages of this revelation are as yet transitory and imperfect as compared with its latest developments.

As a matter of plain honesty and common sense, it ought to be stated that the morality of some passages of the Bible is not in accord with the words of Christ. When we maintain the supremacy of the moral teaching of the Bible we mean the supremacy of that teaching which is stamped by the sanction of consciences which the Gospel has illuminated.

The imperfect insight of an earlier dispensation sanctioned, or at least tolerated, passions, practices, and institutions which the fully enlightened Christian conscience has learnt justly to abhor.

God revealed Himself to man part by part; He lifted the veil fold by fold. It is grievous to recall how many a blood-stained page of history might have been redeemed from its agony and desolation if men had only remembered that the law of the Old Testament was as yet an imperfect law, and the morality of the Old Testament a not yet, in all instances, fully instructed morality.

Such follies and iniquities (of which many find their

pale reflex and faint analogy even in the present day) could never have occurred if men had studied the Bible in the light of the truths which we have just been considering. And those truths were enunciated not only by St. Paul, the great and learned Apostle, but, as we shall see later, by our blessed Lord Himself. He pointed out that the moral conceptions of the Old Testament were but as the starlight compared to the glory of the risen day. If this teaching of Christ be not reverently borne in mind we shall be constantly tempted to that treatment of the Old Testament which runs through whole commentaries, and which, by the straining of words and the invention of hypotheses, aims at concealing all semblance of difference between the tone of a Moses and of a St. John, or between the degree of enlightenment in the moral conduct of a Jael or a Mary of Bethany. Nothing but confusion and retrogression can come of the attempt to elevate the imperfect conceptions of early Judaism to the dignity of Gospel morality. Scripture has itself made clear to us, in words as plain as it is possible to utter, that the degree both of religion and morality which was vouchsafed to the patriarchs was altogether inferior to that which has been granted to us.

It cannot be too distinctly understood that we are free to judge from the standpoint of Christianity every page and every verse of the Old Testament which falls below the rule which Christ set forth. If dark deeds are ascribed to God's command, we, who know that He is of purer eyes than to behold iniquity, can only suppose that, to the defective knowledge of them of old time, those deeds appeared to be in accordance with His will. Nothing can be regarded by us as the message of God which the Spirit of the Son of God has taught us to reject and to condemn.

We must finally repudiate the notion, assumed by the Rabbis and blindly accepted by Christians, that a deed must be right if it was done by a Samuel or a David, and recorded without express condemnation.

The method generally adopted was the method of allegorising. The practice began among the later Jews when they found that there were many things in their Scriptures which could not be successfully defended from the taunts of heathen adversaries.

This was the method adopted by the learned and estimable Jewish philosopher Philo.

He had accepted, not from Scripture but from the Greek philosophers, and especially from Plato, the opinion that inspiration annihilated the activity of the human faculties; and he had fallen under the Eastern Manichean influences which regarded all matter, and therefore the human body, as essentially evil.[1] He thought therefore that there could be no real intercommunion between the divine and the human, and that God could only reveal Himself to man by sinking him into a state of trance and by absorbing the whole soul in such a way as to leave no element of imperfection in the messages which He communicated.

This theory was purely heathen. Nothing which resembled it was to be found in the Bible itself. The Biblical writers make no such claim for ninety-nine hundredths of their utterances. The phrase 'Thus saith the Lord' had no such meaning. It was the common formula of all prophets, and attentive examination shows that the phrase

---

[1] Yet he did not confine inspiration to Scripture, but thought it attainable by good men (*De Cherub.* § 14); himself claims θεοληπτεῖσθαι, and says that every good man is a prophet (*Quis rer. div. hær.* § 52; *De Migr. Abr.* iii. 426; *De Somniis*, ii. etc. See Gfrörer, *Philo*, i. 59, and comp. Ecclus. xxiv. 33, 1. 28.

was simply the natural expression of sincerity and conviction. The voice from heaven which spoke to them was addressed to their own consciences.

No prophet intended to intimate that he had heard the *articulate utterances* of the Eternal, but every true prophet believed that he spoke in accordance with that which the Spirit of the Eternal had revealed. He said 'Thus saith the Lord' whenever he felt himself commissioned to deliver to his people the highest conclusions to which he believed that God had led his thoughts. The Hebrew prophets knew nothing of the notion that they only arrived at truth by the obliteration of their human faculties.[1]

Gradually, however, the fetish-worship to which a faithless religionism constantly tends, and man's vain desire for some infallible authority on all the questions which surround his life, robbed the Jews of the blessed truth that man may hold *constant* communion with his Father in heaven, and substituted for it the hard, mechanical notion that God had put a Book in His own place, and that this Book was a sort of magical amulet which they must surround with artificial reverence. Instead of regarding their Bible as a number of books written for men by men who —though their knowledge was partial and their illumination imperfect—were yet to a high degree under the guidance of God, they gradually described it as a Book altogether supernatural. Philo put the finishing touch to their theories in his Platonic hypothesis, which contradicted alike the plain indications of the Old Testament. 'The spirits of the prophets,' says St. Paul, 'are subject to the prophets.'[2]

Philo applied his alien and baseless theory especially to

---

[1] St. Chrysostom truly says, ὁ δὲ προφήτης . . . εἰδὼς ἃ φθέγγεταί φησιν ἅπαντα (*Hom. xxix. in Ep. ad Cor.*).   [2] 1 Cor. xiv. 32.

the Law, and he identified the Law with the Five Books
of Moses. Of the origin, history, and composite character
of those books he knew nothing. Enough indeed of traditional knowledge was still extant to have told him that the
Pentateuch could never have been 'written' by Moses in its
present form. He could hardly have been unaware that
the Samaritan Pentateuch differed from the Hebrew,[1] and
the Greek translation from both. The Jewish admission
that the Five Books had been 'edited' or even 'written'
by Ezra must have been known to him. It needed no
great acumen to detect the traces of legislative change, the
tessellation of differing documents, and the variations of
literary style. It required a straining even of Philo's
theories to suppose that Moses had penned the record of
his own death. But if he chose to overlook or ignore all
other phenomena, he found enough in the 'Books of Moses'
to show the unsuitability, if not the blasphemy, of asserting
that every word in them had been 'dictated by God.'

Some way of getting over this difficulty was indispensable if his theory was to be saved: and he found the means
ready to his hand. It was the method of 'allegory,' by
which, whenever he chose, he could ignore the literal story,
or the actual expressions, and arbitrarily extort from them
some meaning which he exalted as the 'spiritual' or
'mystic' sense, but with which the actual narratives never
had the remotest connection.[2] His Platonism is anti-

---

[1] The Jewish scholar Geiger has decidedly proved that the text of
the Pentateuch has been in many places modified. The oldest of the
writings which may be classed as 'Talmudic'—the Book of Jubilees
—which was perhaps collected about fifty years before Christ, in
dealing with the main chronology of the patriarchs, and in other
points, agreed with the Samaritan rather than with the Hebrew text
of the Pentateuch (Nöldeke, *l.c.* p. 351).

[2] From the LXX word for 'cakes' (ἐγκρυφίας, Ex. xii. 34) is deduced

5

Judaic—for the Rabbis said, 'Scripture goes not beyond its plain meaning.' The Haggadic formula, 'Read not thus, but thus,' was applied in a quite different way.

This method was equally heathen in its origin with the theory which it was adopted to support. There was not in the Hebrew Scriptures anywhere, and least of all in the Books of Moses, the faintest trace of any such right to 'allegorise' their meaning. But the Stoic philosophers among the Greeks had been confronted with much the same difficulty as that which perplexed Philo and his predecessors among the Alexandrian Jews. The poems of Homer were to the Greeks a sacred book; yet they contained passages about the gods which the Stoics felt to be unworthy and degrading, though they had inflicted no shock on the ruder consciousness of earlier ages. The Stoics got rid of these difficulties by saying that Homer wrote 'allegorically;' in other words, that he said one thing when he meant something entirely different.[1] In this way they had read all sorts of fine moral meaning into the crude glad mythology, and the simple sensuous pas-

---

the duty of esoteric teaching! He calls this explanation a great mystery, *De Sacr. Abel. et Caini* (ed. Mangey, i. 174). This fancy is borrowed by Clem. Alex. *Strom.* v. 694, and St. Ambrose, *De Abrah.* i. 5. For more details see my Bampton Lectures (*Hist. of Interpretation*, pp. 22, 23, 127–158).

[1] The word 'allegory' is derived from ἄλλο ἀγορεύειν, 'to say something else than what is really said.' Socrates, when asked for a solution of the difficulty about an ancient Homeric myth, was content to say, 'The wise are doubtful,' and that he, for his part, had no time for such inquiries. For Philo's views of 'ecstatic trance' see *Quis rer. div. hær.* (*Opp.* ed. Mangey, i. 508), *Quod a Deo mittantur somnia* (id. p. 689), *De Mose* (id. p. 124), *De Spec. legg.* (id. p. 343). For his views and illustrations of allegory see *De Abrahamo* (id. p. 9 sqq.), *De Decem Oraculis* (id. p. 180), and *De Legum Allegoriis, passim.* —Orig. c. *Cels.* iv. 48.

sionate poetry, of an early age. Heracleides of Pontus had reduced their allegorical methods into a system, in a book still extant, 'On the Allegories of Homer.' Philo had read this book, and he found that some previous Jewish writers, now for the most part forgotten, had utilised the hint of the Stoics and applied it to the difficulties of the Law. By the use of this potent alchemy the facts which ought to have proved to Philo the impossibility of his theories of inspiration evaporated at a touch. He borrowed a heathen method to maintain a heathen hypothesis, and thus succeeded in blinding himself to the most obvious facts.

Philo's theory and his method were, however, adopted by many of his countrymen, and were inherited by Christian teachers as a disastrous legacy from the Jewish Church.[1] They were unfortunately accepted by the great and many-sided Christian teacher Origen of Alexandria, and owing to the spell of his learning and genius they exercised an immense influence for many centuries.[2] But

---

[1] In the earliest known New Testament commentary, that of the Gnostic Heracleon on St. John (c. A.D. 170), 'the allegorical method is already full blown' (Sanday, p. 39).

[2] Origen's principles of exegesis were, however, more elaborate than Philo's. He was the practical inventor of the 'threefold sense.' In confirmation of this he referred to Prov. xxii. 20, 'Have I not written unto thee excellent things?' where the Septuagint and Vulgate, following a very doubtful reading, render $\kappa\alpha\grave{\iota}\ \sigma\grave{\upsilon}\ \delta\grave{\epsilon}\ \mathring{\alpha}\pi\acute{o}\gamma\rho\alpha\psi\alpha\iota$ $\alpha\mathring{\upsilon}\tau\grave{\alpha}\ \tau\rho\iota\sigma\sigma\tilde{\omega}\varsigma$ ('Ecce descripsi tibi *tripliciter*,' Vulg.). Even if the reading were correct, there is no reference whatever to any system of interpretation. It would be difficult to find a parallel, even in the misuse of Scripture, for a more amazingly irrelevant inference, founded on a more completely misinterpreted fragment of a text! See Origen, *De Principiis*, iv. § 11; see too *C. Cels.* iv. 43–51, v. 47–60. We find that the pagans already ridiculed the allegorising of Scripture. And this 'threefold sense' was afterwards made fourfold, and every text or story had to be interpreted 'literally, allegorically,

they did not pass without challenge.   One leading Father
wrote a book against the notion that the Prophets only
spoke in a trance, and the theories of verbal dictation and
allegorical meaning were rejected by the soundest and
most learned Christian exegetes, the representatives of the
great School of Antioch.   As late as the ninth century a
Church writer (840) decidedly rejected, and even ridiculed,
the notion that the words used by the sacred writers were
the veritable vocables of God.

Let us show the narcotic spell exercised by this baseless
hypothesis, and by the fatal facility of imaginary interpretations to which it inevitably led.

In a Jewish book called the 'Lekach Tobh' we are told
that all the Law is of equal value from 'I am thy Lord'
(Ex. xx. 2) to 'Timna was the concubine of Eliphaz' (Gen.
xxxvi. 12); and that Moses wrote down completely from
the mouth of Jehovah the whole Law, from 'In the beginning' (Gen. i. 1) to 'all Israel' (Deut. xxxiv. 12).

Rabbi Aqiba said that there was a mystic meaning in
every letter, tittle, and flourish of every letter in Scripture,
just as in every fibre of an ant's foot or a gnat's wing; and
R. Eliezer says that he taught 300 laws based on the text
'A witch shall not live.'[1]

Quenstedt, whom we choose as a type of the post-Reformation dogmatists, says, 'Scripture is the infallible fountain of truth, and is free from all error; everything and

tropologically, and anagogically' according to the old mediæval
jingle—

> Littera gesta docet; quid credas Allegoria;
> Moralis quid agas; quo tendas Anagogia.

For full details on this whole subject see my *Hist. of Interpretation*,
Bampton Lectures, pp. 276–300.

[1] Compare *Sanhedrin*, p. 68, 1; Hershon, *Talm. Miscellany*, p. 261.

each thing in it, whether dogmatic or moral or historic, &c., is most true.'

The celebrated Puritan divine John Owen held that 'the Scriptures of the Old and New Testament were immediately and entirely given out by God Himself, His mind being in them represented unto us without the least intervening of such mediums and ways as were capable of giving change or alteration to the least iota or syllable.'[1] And again, 'Nor is it enough to satisfy us that the doctrines mentioned are preserved entire; every little iota of the Word of God must come under our consideration as being one book from God.'[2]

The late Dean Burgon, not content with asserting the supernaturalness of every book, every chapter, every verse, and every word of the Bible, declared—with nonsensical rhetoric—that 'even every letter' of the Bible was divinely inspired.

Such views we reject. They are disproved by history, philosophy, and criticism; they are burdensome to the reason and repugnant to the conscience.

The teachers who held these views were compelled to deal, on the most absurd principles, with passages which on the face of them were morally imperfect; with stories which Pascal describes as unbecoming; with apparent discrepancies; with distinct contradictions; with duplicate and varying narratives; with untenable chronologies; with details which sometimes seemed to be erroneous, trivial, or unjust. To get rid of phenomena which disproved their theory they had to invent the assertion that all such things were allegories, or to maintain that principles irreconcilably opposed to each other were equally expressive of the Will of God.

---

[1] *The Divine Original &c. of Scripture.*   [2] *Works,* xvi. 303.

Thus Philo, whenever he finds anything in the letter of
the Law which he admits to be 'abject, untrue, contradictory, or derogatory to God,' still maintains his mechanical theory by inventing a set of rules half Rabbinic and
half Stoic. Nothing was easier for him than complete
misrepresentation of all that the Books of Moses mean,
when he started with the assumption that 'the whole or
the greatest part of the legislation is allegorical.' Such
an opinion led him to strange lengths of freedom. 'It
would,' he said, 'be a sign of great simplicity to think that
the world was created in six days, or at all in time!' 'To
take literally the words "God planted a garden in Eden"
is impiety. Let no such fabulous nonsense ever enter our
minds.' Yet so vague and varying is the view of Philo,
that, though he uses these strong expressions about the
letter of Scripture, he tells a story of the condign vengeance
of God upon an offender who scoffed at a minute Scriptural
allusion.[1]

Similarly Origen, insisting—like so many of the Fathers
and Christian interpreters down to recent times—upon a
complete misinterpretation of the verse 'The letter killeth,
but the spirit giveth life,' elaborated his system of the
threefold sense of all Scripture, which reduced its exposition to a sort of divination. This text furnishes us with
another salient instance of the mischief which results from
the old atomistic method, which, in defiance of Scripture
itself, treated Scripture as a congeries of separate supernatural utterances homogeneously inspired and spiritually
equipollent. And since this text has been so enormously
misapplied, we may well pause to ask, The letter killeth—

---

[1] *De Mutat. Nom.* 8. The scoffer was jesting at the change of names,
Abraham and Sarah : but τῆς φρενοβλαβείας . . . ἔδωκε τὴν ἁρμόζουσαν
δίκην . . . ἐπ᾿ ἀγχόνην ἦξεν.

what? The letter killeth—*whom?* Is *all* literal interpretation, then, murderous? If so, why is it ever permissible, and when? And if, in the sense of the Fathers and Schoolmen, the letter kills, why was it not made as vivifying as the Spirit? The real meaning of the text is wholly different. It means that *the letter of the Mosaic law threatened death to those who disobeyed it*, while the Spirit of the Gospel offers life to all who accept it. The phrase made not the faintest reference to the literal or the so-called 'spiritual' meaning of Scripture, though, isolated from its context and its true significance, it was used for seventeen hundred years as the chief 'proof' of the duty and necessity of allegorising Scripture! What connection is there between the laws of exegesis and the statement that the written enactment of Moses punishes disobedience with death?[1] The 'letter' which thus killed was nevertheless meant to be quite literally understood. But Origen's remarks show how little he apprehends the true significance of Scripture. How, he asks, could hearers possibly be edified by the trivialities of Leviticus or Numbers? How could God have given minute regulations about fat and leaven? How could He have said that Abraham betrayed the chastity of his wife? How could He have justified bloody wars or fierce imprecations? The Scripture (he thinks) enweaves into its narrative some things which have never happened, and which in part could not have happened. In all these things we must seek a meaning worthy of the mind of God. How can it possibly advantage any one to read about the drunkenness of Noah?[2] or about

---

[1] See Rom. viii. 8–13.

[2] Strange that Origen, misled by the spirit of system, should have failed to see the profound moral significance of the story of Noah's degrading fall!

Jacob and his wives and concubines? or about the horrid incest of Lot? or about the foul story of Judah and Tamar? All these things, he says, are not facts but 'mystic economies.'[1] He denied their literal truth, or ignored it as something unimportant. 'Where the subject matter involves either turpitude or impossibility,' says St. Jerome, 'we are passed over to higher things;' and 'the paltriness of the letter sends us back to the preciousness of the spiritual sense.'[2]

Let us take the Venerable Bede as another instance of the results which spring from an exaggerated theory of Inspiration necessitating a sham principle of exegesis. 'What is it,' he asks, 'to us monks to be told that Elkanah had two wives? If we only draw such "old things" as the literal sense out of Scripture, we get no spiritual doctrine; but when we understand it allegorically, Elkanah is our Lord and his two wives are the synagogue and the Church'! So far as this is offered as an *interpretation* of the meaning of the Book of Samuel, we can only say that it is pure nonsense. It makes Scripture 'profitable' by attributing to it a sense with which its words have nothing to do. It reduces large sections of the Bible to a mere *abracadabra* to be manipulated by the inventiveness or the self-interest of ignorant interpreters.

So Sixtus Senensis, the author of the once celebrated 'Bibliotheca Sancta,' asks, 'What does it help us to know the wars and seditions of the ancient Jews?' and he makes this a potent argument for the allegoric system. The question shows how radical was that misconception of

---

[1] See Origen, *De Principiis*, iv. §§ 9–27; c. *Cels.* iv. 48; where abundant illustrations will be found. Comp. Aug. *De doctr. Christ.* iii. 10.

[2] See his Commentary on Hosea.

the historic significance of Scripture which had become stereotyped for nearly a thousand years. Under such methods the exquisite human interest of Scripture is evaporated at a touch, leaving a thin residuum of hollow unreality. A specimen or two more, out of the myriads which encumber whole volumes of Fathers, Schoolmen, and Commentators, may suffice to show the reader the extravagances which result from an indiscriminate and unauthorised extension of the allegorical method to passages of which the real meaning is simple and obvious.

Philo's own method of dealing with Scripture, from which all these streams of impossible exegesis derived their ultimate origin, may be judged of from the following instances :

i. 'God did not rain upon the earth.' This implies that God did not shed the perceptions of things upon the senses ! [1]

ii. *Er* means leather, *i.e.* the leathern mass which covers us, *i.e.* the body.[2] Hence the slaying of Er means that goodness condemns the body to death !

iii. 'With my staff I passed over this Jordan.'

Philo is by no means content to understand the verse literally. Jordan means 'baseness;' the staff means 'temperance;' and Jacob intends to say that by discipline he has risen above baseness.[3]

iv. Now let us pass over two centuries and hear one of Origen's allegorical explanations of the New Testament. One will more than suffice. He is explaining (?) the remark of John the Baptist, 'whose shoe's latchet I am not worthy to unloose,' an allusion which requires no more ex-

---

[1] *De Mund. Opif.* (*Opp.* i. 30); *De Legg. Allegg.* (*id.* pp. 47, 68).

[2] *De Post. Cain.* (*Opp.* ed. Mangey, i. 260).

[3] *De Profugis* (*Opp.* ed. Mangey, i. 568); *De Nom. Mut.* (*id.* p. 598).

planation to the simplest reader than the ordinary phrase
'I am not fit to untie his shoe.' But an explanation so
transparently obvious does not satisfy Origen. 'I think,'
he says, 'that one of the shoes is the Incarnation, when the
Son of God assumes flesh and blood, and the descent into
Hades, whatever Hades may be.'[1]

v. Now pass over fifteen centuries and come to Swedenborg. '"*And Rebecca arose*"—hereby is signified an elevation of the affection of truth—"*and her damsels*"—hereby
are signified subservient affections—"*and they rode upon
camels*"—hereby is signified the intellectual principle elevated above natural scientifics.'[2]

Philo and Origen and Swedenborg were great and good
men, worthy of all our reverence. Nevertheless, the common sense of all except the blindest leaders of the blind
has long ago flung such lines of interpretation to the moles
and to the bats. A modern commentator who ventured
to offer such exegesis would make himself the laughing-
stock of Christendom; and yet the manner in which
some modern commentators deal with Scripture needs a
rejection hardly less decisive. Let us, by way of example,
turn to Bishop Wordsworth's remarks on the murder of
Sisera by Jael. Taking the narrative as it stands, we see
that the Bedouin chieftainess, whose tribe was at peace
with Jabin, King of Canaan, seizing the opportunity of the
defeat of his general, Sisera, and feeling no touch of pity
for him in his hour of misfortune, treacherously enticed
him into her own woman's-tent, offered him the sacred
pledges of protection and hospitality (*dakheel*), and promised, at his request, to lie to his pursuers. Next she lulled

---

[1] Origen, *Hom. in Joann.* vi. §§ 18, 23. (Delarue, iv. 134, 139.)

[2] Swedenborg's *Arcana Cœlestia* (quoted by Rev. R. Heber Newton,
The Right and Wrong Uses of the Bible, p. 113).

him to sleep, and, while he lay under her protection in
weary slumber, brutally dashed out his brains with the
tent-peg. She then exultantly proclaimed her treacherous
and bloody deed. It would be absurd to judge this ignorant daughter of a savage epoch by any modern or Christian standard. She may have been impelled by blind
instincts of patriotism which seemed to her to transcend
all the sanctions which otherwise her race regarded as
the most divine. But to laud her murderous deed as
exemplary; to invent a Divine suggestion as having
inspired her ferocity; to invest it with a miraculous character by the strained interpretation of a word; and, finally,
to compare this wild murderess to the Virgin Mary—as is
done by the Bishop—is to adopt a method which has often
been abused by casuistry into opinions which are ultimately
fatal not only to the claims of Scripture but to all honesty
and all morality, and which have been a curse to the
human race. The deed of Jael is but an illustration of
the truth that ' the times of this ignorance God winked at '
(R.V. ' overlooked '), ' but now commandeth all men everywhere to repent.' [1] The story can only profit us by kindling a spirit of gratitude that, in past days, darkness
covered the earth, but the true light has now shined. It
is right to say that Jael must only be judged according to
her lights, and that no one thinks of condemning her as
though she had the remotest conception of the morality of
the Gospel. But it is false to pretend that her deed was
anything but an act of wild and deceitful revenge. The
praise of Deborah, even if it be rightly interpreted into a
moral commendation, is infinitely less authoritative than
the eternal voice of conscience and of the moral law.
Plato taught us many centuries ago that the inevitable

<hr>

[1] Acts xvii. 30.

difficulties of ancient religious literature should in no way be suffered to interfere with moral growth. In his 'Phædrus' we find this striking passage:

'I beseech you to tell me, Socrates,' said Phædrus, 'do you believe this tale?'

'The wise are doubtful,' answered Socrates, 'and I should not be singular if, like them, I also doubted. I might have a rational explanation. There is a discrepancy, however, about the locality. Now I quite acknowledge that these allegories are very nice, but he is not to be envied who has to invent them, and when he has once begun he must go on and rehabilitate centaurs and chimæras dire . . . and numberless other inconceivable and portentous monsters. . . . I say farewell to all this.'[1]

If any choose to maintain the equable and plenary inspiration of the Bible in all its parts they must defend their idol by such means as their conscience permits against the assaults of atheists and the perplexities of Christians. But no one is bound by the Christian verity or the Catholic religion to adopt any such theory. Any Christian may repudiate alike the theory and the scheme of impossible misinterpretation invented to disguise its most flagrant difficulties. Whatever explanation may be offered of the perplexities presented by some parts of Scripture, the fallacious extension of allegory must be rejected as a mere subterfuge.[2]

---

[1] See Jowett's *Translation of the Dialogues*, ii. 106.

[2] In spite of Cardinal Newman's most rash and untenable assertion that 'the mystical interpretation and orthodoxy will stand or fall together' (*Ess. on Development*, p. 344), it was rejected by the School of Antioch (by far the greatest exegetes among the Fathers) and first adopted by the Gnostics. Its excesses are strongly condemned by Eustathius, Basil, Epiphanius, Augustine, Chrysostom, and even by Irenæus (i. 1. 5), and Tertullian (*c. Marc.* iv. 19: Sem-

per hæretici . . . nudas et simplices voces conjecturis quo volunt rapiunt). Mr. Chase, who quotes these and other passages (*Chrysostom as an Interpreter*, p. 60), also quotes the condemnation of 'this deluding art, . . . which maketh of anything what it listeth,' by Hooker (*Eccl. Pol.* V. lix. 2); and by Fuller (*Pisgah Sight*, iii. 2, § 7), 'Is not this rather *lusus* than *illusio?* Such grainless husks, when threshed out, vanish all into chaff.'

CHAPTER V

THE BIBLE IS NOT HOMOGENEOUS IN ITS MORALITY.

'Those points that are necessary God hath made plain; those that are not plain, not necessary.'—Bp. ANDREWES, *Sermon III. on the Nativity.*

'And here I must tell you a great and needful truth, which ignorant Christians, fearing to confess, by overdoing, tempt men to infidelity. The Scripture is like a man's body, where some parts are but for the preservation of the rest, and may be maimed without death; the sense is the soul of Scripture, the latter but the body or vehicle.'—BAXTER, *Catechising of Families,* ch. vi.

SINCE Christ Himself taught us that the morality of the Gospel is infinitely in advance of the morality of the Law,[1] ought we not to apply the principle which He laid down?

i. There are certain Psalms known as the Imprecatory Psalms, which are partly explained away in a non-natural sense, and partly defended by elaborate systems of casuistry. But will any one pretend that the same spirit is breathed by the sweet childlike trustfulness of the 23rd and 91st Psalms, and the sweeping curses of the 59th and 109th? In the blessing pronounced on those who should take the little children of the Babylonians and dash them against the stones, are we to see a supernaturally dictated sentiment of Divine morality, or are we to detect a fierce

[1] Matt. v. 43, 44, xix. 8, &c.

utterance of Jewish hatred which directly contradicts the noble exhortation of Jeremiah?[1] Could it ever have been right for any men, under any circumstances, to pray a prayer so utterly antichristian in spirit as 'let the iniquity of his father be had in remembrance, and let not the sin of his mother be done away'? or 'let there be none to pity him, or to have compassion on his fatherless children'? In the bitterest of these Psalms (cix.) an attempt has been made to represent these awful curses as being the curses of David's enemies, against which he prays. But of what avail is this palliation for Psalms xxxv. lxix. cxl. and others? Can the casuistry be anything but gross which would palm off such passages as the very utterance of God? In such a passage as Psalm lxviii. 22, 23, are we to suppose that the Lord actually said to the Israelites that He would bring them again from Bashan 'that their feet might be dipped in the blood of their enemies, and the tongue of their dogs be red through the same'? Is there no difference between the spirit of this clause and that of Psalm lxvii. 1, 2, 'God be merciful unto us and bless us . . . that Thy way may be known upon earth, Thy saving health among all nations'? One thing is certain; without 'divine imbreathings and aspirations' in our own hearts we shall never understand the true spirit of the Scriptures. We may make of them a mass of propositions; we may torture out of them a dialectic system; we may petrify them into a heap of missiles to hurl at our opponents; but to the proud, bitter, and narrow soul they cease to be a field of manna strewn with the bread of life.

'The popular religion of the day,' it has been said, 'is still full of crude and unassimilated errors which nominally survive, although in practice they have been rendered

<hr>

[1] Jer. xxix. 7.

comparatively innocuous by the selective instinct of common sense. A pseudo-reverence is often the worst stumbling-block in the path of religious progress, and, among men's religious conceptions, childish prepossessions, obsolete ethics, vulgar superstitions, and scientific absurdities often seem to have an equal and sacred right of citizenship. Absolutely inconsistent and mutually destructive beliefs lie side by side in men's creeds like the lion and the lamb of Isaiah's prophecy.' And the curious thing is that the maintenance of worthless survivals is often made an excuse for spiritual conceit and savage anathemas. There are many with whom 'the childish following of Scripture is apt to stand in a huge delight in their favourite scraps of the sacred text, and their favourite blunders of interpretation.' But religion has nothing to do with the maintenance of such opinions; it must be based on that love of truth, and that faith in the God of Truth, which refuses to be tied down to views which the voice of God in History, Science, Reason, and Conscience, has convicted of falsity or error.

ii. We are told of the Ten Commandments that God spake them; and according to Deut. v. 22 'He added no more.' We regard Moses as a great lawgiver and a great prophet; but are we to defend the divinity of passages so morally indefensible as that which directs that a man is not to be punished for smiting his slave, male or female, if only the slave survives for a day or two—'for he is his money'?[1] or can we, as honest men, possibly suppose that such a passage as Deut. xxi. 10–14 was dictated by God? or, again, such a verse as Deut. xiv. 21, 'Ye shall not eat of anything that dieth of itself: thou shalt give it unto the stranger that is in thy gates, that he may eat it; or thou

<hr>

[1] Ex. xxi. 21, 22.

mayest sell it unto an alien.' We may admit that slavery was for a time a tolerated curse; but is it a special proof of piety to regard it, on the authority of Exodus, as a sacred institution? May it not be profitable to remind ourselves of the Indian proverb, 'The holy fire is beaten with hammers if it allies itself with iron'?

iii. In Num. xxxi. 1–18 it is said that Moses, in God's name, bade the Israelites to exterminate the people of Midian. In obedience to this command they 'slew all the males,' but after burning up the cities and appropriating the cattle, they took captive 'all the women of Midian and their little ones.' Thereupon Moses is angry with them, and indignantly asks them, 'Have ye saved all the women alive?' and then, on the ground that heathen women had tempted Israel to sin, he says 'Now therefore kill every male among the little ones, and kill every woman that hath known man. But all the women children that have not known a man . . . keep alive for yourselves.' This is done; and, next, Moses is represented as bidding those who in cold blood carried out this ghastly massacre of women and innocent children to go through certain ceremonial purifications! And the Israelites saved '*for them-selves*' 32,000 virgins (xxxi. 35). If the voice of History sternly condemns the Athenians for their conduct to Scione, Torone, and Melos, are we not to condemn the Jews for their conduct towards the kindred people of Midian? Was that laudable in the Jew which we denounce as execrable in the Athenian? Can we really regard as exemplary the worse than 'Armenian atrocities,' the worse than Sicilian Vespers, which they inflicted on their enemies when they massacred 75,000 of them, as narrated in the Book of Esther? Even if this be not history but Haggadah, can we approve the narration of it with evident satisfaction?

6

'It is,' says Professor Sanday, 'out of the question to say that the Book of Esther is wholly filled with the Spirit of God, and the Book of Wisdom wholly devoid of it.'

Fall back, if you can, on the miserable pleas which have sometimes been urged in favour of the righteousness of the wars of extermination; but if a single word be said in their palliation, can it also excuse the cold-blooded butchery of captive women and innocent little ones, and the retention of others to be slaves and concubines?[1] To the Israelites, it may be that such things did not seem guilty and horrible. If the record be literal history the Israelites may have believed, in their moral ignorance, that by such deeds they were pleasing God and obeying His commands. If such horrors could be recorded without blame—perhaps centuries after the date at which they were supposed to have happened—it is too easy to see that they might have been perpetrated without consciousness of guilt. If so, what does this prove except that the moral views of the desert tribes on such subjects were in this respect very rudimentary?

It is needless to multiply illustrations. The defence of religious truth is in no wise concerned with such passages as these. We condemn them as energetically as any by whom they have been held up to execration. They are in the Bible, and the Bible contains all things necessary to salvation; and the final teaching of the Bible represents the loftiest summits which have been reached by the wings of the purest moral aspiration. But neither these passages, nor any like them, represent to us the true nature and significance of the Bible. We read them as history only. Their instructiveness depends on the warnings and the con-

[1] This subject will be touched upon more fully in ch. xiv. As to the demonstrated impossibility of the *numbers*, I say nothing.

trasts which they involve. In that sense, and that alone, they are profoundly instructive. They prove how slow, in many particulars, was the development of the religious consciousness of mankind. Even in Jeremiah (xlviii. 10), in a denunciation of Moab, we read 'Cursed be he that keepeth back his sword from blood.'

iv. The same remarks apply to some details in the narratives of Abraham, of Jacob, of Jephthah, of David, of many more. The use made of them in the sceptical propaganda is often illegitimate. The Jewish records never intended to represent the patriarchs and kings as faultless. The deceitfulness of Abraham, of Isaac, of Jacob, is narrated, but their *general* faithfulness is rightly held up to admiration as our example. That they were faultless was never maintained even by the Rabbis, till Rabbinic exegesis had sunk to its lowest dregs of folly and falsehood.[1] Many things are narrated in the Bible without blame, as they are in the poems of Homer and other ancient writings, to which there was nevertheless no intention of giving any colour of approval. Supposing it to be admitted that Abraham, in the infancy of religious knowledge, believed that he was bidden by God to offer a human sacrifice : we learn from the sequel of the story it was the will of God to prove once for all that such sacrifices are to be for ever condemned.

v. We see from Scripture itself that the impulse to the same act may, from different points of view, be attributed indifferently to God and to Satan. Thus in the Book of Samuel (2 Sam. xxiv. 1) we are told that '*God tempted David*' to number the people. In the Chronicles (1 Chr.

---

[1] 'Whoever says that Reuben, the sons of Samuel, David, and Solomon sinned, as appears at first sight in Scripture, is decidedly in error.' *Sanhedrin*, ff. 55. 5 (Hershon, *Genesis*, p. 177).

xxi. 1) we are told that *Satan* tempted him. To a Jew there would not seem to be any violent contradiction in such language, because the Jews referred everything to the permission and will of God to such an extent that the Prophet Isaiah does not hesitate to use such language as ' I make peace *and create evil.'* [1] Nevertheless, such phrases must not lead us to forget the truth so plainly set forth by St. James. ' Let no man say when he is tempted, "I am tempted of God," for God cannot be tempted with evil, neither tempteth He any man.' From Lev. xxvii. 28, 29 we see 'that human sacrifices offered to Jehovah were possible to the Hebrews after the time of Moses without meeting check or censure from the teachers or leaders of the nation.'[2] What does this prove except that the conceptions of the nation of serfs who escaped out of Egypt, and of their descendants, continued to be lower in that particular than we could have imagined possible ?

vi. Supposing, again, that Jephthah really burnt his daughter in accordance with his vow, what bearing has that fact on the morality of the Bible as a whole ? Can there be the shadow of a pretence that the Bible holds up his example to our imitation, or does anything more than narrate his wild and pathetic story ? What was Jephthah but a rude, ignorant, half-heathen freebooter who was an instrument in the hands of God to effect His purposes ? It may be that the tradition of the Jews is true; that Phinehas was the priest who offered this human sacrifice, and that the horror of it so roused the indignation of the people that the High Priest was driven from his office. This would account for the priesthood being transferred to the House of Ithamar, the younger branch of the House

---

[1] Is. xlv. 7; compare Amos iii. 6.
[2] See Kalisch, *ad loc.*

of Aaron, in whose hands, without reason assigned, we find it for a long period of years until the older line was restored in the person of Zadok. It is said that Idomeneus, the Homeric king of Crete, in exactly the same way vowed, in the peril of a great storm, that he would sacrifice the first thing that met him if he was saved. He was met by his eldest son, and slew the youth in accordance with his vow. But Crete was at once plunged in ruinous civil war, and Idomeneus was driven from his kingdom by the indignation of his subjects. Why should we suppose that the religion of the half-caste Gileadite outlaw was in this respect superior to that of the grey-haired Cretan king? And if history have any lesson at all, why should this story, with its many touches of redeeming nobleness, have been obliterated from those early annals of an anarchic time? In the deliverance which he wrought for his nation, Jephthah was one of the 'heroes of faith;' but does this imply that he was a model for us in any other respect? Was not Samson, too, one of the heroes of faith? Yet his life was stained for years with every species of sensuality and folly.

vii. Or take the life of David, the favourite hunting-field for those who, in ignorance of what the Bible is, desire on false principles to hold it up to ridicule. This was exactly what the Prophet Nathan foresaw, when he told David that his sins would cause the enemies of the Lord to blaspheme. The Scripture narrative does not gloss over David's crimes. It tells us of his duplicity, of his adultery, of his murder, of his cruelty: and 'this,' say the scoffers, 'is your man after God's own heart'! Now that phrase, like thousands which are currently quoted from the Bible, is entirely misapplied. David is not called in the abstract 'a man after God's own heart;' [1] but is described

1 Sam. xiii. 14; Ps. lxxxix. 20; Acts xii. 22.

in that expression as a king who would accomplish, better than Saul had done, the task for which he was appointed. His errors, like those at which we have been glancing, were more the vices of his age than of the man. Neither his own conscience nor the conscience of his day would condemn him for deceiving Achish; or for having several wives; or for putting the Ammonites under saws and harrows of iron; or even perhaps for recommending Joab and Shimei to the vengeance of his son. He did indeed commit crimes of the most heinous dye, which were seen to be such both by himself and by his people; and for these he repented with a bitter repentance. When a man has repented with all his heart, is he to be taunted with his former sins as though they expressed his real nature or his final condition? Would it be fair to call St. Augustine a thief, a liar, and a debauchee because of the offences of his hot and evil youth? David is our model, not in his wickedness, but in his self-abasement; not in his unworthy fall and failure, but in his devotion, his magnanimity, his conquest over his worst passions, his sense of God's presence, his many impulses of chivalric nobleness. We have in his story an unvarnished narrative, and its straightforwardness makes it all the more instructive. To pretend that he is represented as 'the man after God's own heart' in the sense that his evil deeds were approved, is wilfully to distort the meaning of a fragmentary clause.

viii. It is so necessary to be honest and truthful about these questions, and such deadly evils are resulting from the silence by which men shirk them, that I will next refer to what seems to me the most dubious and dreadful transaction which stains the troubled annals of David's reign.

The kingdom had been devastated by three years'

famine, and David, probably by means of the priests and their Urim and Thummim, 'inquired of the Lord.'[1] The answer which he received was, 'Blood upon Saul and upon his house,[2] because he slew the Gibeonites!' The Gibeonites were a remnant of the Canaanites, who, by trickery, had secured a sworn exemption from the Canaanite extermination and had been taken into the service of the Temple. Saul in his zeal had sought to slay them. David offers them an atonement. They decline any money ransom, and, on David's promise to do anything which they required, they demand that seven of Saul's sons should be hung up 'unto the Lord.'[3] David grants this request, and makes his selection, choosing five of the nephews of his former wife Michal,[4] and two sons of Rizpah the concubine of Saul. The seven hapless youths were slain, and impaled together on the top of the hill, and 'after that God was intreated for the land.'

What are we to make of this terrible story? Are we to regard it as a laudable human sacrifice? Are we to consider it as truly expressive of the mind and will of God?

For my part I regard it as a true fragment of the annals of David's reign, conveying exactly such lessons as are conveyed in all true history; for History, too, is a book of God. Many years ago one of our ablest judges told me that, at a gathering of working men, an intelligent artisan got up, narrated the story, and asked 'whether it was not meant to imply that God was pacified by the blood of innocent human victims?' To all appearance it *is* a story

---

[1] Lit. 'sought the face of the Lord' (2 Sam. xxi. 1).
[2] So the Septuagint reads.
[3] *I.e.* impaled or crucified in public.
[4] The true reading in 2 Sam. xxi. 8 is, 'Merab, Michal's sister' (see 1 Sam. xviii. 19). The chronicler omits the story altogether.

of human sacrifice, and one which contains some very lurid elements. It has probably been preserved out of admiration for the motherly devotion of Rizpah the daughter of Aiah, watching the corpses of Armoni and Mephibosheth—

> Her two strong sons
> Dead in the dim and lion-haunted ways.

But in what sense can it be said that it is a 'word of God' to us?

May we not find some light in dealing with such passages when we notice the peculiar forms of speech adopted in Old Testament History, and see that they are not to be pressed to extreme conclusions? Thus in 2 Sam. xxiv. 1 we read, 'And again the anger of the Lord was kindled against Israel, *and He moved David against them*, saying, Go number Israel and Judah.' Yet though the temptation is attributed to God, we read in verse 10, '*And David's heart smote him*, and he said unto the Lord, *I have sinned greatly.*'

Is it in accordance with anything which God has revealed as to His will and nature, if, taking the expressions with a literalness which does not accord with ancient and Oriental modes of phraseology, we assume that the blood of seven innocent young men, five of them in the third generation, was required to prevent Him from continuing to afflict an innocent people for the long-past crime of their dead king? 'If this would be barbarity below,' says Dr. Martineau, 'it cannot be holiness above. It would be no more possible that what would be evil in man should be good in God than that a circle on earth should be a square in heaven.'

Be this as it may, is it not quite sufficient, so far as the

Bible is concerned, to lay down the broad indisputable principle that 'belief in Divine guidance is not of necessity belief that such guidance can never be frustrated by the laxity, the infirmity, the perversity of man, alike in the domain of action and the domain of thought'?[1]

Whenever the Old Testament historians narrate certain facts about kings and Prophets, whether with or without reprobation of those deeds when they are evil, it is as true as of the whole story of the Israelites, that 'these things are written for our admonition;' and that in these things they were figures for us 'to the intent that we should not lust after evil things as they also lusted.'[2]

So that, again and again, we fall back on the proposition that the Old Testament contains some very heterogeneous elements. It is, as Heine said, 'the great family chronicle of the Jews.' We find in it 'snatches of rude song, fragments of custom-made law, tradition, history, legislation, theology, ethics, proverbs, idyls, poetry, letters—authentic, anonymous, pseudonymous—all mingled together and collected from a space of years as widely separated as the days of King Alfred from the days of Queen Victoria.' In such an anthology of fragments is it not inevitable that there should be some discrepancies and divergent points of view? Supposing, it has been said, that a man should try to represent the biography of the English people, and in order to do so should make a compilation from the fragments of Saxon sagas and Witenagemot decisions, with some paragraphs of the Venerable Bede, of Gildas, of Beowulf, some poems of Caedmon, of Walter Mapes, of Chaucer and Drayton and Skelton and Thomas

---

[1] Mr. Gladstone in the *North American Review.*
[2] 1 Cor. x. 5, 11.

Tusser, some chapters of Froissart's Chronicles, and of William of Tyre and the Gesta Dei per Francos, and the historic plays of Shakespeare, Spenser's Epithalamion, and parts of Milton and Bacon, ending with selections of Pope, Cowper, Wordsworth, Tennyson, and Browning—would it not be absurd to suppose that all would be exactly on the same level of moral insight?[1]   Yet *externally* such a collection would offer some slight analogy to the Old Testament.   And why would it not as a whole be a sacred book?   Not because the hand of God is less visible in the history of England than in that of Israel; not because the inspiration of God's Holy Spirit has been exclusively confined to the sacred writers; but because such a collection would have no truth to make known to us respecting the ways and the will of God which is not already implicitly revealed in Scripture.

The whole history of England, and of all the greatest modern nations, has been moulded and influenced by the ideas set forth in the Bible, which lays before us the record of the Divine education of the earlier race of man.   There was granted to the teachers and prophets of Israel, even before 'God spoke unto us by a Son,' a degree of illumination which, though fitful and partial, was incomparably more intense as a whole than any which is found in the greatest of pagan writers.   The literature of the Jews is far more exclusively religious than was the case in any other people   Their books are, as a whole, more sacred,

---

[1] 'Ainsi se forma . . . par le mélange des éléments les plus divers, ce conglomérat étrange où se trouvent confondus des fragments d'épopée, des débris d'histoire sainte, des articles de droit coutumier, d'anciens chants populaires, des contes de nomades, des utopies, de légendes, . . . des morceaux prophétiques.'—Renan, *Hist. du Peuple Israël*, iv. 112.

more exalted, more precious, more universal, more diffusive and penetrating, more indispensable to the human race, more 'profitable for doctrine, for reproof, for correction, for instruction in righteousness, that the man of God may be perfect, thoroughly furnished unto all good works,'[1] than any other books which the world has ever seen or known. They contain, as no other books contain, all things necessary to salvation; they reveal, as no other books reveal, the will of Heaven. Amid much which they themselves teach us to regard as transitory and imperfect, even as 'weak and beggarly,'[2] they enshrine more clearly and more authentically than any other writings the messages of God. This is true of the books of the Old Testament. It is incomparably more true of the New Testament, from which we learn the glad tidings of eternal life.

[1] 2 Tim. iii. 16.

[2] Gal. iv. 9; Rom. viii. 3; Heb. vii. 18. The line of thought in this chapter is found in not a few of the Fathers. For instance, St. Chrysostom, speaking of Ps. cxxxvii., says, exactly as I have done, *'Though these words are pregnant with rage and vengeance they are the expression of the fury of the captives. The prophets often do not speak their own mind, but represent the passions of others.'* Elsewhere he gets over the difficulty (*e.g.* in Ps. cix.) by calling it 'a prophecy in the form of a curse' (see Chase, pp. 55, 72).

CHAPTER VI

ANTITHESES OF SCRIPTURE.

'What is the straw to the wheat? saith the Lord.'—Jer. xxiii. 28.

'Amid changing interpretations (our aim is) not to add another, but to renew the original one; the meaning, that is, of the words as they first struck on the ears or flashed before the eyes of those who heard and read them.'—JOWETT.

THUS far we have spoken mainly of the Old Testament, and it would be possible indefinitely to expand the proof that it contains some elements which reflect the lower standard of rude ages, and that its moral teaching and spiritual nobleness are not on one uniform level.

It will be sufficient to touch on but one more illustration —namely, the marked difference between the Law and the Prophets; between Mosaic and Gospel principles; between Levitism and spiritual religion.

i. When we read the books of Numbers and Leviticus we can hardly wonder that Pharisees thought that the whole world 'depended on the right burning of the two kidneys and the fat.' Turn to the Prophets, and we find an almost contemptuous disparagement of the rites and sacrifices of the current ceremonialism.[1]

[1] Is. i. 11–14; Hos. vi. 6; Jer. vi. 20, vii. 21–23; Amos v. 21–24; Mic. vi. 6–8, &c. I do not quote Ezek. xx. 25, as the meaning is uncertain.

It is from among the antitheses, and even the antinomies of the Bible—which are in themselves relative and fragmentary, but are often supplementary and complementary to each other—that we must gather its final revelation.

ii. Even if we turn to the New Testament we find distinct differences in the modes of representing the truth. No one can read the Fourth Gospel after the first three without observing the impress of a different mind. The old Fathers were broadly right when they described the first three as 'bodily,' and the fourth as the 'spiritual' Gospel.

iii. Again, from the dawn of criticism, all readers have noticed the marked differences of standpoint which separate the teaching of St. James from that of St. Paul, and the teaching of St. John from that of both. There is no irreconcilable contradiction, but there is wide divergence in the method of presentation.

Luther, with the self-confidence which marked some of his utterances, said bluntly that St. Paul taught 'We are saved by faith,' and St. James 'We are saved by works,' and that it was nonsense to pretend to harmonise the two utterances. But that depends entirely on the question whether the 'faith' and the 'works' meant exactly the same thing on the lips of St. James and of St. Paul; and we know by careful examination that they did *not*.

iv. But it is when we contrast the Old Testament with the New that we perceive most fully the chasm which separates some portions of Scripture from others. We can no longer be surprised that books should have been written like the Antitheses of Marcion to set forth these apparent oppositions.

Many sects of the early heretics felt themselves so entirely unable to adjust the balances of revelation, or to understand the contrasted presentations of the Jehovah of the Hebrews and the God and Father of our Lord Jesus Christ, that they abandoned the Old Testament altogether. They represented it as the work of an inferior or even of an evil deity, whom they called the Demiurge or Creator of the World. Marcion's book was composed of texts which he regarded as irreconcilably in contradiction with each other—such as, on one side, 'An eye for an eye, and a tooth for a tooth,' and on the other, 'I say unto you, Resist not evil;' or, on one side, 'Cursed be he who keepeth back his sword from blood (of the Moabites),'[1] and on the other, 'I say unto you, Love your enemies.'

Can any amount of sophistry maintain that there is *not* an immense chasm between the spirit of the dying prayer of Zachariah the son of Jehoiada, 'The Lord look upon it and require it,' and the dying prayer of St. Stephen, 'Lord, lay not this sin to their charge'? And do we not see the chasm bridged by the prayer of Christ as He was nailed to the Cross, 'Father, forgive them, for they know not what they do'?

Marcion, by the admission of his opponents, was an able and honest man, however deeply he was mistaken. Had he and others like him been able to grasp the fact that the Old Testament contains only the record and the outcome of a multifarious, fragmentary, and progressive revelation, they might have been saved from falling into false and Manichean views.

v. But even in the Old Testament is there no difference in the point of view between 'Noah offered burnt offerings; and the Lord smelled a sweet savour, and said in His heart,

---

[1] Jer. xlviii. 10.

I will not again any more curse the ground' (Gen. viii. 21), and 'Thou desirest not sacrifice, else would I give it Thee, but Thou delightest not in burnt offerings' (Ps. li. 16); or 'Sacrifice and offering Thou didst not desire' (Ps. xl. 6)? Or between the injunctions of the Pentateuch (*e.g.* Num. xxix. 1–40) and such passages as Is. i. 11–14, Jer. vii. 21–23, Hos. vi. 6? I do not say that the points of view are wholly irreconcilable, but undoubtedly they differ.

vi. And it was strange that men did not learn from the New Testament itself the true way to remove their perplexities.

While the Rabbis were teaching that the world was only created for the sake of the Mosaic Law; that every jot and tittle of it was divinely stored with supernatural mysteries; that God Himself wore phylacteries, and daily repeated the Sh'ma—Paul was teaching, as a fundamental position of the Gospel, that the Levitic Law was typified by the bondwoman and her son who were to be cast out, and not to share with the son of the freewoman; and by 'Mount Sinai in Arabia which gendereth to bondage.' It was a ministry of the letter and of death; at the best a transitory flash, an evanescent glory.

One of the earliest sub-Apostolic writers, the author of the Epistle of Barnabas, whose book was regarded as so sacred that it is appended to the Sinaitic manuscript of the New Testament and was read aloud in public worship, was so filled with the hatred of Judaism that he went much farther than St. Paul. He argued at length that the Levitic dispensation had only been enforced upon the Jews in anger and as a positive evil; and that the practice of circumcision, which the Law commanded on pain of Divine vengeance, had never been anything but *concision*, a vile personal mutilation, into which the Jews had been misled by the deception of an evil angel.[1]

vii. But while this view was entirely false, it is extraordinary how entirely Christians have failed to grasp the Gospel teaching, that the whole Levitic Law, which had been regarded for centuries as the most sacred essence of the Old Dispensation, was imperfect, transitory, and no longer worthy of observance.[2]

It was in reliance upon this Divine estimate that Luther says, 'We will neither see nor hear of Moses; for Moses was given only to the Jewish folk, and does not extend to us Gentiles and Christians.' And again, in that sweeping tone which often sounds irreverent, 'If any one brings up Moses with his laws and will compel you to keep them, say "Go to the Jews with your Moses. I am no Jew; leave me unperplexed with Moses."'[3] With more reverence but with equal clearness the saintly Richard Baxter speaks of the Old Testament as the imperfect vehicle of a revelation as yet imperfect, 'so that faith is not injured by doubts of the truth of some words of the Old Testament, or of some small circumstantials in the New.'

viii. Let us consider some further illustrations of this important subject.

(a) A large part of the Levitic Law is taken up by the distinction between clean and unclean meats, to which immense importance is attached, and which profoundly affected—as it does to this day—the life of the orthodox

---

[1] See Ep. Barn. ii. xv. &c. One main object of the Epistle is to show that ceremonial Judaism was not an ordinance of God at all, but due to the seduction of an evil spirit.

[2] Heb. viii. 13, x. 1; Rom. iv. 13, viii. 13; Gal. iv. 9, &c.

[3] *Werke*, ed. Halle, xx. 203, iii. 10; Köstlin, *Luthers Theologie*, ii. 84; Ladd, *Doctrine of Sacred Scripture*, ii. 160.

Jew. Out of this and similar regulations the Scribes, Rabbis, and Pharisees had constructed an iron network which cramped and entangled the souls of their votaries, and tyrannously dominated over their minutest actions from the cradle to the grave. As it were with one wave of the hand, our Lord sets all this triviality aside. He called the multitude and said, '*Not* that which goeth into the mouth defileth a man;' and 'this He said, making all meats clean.'[1] It is not externalism, it is not bodily exercise, which has the smallest intrinsic importance in the sight of God, but moral righteousness and a holy heart.

(*b*) How completely, too, did Christ disparage the whole laborious system of Pharisaic ablutions, when He said of moral offences, 'These are the things which defile a man; but to eat with unwashen hands defileth *not* a man.'[2]

(*c*) And with what small sympathy does the Evangelist speak of 'the washing of cups, and pots, and brazen vessels, and of tables,'[3] which fills one entire treatise of the Mishna and occupies many pages of the Talmud!

(*d*) And there was another respect, even more fundamental, in which Christ not only annulled the Mosaic rules, but treated them as concessions to immaturity and evil passions. In the Mosaic Law both polygamy and divorce had been directly sanctioned. Our Lord passed His condemnation upon both as being untrue to nature and to God.

(*e*) Once more, the Jews had done much by their traditions to render nugatory the blessed and primeval ordinance of the Sabbath. By an elaborate system of childish outward regulations known as *aboth* and *toldoth*, or pri-

---

[1] Mark vii. 19 (according to the true rendering).
[2] Matt. xv. 20.   [3] Mark vii. 4, 8.

7

mary and derivative rules—rules which they themselves constantly evaded, when it served their purpose, by deceptive tricks and specious semblances—they had turned the Sabbath day into a burdensome fetish. To them the poor hungry Apostles were guilty of a flagrant 'scandal' when they plucked the ears of corn and rubbed them in their palms, to satisfy the cravings of nature while they walked through the cornfields. How sharply did our Lord rebuke their officiousness! How thoroughly did He expose, in this and many other particulars, the depth of their hypocrisy! How plainly did He demonstrate on many occasions the peril of turning the Law of Moses into a pernicious idol by exorbitant inferences and multiplied minutiæ! How overwhelmingly did He convict the Priests and Pharisees, who were blind leaders of the blind, of ostentatiously deifying the trifles of religionism while they were constantly obliterating the fundamental truths of religion!

Whatever be the origin of the non-genuine addition to the text of Luke (after vi. 5) in the 'Codex Bezæ,' the writer of it, unless he was incorporating some 'unwritten dogma' or unrecorded tradition, shows how thoroughly he had grasped the spirit of Christ's teaching in these respects.[1]

'The Law,' says St. John, 'was given by Moses; grace and truth came by Jesus Christ.'

(*f*) Nor were these the only utterances by which Jesus showed that the system of Judaism was waxing old and

---

[1] See the author's edition of St. Luke in the *Cambridge Bible for Schools* (Greek, p. 179). The addition is, 'The same day He saw a man working on the Sabbath, and said to him, Man, if thou knowest what thou art doing, blessed art thou: but if thou knowest not, thou art cursed, and a transgressor of the law.'

was ready to vanish away. When James and John, the sons of Thunder, wished to call down fire from heaven on the offending village of En Gannim, they doubtless thought that their fierce intolerance was justified by the example of so splendid a Prophet as Elijah, who was narrated to have destroyed in succession two captains of fifties with their fifties. How swiftly decisive was our Lord's reply! How total His repudiation of the precedent! How unmistakable His enunciation of an order of things which reversed and condemned the tone which runs through parts of the Old Testament records! He turned and rebuked the two Apostles, and said, 'Ye know not what manner of spirit ye are of. For the Son of Man is not come to destroy men's lives, but to save.' Had that single utterance been rightly understood, what a flood of light would it have thrown on the true interpretation of Scripture!

Here let me place side by side two anecdotes.

1. Réné, Duchess of Ferrara, daughter of Louis XII., was a thoughtful and pious princess, and a warm admirer of Calvin. In a letter to the great Reformer of Geneva she made the wise remark that 'David's example in hating his enemies is not applicable to us.' It might have been supposed that Calvin would at once have endorsed a sentiment which only echoed the teaching of Christ. 'It was said to them of old time, Thou shalt love thy neighbour and hate thine enemy; but I say unto you, Love your enemies, bless them that curse you, and pray for them that despitefully use you and persecute you.'

But Calvin was shocked by the remark of the Duchess! He curtly and sternly answered her that 'Such a gloss would upset all Scripture;' that even in his hatred David *is* an example to us, and a type of Christ; and 'Should we presume to set ourselves up as superior to Christ in sweetness and humanity?'[1]   The Princess was wholly right, the theologian disastrously in the wrong.   It would have been better for Calvin had he more truly understood the teaching of Christ and the inferior standard of the Old Testament.   Had he done so, he would have been saved from the worst errors of his life—the burning of Servetus, the recommendation of persecution to the Protector Somerset, and the omission to raise his voice in aid of the miserable and exiled congregation of John à Lasco.   But, as Grotius truly said, the Calvinists were for the most part as severe to all who differed from them as they imagined God to be severe to the greater part of the human race.   And, unhappily, the Pilgrim Fathers and their earliest descendants imbibed these perilous errors, and though they were themselves fugitives from kingly despotism and priestly intolerance, they tortured harmless old women whom they called witches, and treated saintly, if misguided, Quakers with remorseless fury.

2.   When, in 'Old Mortality,' Balfour of Burley proposes to massacre the inhabitants of Tillietudlem Castle, 'By what law,' asks Henry Morton, 'would you justify the atrocity you would commit?'

'If thou art ignorant of it,' replied Burley, 'thy companion is well aware of the law which gave the men of Jericho to the sword of Joshua the son of Nun.'

'Yes, but we,' answered the divine, 'live under a better dispensation, which instructeth us to return good for evil, and to pray for those who despitefully use us and persecute us.'

Surely the humble minister in the fiction spoke deeper wisdom than the world-famous Reformer!

---

[1] 'When I come to such Psalms wherein David curseth his enemies, oh! then let me bring my soul down to a lower note, for these words were made only to fit David's mouth.'—Thomas Fuller.

Does the fact that elements of imperfect morality and narratives capable of misuse occur in the Bible, destroy its eternal value? Let me quote on this subject the excellent remarks of an American writer. 'It is,' he says, 'no argument against its greatness that men should misuse it as they have done so often, any more than it is a fair argument against the ingrain worth of good corn or wheat that so much of it should be turned into whisky. We have drawn from it the power to save men and to slay them, to establish peace and to mass artillery, to be Christians of the noblest type and bigots of the direst. It is the text-book alike of your iron-clad Calvinism and your sunny and most generous Universalism; the volume in which the Quaker finds food for his quietness, and your Millerite of all brands for his craze. It was the corner-stone of the great Puritan foundation which underlies our nation's life; it was also the book from which the Puritan drew his infernal power to hang the Quakers, whip and banish the Baptists, and to burn the witches; while the advocates of human slavery, in the times I easily remember, found proof in it to show that slavery was a divine institution, and men like Garrison that it was accursed of God and man. Always in the Bible we may find this power for good and evil, the inspiration of life unto life and of death unto death. The fine wheat of it even has been turned into a sour mash, and so distilled through the twisted worm of bigotry and intolerance that men have become drunk thereby and insane, and that things have been done in the name of God and the Holy Book which are the disgrace of God and the Holy Book.'

That the Bible has been fatally perverted by ignorance and self-interest no more condemns it than does the misuse of a nominal Christianity condemn the perfectness of the

Gospel. 'Lies have been propagated in its name; swarms of vile creatures have made it an inexhaustible prey, and have heaped upon its head abuses scandalous and loathsome. It has had to contend with the desolation of barbarism, the selfish pretences of kings and priests, and the stupefied spirits of a downtrodden populace; but it has lived through all. It has suffered that which would have been tenfold death to aught less Divine; and it has even given life and beneficent power to institutions in themselves deadly.'[1]

It would be as senseless to condemn Christianity as to condemn the Bible for the gross perversions to which they have alike been subjected.

It will be observed that 'Biblical difficulties' arise all but exclusively from incidental passages in the Old Testament. From the days of St. Peter downwards men have racked and tortured Scripture—stretched and twisted it as it were with a windlass ($\sigma\tau\rho\epsilon\beta\lambda o\tilde{\upsilon}\sigma\iota\nu$, 2 Pet. iii. 16) to their own destruction. Hence the misuse of its isolated texts to sanction the deadliest crimes against the sacred rights of mankind, and to block up with anathemas, and shouts of 'infidel' or 'heretic,' the path of advancing knowledge. But we may lay down the two rules: (1) that there can be no deadlier desecration and perversion of the true purpose and meaning of the Bible than when it is used to justify slavery, or religious persecution, or intolerant bigotry, or any form of false religion and false morality; (2) that it is always rightly used when its teachings are applied to make men more noble and more happy. There is surely a most luminous principle enshrined in the words of St. John: 'The Law was given by Moses, *but grace and truth came by Jesus Christ.*'

<hr>

[1] Howitt.

'No doubt,' says Bishop Westcott,[1] 'we have often used the Scriptures for purposes for which they were not designed. We have treated them too often as the one mechanical utterance of the Spirit, and not as writings through which the Spirit Himself still speaks. There is an immeasurable difference between making the Bible a storehouse of formal premises from which doctrinal systems can be infallibly constructed, and making it, in its whole fulness, the final test of necessary truth.'

[1] *The Revelation of the Father*, p. vii.

CHAPTER VII

'He that takes away Reason to make way for Revelation, puts out
the light of both.'—JOHN LOCKE.

WHAT has been already said should decisively prove that
the theory of a 'verbal dictation' of the Bible by God flies
in the face of the most obvious phenomena which meet us
when we open the sacred page. Each separate writer
shows that he is human and a man 'of like nature' with
ourselves.[1] Each several writer has his own style, his own
phrases, his own methods. One is fervent and impassioned,
another is prosaic and cold. One writes in swift arrowy
sentences, another in flowing rhetorical periods. One is
annalistic, another diffuse. Take the Prophets. The language, the imagery, the form, the structure are different
in each prophetic book. The character and temperament
of the Prophets are stamped upon their writings, and they
are seen to be men of essentially different types.[2] Godet
imaginatively compares Isaiah to a majestic and over-
shadowing oak; Jeremiah to a weeping-willow in a de-

[1] Acts xiv. 15; Jas. v. 17.

[2] Jerome criticises the '*rusticitas*' of some of the Prophets (Prooem.
in Es., Id. in Jer.). He also (*ad Galat.* iii. 1) speaks of the 'solecisms'
of St. Paul.

serted fortress; Ezekiel to an aromatic shrub; Daniel to a
solitary tree in the midst of a mighty plain.   Or take the
Psalms, in which, as Calvin says, 'the Prophets themselves
hold converse with God' and lay bare their inmost feelings
and infirmities.   'In many passages,' he says, 'we may see
the servants of God so tossed to and fro in their prayers
that, almost crushed at times, they only win the palm after
arduous efforts.   On the one side the weakness of the flesh
betrays itself : on the other the power of faith exerts itself.'
In the face of such phenomena, does not the 'verbal dictation' theory become absurd, and almost repellent?   Did
the Divine voice of the Eternal simulate human individuality and human imperfections?   Of the Bible we are
forced to see that 'its text is not infallible; its grammar
is not infallible; its science is not infallible; and there is
a grave question whether its history is altogether infallible.'[1]

It might seem incredible that, in the nineteenth century,
any could still profess a theory so crude and so unscrip-
tural.   It is in opposition to all the evidence of facts
which show that it was God's will to reveal Himself in the
Old Testament not immediately and completely, but
mediately, indirectly, progressively, partially, as we could
alone receive the manifestation of His will.[2]

Direct supernatural dictation was, however, the asserted
doctrine of some of the later Reformers, and it continued
to be held for many years.

It is distinctly stated in the 'Helvetic Confession,' drawn
up in 1675.   'The Hebrew text,' says this document, 'both
as regards consonants and as regards vowels—whether the
vowel points themselves, or, at least, the significance of the

<hr>

[1] Sanday, *Oracles of God*, 36.
[2] Compare Ezek. xx. 19, xxxiii. 18–23; 1 Cor. iii. 2.

points—is divinely inspired.'[1]　It would be difficult to formulate a proposition more glaringly in violation of the known facts as to the sacred text.

Some post-Reformation theologians went to incredible lengths of folly in their endeavour to erect the Bible into a sort of uncreated idol; a 'Fourth Person of the Trinity' to which the Holy Spirit had abdicated His own agency. The Hellenistic Greek in which the New Testament is written is a decadent form of Greek, but they treated it as 'holy Greek,' a form of the language peculiar to God!　In some passages the Greek of the New Testament writers betrays provincialism, and the Book of Revelation is sometimes startlingly ungrammatical.　Yet men like Quenstedt, Hollar, Calovius, and the Wittenberg theologians in 1638, decreed that to speak of barbarisms and solecisms in the New Testament would be a blasphemy against the Holy Ghost!　As far back as A.D. 600 Gregory the Great speaks of the sacred writers, not as penmen, but as 'living and writing pens' of the Holy Ghost.　The phrase was adopted and amplified, and it became the fashion to talk of the Scripture writers as 'amanuenses of God, hands of Christ, scribes and notaries of the Spirit.'　Such language can only spring from inadequate conceptions, and it collapses in every direction at a touch.

1. 'There is such a thing as weakening a good cause by overstating it, and there have been instances in which disgust and rebellion have been provoked by rulers unwisely laying claim to unlimited authority, when by making more moderate claims they would have placed themselves in an unquestionable position of command.　Even so we are convinced that it is better for Christianity, which is "the

---

[1] See Buxtorf, *Tract. de Punct. Vocal.* ii. v.　Lee, *On Inspiration,* p. 447.

truth," to base the authority of Scripture on a consideration of that wisdom which reflection will abundantly
vindicate for the Old and New Testaments, than to rest a
stupendous assertion of the Bible's Divine authority on an
idea of Biblical infallibility, which reason does not uphold,
and which every fresh perusal of the sacred volume gives
us some additional proof is untenable.'

Yet this theory will find maintainers until men get rid
of that heresy of heresies, the worst and most fundamental
of all heresies, which lives and talks as if God had withdrawn Himself into silence since the days of old, and as if
men, instead of living and moving and having their being
in Him, have to get on as best they can, not with the abiding presence of the Holy Spirit, but with upheaped masses
of Church tradition and the manifold perplexities of a
fragmentary ancient literature.

Can any one with whom the love of truth is a supreme
law refuse to believe that nothing which would be posi-
tively wicked in man can have been directly sanctioned by
God?[1] If there be, as no sane scholar denies, a human
element in Scripture, can it be free from human limitations
and infirmities? Let any humble and devout Christian,
who has endeavoured to form an adequate conception of
God's supreme and unspeakable holiness, study the Holy
Volume, and ask himself whether it does not contain many
passages which can only be read *historically*, and with
direct reference to their place, origin, and literary expression. Are there not many passages which we cannot think
that God in any sense dictated, without signally dishon-
ouring His majesty and holiness? The theory of verbal
dictation is not holy, but—however unconsciously—irreverent. It does not tend to devotion, but to idolatry and

[1] See Jas. i. 13.

materialism. So far from exalting the Bible it degrades it into a hollow Memnon's head for the passage of a voice, and robs it of its most precious elements, both human and divine.

2. Even were we to adopt the proposition, which involves a constructive blasphemy, that God had verbally dictated the whole Bible, such verbal dictation would long ago have become worse than useless. For the text has undergone thousands of variations, of which some affect questions of extreme importance.[1] Some passages have been interpolated; others have ceased to be comprehensible; some have been falsified; in a few the text is hopelessly corrupt. All this is now a matter of certainty: yet so great a man as Dr. John Owen condemned the Complutensian Polyglot for its various readings, and said 'the notion that the Bible had not been properly protected bordered, in his opinion, upon Atheism'![2] The vowel points, which constitute a running commentary on the entire Hebrew text, and which the post-Reformation divines vehemently asserted to be divinely inspired, are now known to be comparatively modern. A text verbally dictated could be of no use to the majority of mankind, who have to be content with translations, *all* of which are imperfect, and some of which are erroneous in hundreds of particulars.[3] St.

---

[1] Even Bishop Wordsworth admitted (on 2 Cor. iii. 3) that 'explanatory interpolations have been a fertile source of error in some MSS. of the sacred volume.' Nor would it be true to say that the variations of the text are always unimportant (see Rom. ix. 5; 1 Tim. iii. 16; 1 John v. 7, 8, &c.).

[2] See Dr. Ginsburg, *The Revised Version*, p. 9.

[3] Errors in numbers may be of little importance. But there are grave variations of the text in John i. 18, Acts xx. 28, and there cannot be inerrancy in the present text of the genealogies of Caleb and Saul; in the discrepant account of David's introduction to Saul; in

Augustine, writing to St. Jerome, says that when he comes across anything at variance with the truth he can only suppose either that his copy is faulty, or that the translator has erred, or that he has mistaken the meaning. But since all except a fraction of mankind have to depend on faulty copies, erroneous translations, and highly fallible as well as grossly erroneous expositions, of what avail would verbal dictation have been to them, even if it had ever been vouchsafed?

3. Indeed, it might seem as if the plainest facts which lie on the surface of the Scriptures were meant to render *impossible* so mechanical a superstition. For the writers in all cases show themselves entirely indifferent to verbal fidelity.

i. For instance, we find the 18th Psalm both in the Psalter and in 2 Sam. xxii., but though the substance is the same, the wording is by no means identical, and the one version is very inferior to the other. In ancient days the notion of literary property was non-existent, so that the Prophets, in many instances, make use of each other's writings in a way which in modern times would have been described as plagiarism; but they are not in the least degree particular to reproduce the exact expressions. Sometimes, in the Bible, quotations are referred to wrong names; and are applied in shades of meaning which ignore their context and their primary significance. There is *verbal* variation in those narratives and utterances which might seem to be of all others the most intensely sacred. In the Old Testament there are duplicate narratives of the

divergent chronologies; in separate allusions such as Mark ii. 26, Matt. xxiii. 35, &c. And in St. Stephen's speech Alford reckons several mistakes (Acts vii. 6, 7, 14, 16) and seven allusions to the Haggadah (2, 4, 14, 16, 22, 23, 42, 53).

Creation; duplicate accounts of the Flood; duplicate versions even of the Decalogue.

ii. In the New Testament, if any words *as* words are immediately Divine they are surely those of the Lord Christ. Yet the discourses of Christ are not reproduced by the Evangelists with verbal identity. The reports of them differ in expression. Take the words in which Christ instituted the Last Supper, and His last words to His disciples before His Ascension, and the inscription on the Cross, and the Lord's Prayer. Amid perfect unity of substance there is no identity in the verbal details, but omissions, additions, and verbal variations; and in St. Luke and St. Matthew we have variant records even of the Beatitudes and the Sermon on the Mount.[1]

iii. Further, the sacred writers describe to us, in some cases, their own methods of composition; and so far from claiming that their books were dictated by God, they acknowledge their indebtedness to previous documents and authorities, like other historians. What can be more sacred than the Gospel history? Yet St. Luke, the author of that infinitely precious Gospel which has been justly described as ' the most beautiful book in the world,' in telling us how he wrote, gives no hint of miraculous guidance, but only claims the merit of a painstaking historian. It is evident that to him the Divine revelation consisted in the truths recorded, not in the words by which they were described.[2]

iv. Once more, so little careful were Apostles and Evangelists of the actual words of the Old Testament writers

---

[1] See the comments of Origen and Augustine on Matt. xxvii. 9. Augustine says that the Evangelists wrote 'ut quisque meminerat, et ut cuique cordi erat.' *De Cons. Evv.* ii. 5.

[2] ' It seemed good to me also.' The words ' and to the Holy Spirit' are a late interpolation.

that they most frequently rely upon the Greek translation (the LXX). It is a translation made 'at different times, by different authors, with no unity of execution and no authoritative revision.' They freely use this version, though it is sometimes altogether erroneous, sometimes untrustworthy. The LXX translators often show the bias of Alexandrian philosophy, and make changes in accordance with it. They are sometimes influenced by Jewish legends (the Haggadah) and Jewish ceremonial traditions (the Halacha).[1] Some of them were imperfectly acquainted with Greek, some with Hebrew, and one or two of them with both. In many places they have not understood the original; in others they tamper with it; in others they follow a text unknown to us.[2] If there were the least truth in the doctrine of verbal dictation we should have to claim it for the Septuagint also, as Augustine[3] did; but that is a proposition so flagrantly absurd that it has been universally abandoned. Out of 228 passages quoted from the Old Testament, in the New there are but 53 which agree accurately with the original Hebrew. In 76 the New Testament differs from both the Greek and the Hebrew; and in 99 the New Testament, the Greek, and the Hebrew are all variant.[4] Could there be a more decisive

---

[1] See Hody, *De Bibl. text orient.*, passim; and Frankel, *Ueber d. Einfluss d. Pal. Exeges. auf d. Alexandr. Hermeneutik*, §§ 7, 17, 23.

[2] The version of Aquila, a Jewish proselyte of Pontus, was expressly made (about A.D. 130) because the Jews desired a more literal Greek version than the Septuagint.

[3] Aug. *De Civ. Dei*, xv. 43; Frankel, *Vorstudien*, i. 258–267.

[4] See the full analysis in Turpie, *The Old Testament in the New*. Mill (on Heb. xiii. 25) says that the Apostles sometimes quote the Septuagint in places where 'si reponerentur Hebræa, non modo periret vis argumentationis Apostolicæ, sed ne ullus quidem foret argumentationis locus.' So Chrysostom, on Ps. cix. (*Opp*. Montfaucon,

proof that the gross material notion of 'verbal dictation' was entirely unknown?

v. In some cases, too, the Apostles appear to quote passages which do not occur at all in Scripture. Thus St. James says, 'Think ye that the Scripture speaketh in vain? Doth the Spirit which He made to dwell in us long unto envying?' Similarly, the quotations in Eph. v. 14, 1 Cor. ii. 9 have been referred to an 'Apocalypse of Elijah.' In Luke xi. 49, 51 and John vii. 38 the passages quoted come from the Old Testament, but they are freely intermingled and adapted. These and other passages, together with St. Jude's quotation from the Book of Enoch, without the least intimation that it is apocryphal, show both the freedom with which the words of Scripture were treated and the fact that the formulæ of Scripture citation must not be pressed into unwarrantable inferences.

vi. It is useless to waste any further time over the slaying of a theory which has been slain ten thousand times by the force of facts. 'Catholics,' says the Bishop of Amycla, 'are under no sort of obligation to believe that inspiration extends to the words of Holy Scripture as well as to the subject matter which is therein contained.' Further, may we not learn from the teaching of thousands of years of history that God could never have intended us to possess hundreds of pages 'verbally dictated' by Himself? For there could have been but one object for so stupendous a miracle—namely, that man should be in possession of an enormous mass of infallible truth. Such a miracle could not have been wrought with purely

---

v. 245), admits that some of the N.T. quotations are *applications*. Bengel on Matt. i. 22, ii. 15, 18, and on Heb. ii. 6, '*non interpretationem sed exornationem adducit.*' See other passages in Tholuck, *Das A. T. in N. T.*, pp. 2–6.

nugatory results. The revealed truths on which all Christians are agreed could easily be written on a single page; and that Divine revelation is a sufficient guidance for their lives. But the points of Biblical interpretation on which churches are able only to form the most opposite conclusions, are to be counted on many a page of Scripture. Men in all ages have twisted Scripture *ad infinitum* into accordance with their preconceived prejudices, and refused to read in the Bible any truths except those which they brought to it ready made. Others, who have known better, have often, from timidity or self-interest, remained silent.[1]

[1] The Archbishop of Canterbury, writing to Dr. Tait, when he was Bishop of London, speaks of 'that mistaken reticence, which, go where I would, *I perpetually found destroying the truthfulness of religion*' (*Life of Archbishop Tait*, i. 292).

CHAPTER VIII

'PLENARY INSPIRATION.'

'Every word of God is pure.   Add thou not unto His words, lest
He reprove thee, and thou be found a liar.'—Prov. xxx. 5, 6.

'Nemo vir magnus sine aliquo afflatu divino unquam fuit.'—Cic.
pro Arch. 8.

BUT since the same human invention about the Bible
reasserts itself in other vague and unauthorised phrases,
it is necessary to add that no obligation to accept and
defend every text of Scripture is to be deduced from any
assertion that it is 'plenarily inspired.'

The word 'inspiration' is a word of the most indefinite
character, and so many different senses have been attached
to it that it can hardly be used without introducing a pos-
sibility of confusion.

What is inspiration ?[1]

If by 'inspiration' be meant the influence of the Spirit
of God upon the mind of man—dilating, strengthening,
elevating, revealing—then we must believe that every pure
and sweet influence upon the soul—all that is best and
greatest in philosophy, eloquence, and song—is due to the

---

[1] The term ($\pi\nu\epsilon\upsilon\mu\alpha\tau o\phi\acute{o}\rho o\iota$) as applied to the New Testament writers
is perhaps first found in Theophilus of Antioch, A.D. 181.   The
word ($\theta\epsilon\acute{o}\pi\nu\epsilon\upsilon\sigma\tau o\varsigma$) of the N.T. occurs in Clement of Alexandria.
Sanday, *Inspiration*, p. 33.   But see 2 Pet. i. 21.   Philo speaks of
the $\theta\epsilon\acute{o}\chi\rho\eta\sigma\tau\alpha$ $\lambda\acute{o}\gamma\iota\alpha$, and in 2 Macc. vi. 23 we read of the $\theta\epsilon\acute{o}\kappa\tau\iota\sigma\tau o\varsigma$
$\nu o\mu o\theta\epsilon\sigma\acute{\iota}\alpha$.

inspiration of the Holy Spirit of God. 'Every good gift and every perfect boon is from above, and cometh down from the Father of Lights, with whom is no variableness, neither shadow cast by turning.' There is therefore an ethnic as well as a Jewish and a Christian inspiration. The best of the Fathers acknowledged this. They did not deny the gifts of the Spirit to the wise thinkers and writers of Greece and Rome. They admit that the great pagans 'knocked at the door of truth.' One of the earliest Christian writers, St. Justin Martyr, borrowed from Plato the beautiful belief in a germinal word—the *Logos spermatikos* —of which all are partakers in various measure, and which is the source of all enlightenment. He held that—

> —in all ages and on every sod
> Whatever truth man troweth is of God.

It is the teaching of Solomon that 'the spirit of man is the candle of the Lord.' It is the doctrine of St. John that there is a light ever coming into the world, which lighteth every man. It is the truth, recognised in the greatest book of the Apocrypha, that 'the Spirit of the Lord filleth the world.'[1] Wisdom is 'the brightness of the everlasting light, the breath of the power of God, and a pure influence flowing from the glory of the Almighty,' which 'being but one can do all things, and remaining in herself, regenerateth all other powers, and maketh all things new;' and 'in all ages entering into holy souls, maketh them friends of God and prophets.'[2]

---

[1] Wisdom i. 7, lit. 'hath filled and still fills.' Compare Jer. xxiii. 24. So Philo, 'God hath filled all things, and hath penetrated all things, and hath left nothing empty or void of Himself' (*De Legg. Allegg.* iii. 2).

[2] Wisdom vii. 25-27. Compare Ecclus. xiv. 22-27.

The same belief was shared by the greatest of the Jews and of the heathen.[1]   Philo, lofty as were his conceptions of inspiration, yet, in more than one passage, claims it for all truly good and earnest men.

1. It is in this sense—not in any special sense exclusively applied to Scripture—that the best English writers have always used the word 'inspire.'   Thus Milton prays—

> And chiefly Thou, O Spirit that dost prefer
> Before all temples the upright heart and pure,
> Instruct me, for Thou knowest . . .
> 　　　　　　what in me is dark
> Illumine; what is low, raise and support.

And again—

> So much the rather, Thou, celestial light,
> Shine inward, and the mind through all her powers
> Irradiate: there plant eyes, all mist from thence
> Purge and disperse, that I may see and tell
> Of things invisible to mortal sight.

And again he speaks of Urania, his celestial patroness, who

> Dictates to me slumbering, or inspires
> Easy my unpremeditated verse.

And prays—

> Inspire as Thou art wont
> My prompted song else mute.

And even Pope, at the beginning of his 'Messiah,' writes—

> Do Thou my soul inspire,
> Who touched Isaiah's lips with hallowed fire;

and Herrick says that he can only write

> when the Spirit fills
> The fantastic panicles
> Full of fire.

---

[1] See Plato, *Ion.* pp. 533, 544; Tim. p. 72; Arist. *De Mundo,* 4; Cic. *de Div.* i. 50; Livy, v. 15; Verg. *Æn.* vi. 47, &c.

2. We are assured by Professor Abraham that even among the Jews there is no single opinion on the question of inspiration which can be called the Jewish opinion. And the Christian Church never attempted to define either the nature, the action, or the limits of inspiration. In *every* instance in which the word is used in our Prayer Book it tends directly to exclude the notion that inspiration is confined to Scripture, or that the Bible is the product of an exhausted energy, the sepulchre of a dead influence. On the contrary, being deeply penetrated with the truth that Christ is a living, not a dead Christ, a present, not an absent Christ—that He has promised to be with us always, and that He giveth His Holy Spirit to them that ask Him —the Prayer Book *always* refers to 'inspiration,' not as an exceptional gift of infallibility, but as the continuous method of divine guidance. Thus the Church teaches us to pray to God that 'by Thy holy inspiration we may think those things that be good;'[1] and 'cleanse the thoughts of our hearts by the inspiration of Thy Holy Spirit;'[2] and

> Come, Holy Ghost, our souls inspire,
> And lighten with celestial fire.[3]

We beseech God 'to inspire continually the universal Church with the spirit of truth, unity, and concord.'[4] One Article speaks of 'Works done before the grace of God and the inspiration of His Holy Spirit.' Again, we pray to God, 'Grant us by the same Spirit to have a right judgment in all things.' But which of us so stupidly extends and perverts the words as to suppose that the answer to our prayers will make us universally infallible?

[1] Collect for Fifth Sunday after Easter.
[2] Collect of Ante-Communion Service.
[3] Hymn in Ordination Service.
[4] Prayer for the Church Militant, &c.

It is clear therefore that the view of the Church of England was that expressed by Milton in the 'Animadversions': 'And as Thou didst dignify our fathers' days with many revelations, so Thou canst vouchsafe to us (though unworthy) as large a portion of Thy Spirit as Thou pleasest. For who shall prejudice Thy all-governing will, seeing the power of Thy grace is not passed away with the primitive time as fond and faithless men imagine, but Thy kingdom is now at hand and Thou standest at the door.'[1]

Indeed, the whole grandeur of Milton's ideal and of Milton's verse was based on the conviction that God 'sends His Seraphin with the burning coal from off the altar to touch and hallow the lips of whom He will.' He was conscious that though he was in no sense of the word infallible, he was (as Dr. Arnold said of him) not surely uninspired by that Holy Spirit to whom his devout prayers were constantly addressed.

3. And with this accords the view expressed in Scripture itself. It uses the word 'inspiration' of that manifold and perpetual—but neither extinct nor abnormal—enlightenment, which is not confined to any one period or any one set of men. 'There is a spirit in man,' says the Book of Job, 'and the inspiration of the Almighty giveth him understanding.'[2] 'See, I have called by name Bezaleel,' so we read in the Book of Exodus, 'and I have filled him with the Spirit of God in wisdom, to devise cunning work, to work in gold and in silver and in brass.' Do those expressions imply that man is therefore infallible? or that Bezaleel the son of Uri was the divinest artist whom the world has seen?

Indeed, this gift of inspiration, which is never confused

<hr>

[1] *Animadversions.*   [2] Job xxxii. 8.

with supernatural infallibility, is recognised alike in Scripture, in heathen and in secular Christian literature. 'I am moved,' said Socrates, 'by a certain divine and spiritual influence.' It was said of the sculptor Scopas, that, 'impelled by a certain inspiration, he threw himself with divine fervour on the making of his statues.' Plato says that philosophers 'would not venture to teach others, unless they were excited thereto by God Himself.' Cicero speaks of poets as inspired by a certain divine influence, and of all great men as influenced by some kind of divine imbreathing in the soul. In Scripture, though the word 'inspiration' occurs in it but twice, yet the influence of the Spirit is freely ascribed to heroes so imperfect as Gideon, Jephthah, and Samson; to rulers like Othniel and David; [1] to wise men in general; [2] to such erring men as Balaam and Saul.[3] Nay, even the discretion of the ordinary plowman is attributed to the instruction of God.[4]

And nothing is commoner in ordinary Christian literature than the prayer 'Do Thou my soul inspire.' Sir W. Raleigh says that great souls are stirred up by 'the Infinite Spirit of the Universal;' just as Carlyle says that 'Great men are the inspired (speaking and acting) texts of that Divine book of Revelations, whereof a chapter is completed from epoch to epoch and by some named history.' [5] 'The gifted man,' says Fichte, 'becomes the mediator of the Divine Spirit. The real man of God is conscious of being seized on by a might superior to his own, to whose behests

---

[1] 1 Sam. xiii. 14.

[2] Dan. ii. 22.

[3] Num. xxiv. 2; 1 Sam. x. 6.

[4] Is. xxviii. 23–26, 'For his God doth instruct him [the plowman] to discretion, and doth teach him.'

[5] *Sartor Resartus*, p. 108.

he consecrates himself.'[1]   Haydn said of his mighty chorus in the 'Creation,' 'Not from me, but from above it all has come!' With this view of an inspiration, which yet is wholly different from infallibility, the Christian Fathers and our own Homilies agree. Speaking of Cicero's remarks about the moral law, Lactantius says (*Institt.* vi. 8) that he must look on such men 'as divinely moved by the Spirit.' Our Homily for Whitsunday says, 'It is the Holy Ghost and no other thing that doth quicken the minds of men.'[2]

No theory of Scriptural inspiration is taught by Christ or His Apostles. Indeed, so far as they speak of it, they tell us that it is granted to all believers. No exclusive inspiration is claimed by the Scripture writers, as a whole, for themselves or for all their writings; nor is it authoritatively asserted for them all by any one of their number. It is only said in the most general way in 2 Pet. i. 21, that 'Men spake from God, being moved by the Holy Ghost;' and by St. Paul that 'Every scripture' (*i.e.* every writing) 'inspired of God is also profitable.'[3]

4. 'Plenary inspiration' is one of those phrases which may be mischievously perverted because it is completely undefined. It is impossible to say what 'plenary' inspiration means, until we know what 'inspiration' means, and

---

[1] Fichte, *Spec. Theol.* p. 653.

[2] For this paragraph I am indebted to Griffith's *Fundamentals*, p. 172. Mr. W. R. Greg, in the *Creeds of Christendom*, defines inspiration as 'that elevation of all the spiritual faculties by the action of God upon the heart, which is shared by all devout minds in different degrees, and which is consistent with many errors.'

[3] That this is the true meaning and translation of 2 Tim. iii. 16 (as in the R.V.) may now be regarded as certain; but even if the translation of the A.V. were correct the general expression would make no difference to my argument.

this has never been laid down in any creed. Unfortunately, instead of trying to discover the nature of Scriptural inspiration by induction from the phenomena of the books themselves, men have first made their own definition of the word, and then tortured the facts of Scripture into conformity with it. Had they followed the wiser course they would have found that 'as inspiration does not suppress the individuality of the Biblical writers, so it does not altogether neutralise their human infirmities or confer upon them immunity from error. Too often the explanations offered of these discrepancies, and of the moral difficulties presented by the Old Testament, leave much to be desired, and are adapted rather to silence doubt than to satisfy it.'[1]

Four well-marked theories on the subject have been held unchallenged within the pale of the Christian Church alone, and that by men of eminent authority and earnest faith.

i. The first may be called the *Organic*, mechanical, or 'dictation' theory, which, when universally professed, was not held with any consistency even by Rabbis and Fathers.[2]

ii. The second theory has been called the *Dynamic*. It maintains that the Bible, though not dictated by God, was yet written under the immediate indefeasible guidance of the Holy Spirit. This view recognises the divine energy, but does not entirely annihilate the human co-operation.[3] It says, as St. Chrysostom says of St. Paul (εἰ καὶ Παῦλος

---

[1] Professor Driver, Church Congress speech.

[2] If, for instance, Papias had held it respecting even the Evangelists, he would not have written about St. Mark as he did (Euseb. *H. E.* iii. 39, 15). Origen and Augustine are compelled to relax the stringency of their mechanical dogma with reference to the variations of the Evangelists in order and phraseology.

[3] Origen in Matt. iii. (συνεργοῦντος καὶ τοῦ ἁγίου Πνεύματος).

ἦν ἀλλ' ἄνθρωπος ἦν), 'Even though he was a Paul he was yet but a man.'

iii. The third may be called the theory of *Illumination*, which confines the divine guidance to matters of faith and doctrine. It recognises *degrees* in inspiration. Romish theologians distinguish between antecedent, concomitant, and consequent inspiration—the latter involving nothing but 'a grace of superintendency' which prevented the writer from grave errors—as distinguished from the graces of elevation, direction, suggestion. Some of the Jews discriminated between different kinds of inspiration. They drew a marked distinction between the spirit which inspired the Law and the Prophets and that which was recognised in the other books (Kethubim or Hagiographa).[1]

iv. The fourth theory may be described as that of *general* inspiration. Those who hold it do not regard the inspiration of the sacred writers throughout the *whole* extent of Scripture as more extraordinary, transcendent, and supernatural in kind, nor even always in degree, than that which is vouchsafed to other noble and holy souls. This view, of which Schleiermacher may be regarded as the foremost representative, looks upon Biblical inspiration as a thing entirely subordinate in the divine economy. It regards the New Testament as simply the truthful record of the life and doctrine of Christ, and does not consider that the action of the Holy Spirit on the heart of its writers was specifically distinct from the analogous influence which (as all admit) He exercises on the heart and intellect of all true Christian men. They believe that, by

---

[1] See Maimonides, *More Nevochim*, ii. 37, 45. The Law was said to be inspired by the 'mouth to mouth' or highest form of inspiration. On its Talmudic superexaltation see Weber, *Syst. d. altsynag. Theol.* pp. 1–60.

its witness to Christ, the Bible animates and awakens the religious consciousness of men, but they attach no attribute of infallibility or supernatural sanctity to all its particular phrases or incidental references. This view has been more or less supported by theologians so different as Erasmus, R. Simon, Grotius, Le Clerc, Pfaff, Perrone, Döllinger, Warburton, Horsley, Lowth, Paley, Clarke, Doddridge, Laud, Baxter, Tillotson, Thomas Scott, Whateley, Hampden, Thirlwall, and Alford, and an ever-increasing multitude of living scholars.

5. It is clear, then, that the maintenance of the opinion that the Bible is, in every text and utterance, inerrant, is no part of the Christian faith. The majority of Christians hold that it is throughout human as well as divine; or that it is only illuminated in differing and intermittent degrees; or that it is divine only in matters of faith; or that it is divine only in that sense in which all else is divine which is good and noble. Any one may denounce the latter theories of inspiration, but no one can alter the fact that each of these theories has been held by divines of accredited faithfulness in every branch of the Christian Church. It is certain that had a doctrine so stupendous as the supernatural dictation of the Bible been in any sense true, it would not have been so completely omitted from Scripture itself, or only so faintly, obscurely, and, as Coleridge expresses it, 'obitaneously' declared, seeing that 'In infallibility there are no degrees.' St. Augustine says of St. Paul that he was 'inspiratus a Deo sed tamen homo,'[1] but to be human connotes multitudinous limitations. 'How can absolute infallibility be blended with fallibility? How can infallible truth be infallibly conveyed in defective and fallible manuscripts, in defective and fallible expressions, or in translations which are liable to every kind of error?'

[1] Aug. *De Consens. Ev.* ii. 28.

6. Assuredly one or other of the latter theories is alone in accordance with all the facts. 'Inspiration,' as Scripture exhibits it, does not exclude human infirmity or error. The Apostles received the outpouring of Pentecost, and were 'full of the Holy Ghost,' yet they do not conceal from us that they could and did err, and that they were men 'of like nature' with their heathen hearers,[1] and capable of serious mistakes both in judgment and in practice. St. Paul freely admits his own hesitations and uncertainties. On one occasion he has a serious quarrel with Barnabas; on another he was compelled to withstand even Peter to his face because he stood condemned. He does not pretend to bow in abject reverence to the dicta and opinions of his inspired brother Apostles.[2] The guidance of the Spirit was promised to them. They were inspired, but do not claim any complete infallibility. They were inspired only as to essential truth, and in varying degrees, and with individual differences.

7. Except by a slavishly literal interpretation, by fallacious extensions of applicability, and by inferences which violate every sane principle of interpretation, there is no passage of Scripture which can be made to bear the immense weight of meaning laid upon it by those who maintain that all Scripture, down to its minutest particulars, is plenarily or supernaturally inspired.[3]

8. The word 'inspiration' is, as we have seen, so vague in meaning that for all who desire clearness of thought it

---

[1] Acts xiv. 15 (comp. Jas. v. 17).   [2] Gal. ii. 6.

[3] See some excellent remarks in Sanday, p. 87. Driver, *The Expositor*, 1889, i. 15. Such passages as Matt. v. 18, John x. 35, 2 Tim. iii. 16, 2 Pet. i. 20, 21 can only be forced into assertions of the entire inerrancy of every line of Scripture in violation of every principle of literary expression and even of common sense. 'My heart,' says Coleridge, 'would turn away with angry impatience for the captious

would be a boon if some less ambiguous word could be adopted. In these shadows of words used in many different senses there lurk multitudes of errors and controversies. The Alexandrian Jews and the Fathers say with one voice that Holy Scripture is 'inspired,' and we accept the phrase because it corresponds with our own conviction that the Scriptures as a whole are supreme in religious authority, priceless in their divine revelation, unique in holy influence, the choicest outward boon which God has granted to mankind. But when we find Philo saying that 'the Holy Word bestows the gift of prophecy upon every notably wise man,'[1] and when we find some of the Fathers attributing inspiration to the LXX and to the Sibyls and to Hystaspes, their use of the phrase becomes valueless for any purpose of help.

These ancient authorities are often quoted as though they proved that the post-Reformation dogmas of the infallibility of the Bible had always been the belief of Christians. We have no right to quote them for this purpose unless we quote them to prove the infallibility of some spurious and even valueless writings to which they also attributed a Scriptural authority.[2]

9. When we ask our divines what inspiration means, we are disappointed by the unanimity with which they

mortal who the moment I had been pouring out the love and gladness of my soul while book after book were passing my memory should ask me if I were thinking of the Book of Esther, or of Ps. xix. 6, 20, or Ps. cxxxvii. 9.'

[1] *Quis rer. div. her.* 52. He calls Plato 'most sacred' (ἱερώτατος), and even claims occasional inspiration for himself. *De Cherub.* 9; *De Migr. Abr.* 7; Schürer, *Gesch. d. jüd. Volkes,* ii. 868; Sanday, p. 94.

[2] Any reader of Clemens Romanus or the Epistle of Barnabas will see at once that their strong phrases about inspiration by no means exclude a very free handling of the Old Testament.

refuse to help us by anything approaching to a definition. No one will question the 'orthodoxy' of Hagenbach: yet Hagenbach wrote, with perfect truth, that 'the Bible is a book which with all its divinity is still written by human hands for human beings, for a human eye, a human heart, a human understanding; a book which, though written for all times, still refers to certain times and occasions, and must from these given times and occasions be interpreted.'

'The Bible,' says Dr. Pope, 'is a divine-human collection of books, the precise relation of human and divine in which is a problem which has engaged much attention, and has not yet been adequately solved. We have to construct our theory from the facts, and our theory must face those indisputable facts as it finds them.'[1]

The Archbishop of Canterbury, in his essay on 'The Education of the World,' says: 'If geology proves to us that we must not interpret the first chapters of Genesis literally; if historical investigations shall teach us that inspiration—however it may protect doctrine—yet was not empowered to protect the narrative of the inspired writers from occasional inaccuracies; if careful criticism shall prove that there have been occasionally interpolations and forgeries in that Book as in many others, the result should still be welcome. The substance of the teaching which we derive from the Bible is not really affected by anything of this sort.'

Dean Bagot, in a little book on the 'Inspiration of Scripture' (1878), written mainly to support the old views, says: 'There are seven gateways through which the material which the Bible contains has come—Observation (as in John xix. 34, 1 John i. 1, 3); Information (Luke i. 1, 2); Compilation (as in the Old Testament historic books);

____
[1] *Comp. Theol.* i. 175, 191.

Meditation (as in Psalms v., xix. &c.); Imagination (as in the Psalms and Isaiah); Argumentation (as in the Epistles of St. Paul and Revelation).' He explains the occurrence in the Bible of objectionable sentiments, as in the Imprecatory Psalms, to 'the outpouring of the sinful nature and carnal minds of those who uttered them.'

10. This being so, it is clear that from the word 'inspiration' no inflexible dogma can be extorted. It cannot be made to mean the same thing as supernatural perfection. It is an indeterminate symbol used by different men in different senses, which none of them will define.

11. With the results at which we have thus arrived accord the dictates of reason, which Tertullian calls in itself 'a divine thing.' Is it not wrong that millions should be asked to accept as a direct transcript from Divine dictation books which, like those of the Apocrypha, abound in false history and dubious morals; books of doubtful authorship and secondary authority; books which, like Canticles and Esther, do not once mention the name of God, and were only admitted into the Old Testament Canon after serious hesitation; passages which are completely mistranslated or which convey to modern ears a sense wholly unlike that of the original; passages which were once universally accepted as genuine Scripture, but which are now deleted as the glosses, interpolations, and additions of unauthorised copyists?

12. If it be asked, How, then, are we to know what is the Word of God contained in Scripture? or if it be argued that it is impossible for us to disintegrate the word of God from the word of man, the answer is that this is exactly what Christians have already had to do again and again. They have been thrown, just as the Jews were, on the ordinary means of criticism and spiritual discernment to

discover what entire books did, and what did not, deserve
the title of Canonical; and their decision has repeatedly
shown itself to be fallible.[1] To this day the millions of
the Roman Church accept, as canonical, books of the
Apocrypha, some of which lie far below the level of many
writings both heathen and Christian. For some centuries
books were admitted into the Canon which are now excluded from it; or books excluded from it which are now
admitted to belong to it. The question 'How, then, are
we to recognise the Word of God?' is an entirely faithless
one. We recognise it precisely as the Christian Church
has always done. All Christians have set aside large sections of the Old Testament as belonging to an abrogated
dispensation. They even treat some passages of the New
Testament as not binding upon them in the letter. They
set aside no small part of Scripture as having been relative
and transient. They recognise that the Tabernacle was a
glorious symbol, but do not find anything which specially
reaches them in long chapters about its upholstery and
joinery, 'its boxes and tables, and rings and lamps, and
loops and bowls, and curtains and candlesticks, and ram

---

[1] 'You must first ascertain the historical proof of books of Holy
Scripture by the ordinary methods of criticism before any question
of their inspiration can ever arise.' 'That is not an act of religion,'
says Whichcote, 'which is not an act of the understanding: for that
is not a religious act which is not human;' and again, 'They are
greatly mistaken who in religion oppose points of reason and matters
of faith: as if nature went one way and the author of nature went
another.' See Bishop Westcott's *Rel. Thought in the West*, pp. 362–
397. Whichcote also says, 'Men have an itch rather to make religion than to use it;' and 'We are more concerned for that which is
our own in religion than for that which is God's.' He hated intolerance, and said, 'I do believe that the destroying this spirit of persecution out of the Church is a piece of the reformation which God
aims at.'

skins and badgers' skins, and pans and shovels, and basins and clothes'—quite irrespective of the question whether they emanated from Moses, or whether, as many critics suppose, they are not much older than the era of the Exile. In spite of the Council of Jerusalem which claimed the direction of the Holy Spirit they do not abstain from blood, or from things strangled. In spite of St. James they do not anoint the sick with oil. If they were not constantly falling into the error of forgetting that Christ is 'alive for evermore'—if they believed His promise that the Spirit should lead them into all essential truth, they would not try to dethrone Him and set up a book in His place. Is it indeed the case that we have nothing to guide us with certainty about the way of salvation unless we put a genealogy of Chronicles or a chapter of Numbers or Esther on the same level as the Sermon on the Mount? Did not St. John tell us to *try* the Spirits?[1] Did not St. Paul say, 'Prove all things: hold fast that which is good'?[2] Did not our Lord Himself ask, 'Why even of your own selves judge ye not what is right?'[3] 'To those who follow their reason in the interpretation of the Scriptures,' said Lord Falkland, 'God will either give His grace, or assistance to find the truth, or His pardon if they miss it.' 'If after using diligence to find truths we fall into error,' said Chillingworth, 'where the Scriptures are not plain there is no danger in it. They that err and they that do not err shall both be saved.' 'God,' says Erskine of Linlathen, 'judges that He may teach, not teaches that He may judge.' Have we no reason lighted by God and lighting to God, *res illuminata, illuminans*—Reason which is a daughter of Eternity, and therefore before Antiquity,

---

[1] 1 John iv. 1.   [2] 1 Thess. v. 21.
[3] Luke xii. 57.

9

which is the daughter of Time? Could not even a heathen say with truth, *Est Deus in nobis, agitante calescimus illo?* [1] Have we within us no voice of conscience, 'that aboriginal vicar of Christ, a prophet in its informations, a monarch in its peremptoriness, a priest in its sanctions and anathemas'? Has the Spirit of God abdicated His office since the days of St. John, or at any rate since the days of St. Augustine? Have we ceased to believe in the Holy Ghost? Is it not enough that God's word to us is the inward teaching of Him who is the Word of God? Do we or do we not believe that there is a spirit in man, and the inspiration of the Almighty giveth them understanding? [2] Were St. Irenæus and St. Augustine wrong when they spoke of those who 'without paper and ink have salvation written on their hearts by the Spirit'? If so, was St. Paul wrong when he spoke of the invisible things of God being clearly manifested by the things that are seen; and of the Gentiles as having the law written on their hearts, and knowing God, and the judgment of God? and was St. Peter wrong in saying that God had *in every nation* them that were acceptable to Him because they fear Him and do righteousness? Is it not a plain and simple rule that anything in the Bible which teaches, or is misinterpreted to teach, anything which is not in accordance with the love, the gentleness, the truthfulness, the purity of Christ's Gospel, is *not* God's word to us, however clearly it stands on the page of Scripture? And need we fear lest we should be led astray in anything essential by the light from heaven? There is no need for such fears. 'To the law and to the testimony: if they speak not according to this word, it is because there is no light in them.' [3] 'Where the doctrine is necessary and important,' says

---

[1] Ovid, *Fasti*, vi. 6.   [2] Job xxxii. 8.   [3] Is. viii. 20.

Whichcote, 'the Scripture is clear and full.' And if the Scripture is sometimes ambiguous, Locke has told us with his serene wisdom that 'he who makes use of the light and faculties which God hath given him, and seeks sincerely to discover truth by those helps and abilities, will not miss the reward of truth.   He that doeth otherwise transgresses against his own light.'

13. God everlastingly reveals Himself to earnest souls.[1] 'It is,' says Mr. Ruskin, 'a grave heresy (or wilful source of division) to call any book, or collection of books, the Word of God. By that Word, or Voice, or Breath, or Spirit, the heaven and earth and all the host of men were made, and in it they exist. It is your life and speaks to you always as long as you live nobly; dies out of you as you refuse to obey it; leaves you to hear and be slain by the word of an evil spirit instead of it. It may come to you in books, come to you in clouds, come to you in the voice of men, come to you in the stillness of deserts. You must be strong in evil if you have quenched it wholly, very desolate in this Christian land if you have never heard it at all.'[2]

The Rabbis were right in the Haggadah, which told that the voice of God reached the people of Israel, but they could not find exactly whence it came by turning either to the north or south, or east or west, or to the depths of the earth. The voice of God speaks to us out of Holy Writ, far more intensely than out of any form of human speech,

---

[1] When Melanchthon asked Luther the meaning of the prophetic formula 'Thus saith the Lord.' Luther answered that 'because the Prophets were holy and serious people, therefore God spoke with them in their consciences, which the Prophets held as sure and certain revelations.'   *Table Talk*, 549 (Sanday, *Oracles of God*, p. xii.).

[2] *Fors Clavigera.*

and, if only we have the courage to be sincere, it will always speak directly and unmistakably to our inmost hearts and consciences. We shall hear it each according to our capacity and our power to receive it, and we shall hear it all the more surely in exact proportion to the measure in which we have arrived at 'truth in the inward parts.'

CHAPTER IX

THE HIGHER CRITICISM.

'True faith and reason are the soul's two eyes.'—QUARLES.

I WILL pause here to say a few words about what is known as 'the Higher Criticism,' which has caused such needless alarm, and of which even the most certain results—such as the composite character of the Pentateuch, and the late origin of the Book of Daniel in its present form—are still resisted, with bitter attacks on those who feel that by refusing to accept its main conclusions they would be fighting against God and offering to Him the unclean sacrifice of a lie.

1. The 'Higher' criticism is not, as many imagine, an arrogant and self-laudatory title.[1] It merely means the criticism which is not purely linguistic or philological, but also takes into account the discoveries of history and archæology, the teachings of comparative religion, and the

---

[1] The name was invented by Eichhorn when the researches of many such scholars as Morinus, Walton, R. Simon, Kennicott, Mill, Bentley, Griesbach, &c., had made *textual* criticism the almost exclusive method. The term merely implies that 'the study of the contents of a book is a higher study than that of the words in which the contents are expressed' (Dr. Cave, *The Battle of the Standpoints*, p. 8).

consideration of the ordinary laws of evidence, of documentary transmission, of psychology, and of human literature.[1]

2. The arguments on which the main conclusions of the Higher Criticism are based are so strong that, as a simple matter of fact, they have convinced nearly all the leading theologians of Germany. I could not refuse to recognise their cogency without the wilful abnegation of the divinest of our natural prerogatives. No consensus of popular opinion can have the smallest weight against the truths which the heaven-directed advance of knowledge reveals. This has ever been the view of our soundest and most orthodox divines.

'That authority of men should prevail with men,' says Hooker, ' either against or above Reason, is no part of our belief. Companies of learned men, be they never so great and reverend, are to yield unto Reason.'[2]

3. Let us recapitulate a few obvious and undeniable facts. No one will deny

(*a*) That to millions of mankind the Bible never has been nor can be known except in translations.

(*b*) That, from the nature of things, no translation can be perfect, because language, with all its subtle mystery, is but an imperfect vehicle of thought, and the different connotation of words in different languages renders it impossible to secure the minutely exact transfusion of thought from one tongue into another.

(*c*) That, as a matter of fact, there is not a single trans-

---

[1] 'The Higher Criticism is but a name for scientific scholarship scientifically used. If the Scriptures are fit subjects for scholarship, then the more scientific the scholarship the greater its use in the field of Scripture.'—Dr. Fairbairn.

[2] *Ecclesiastical Polity*, Book II. ch. vii. 6.

lation of the Scriptures which does not contain errors.
The Septuagint, the Vulgate, Luther's Bible, our Authorised Version, the Douai Bible, and every other known
translation contains grave and numerous errors of translation.[1] Our Revised Version, which has utilised the
knowledge and research of all the ages, is probably the
most correct translation of the Bible in existence, yet even
our Revised Version is by no means exempt from imperfections.   Thousands of years ago it had been recognised
that 'the same things uttered in Hebrew and translated
into another tongue have not the same force in them; and
not only these things, but the law itself and the prophets,
and the rest of the books, have no small difference when
they are spoken in their own language.'[2]

(*d*) Alike in the Old and the New Testament there are
thousands of various readings; important variations occur
in the oldest MSS. and versions; in some books of the
Sacred Writings the genuine text is uncertain, inaccurate,
interpolated, and in a few verses absolutely irrecoverable.[3]

(*e*) When we have obtained the best text at our disposal,
'the form in which the revelation has come down to us—
what seem gaps on the one hand and repetitions on the

---

[1] Consider even the theological importance of the inaccurate renderings in our Authorised Version in Matt. vi. 13, Mark vii. 19, John x.
16, xiii. 10, Rom. iii. 25, xii. 16, Gal. ii. 16, Eph. iv. 32, Phil. ii. 6, Col.
ii. 23, Jas. ii. 14, 1 Tim. vi. 10, 2 Tim. ii. 26, iii. 16, iv. 14, Heb. i. 1,
Jude 22, and many more passages. Our O.T. version of Ex. xxxiv.
33, Deut. xxxiii. 6, Is. vi. 13, xviii. 2, xxi. 7, xxx. 7, Dan. vii. 9, and
in many passages of the Psalms is obscured by errors. The meaning
of the magnificent passage Is. ix. 1-5, which forms our First Lesson
for Christmas Day, is in our A.V. almost reversed.

[2] Prologue to Ecclesiasticus.

[3] As single specimens take the doubt as to the reading μονογενὴς
Θεός in John i. 18.

other—shows that here we have a human literature, embodying a divine message not to be discerned at a glance, but which *makes* us think, compare, examine, weigh, judge.'

(*f*) The history of interpretation shows how many meanings may be attached even to the simplest passages.

(*g*) Hence 'he who holds that these books are indeed the Word of God is *compelled* to examine into their form and structure; to inquire in what sense, to what degree, God may be said to speak, *e.g.* in the Book of Job, in the speculations of Ecclesiastes, in the visions of the Apocalypse. He is compelled by the very variety of form, and complexity of the questions raised, to think and to distinguish, if he would understand and rightly receive the divine message.'

(*h*) 'The question as to the nature of inspiration is raised by the acknowledged fact of the *progressive* character of the divine revelation herein contained. The unity of the Bible is not mechanical, but organic—represented by the growth and development of the plant, not by the erection of a monolith.'[1]

4. These truths are so obvious that every candid man is compelled to admit them. Mr. Gladstone has written much and earnestly on the grandeur and inestimable worth of Holy Writ. Yet, as an honest inquirer, he admits in the sacred writers,

i. Imperfect comprehension of that which was divinely communicated.

ii. Imperfect expression of what had once been comprehended.

iii. Lapses of memory in oral transmission.

iv. Errors of copyists in written transmission.

v. Changes with the lapse of time in the sense of words.

[1] Professor Davison.

vi. Variations arising from renderings into different tongues.

vii. Three variant chronologies of the Old Testament (the Hebrew, the Septuagint, and the Samaritan Pentateuch).

viii. The inspired writers of the New Testament varied in the text they used for citations from the Old Testament, and did not regard either the Hebrew or the Greek as of exclusive authority.[1]

5. Is it not, then, clear that we *must* inquire into the structure and peculiarities of the Sacred Books? that we should be acting with craven unbelief if we refrained from doing so?   Those inquiries have convinced every profound critic and theologian of any eminence that some of the books of Scripture are an amalgam of two or three books, and that other books have been compiled from various sources, and edited and re-edited by later hands.   There is nothing whatever in such conclusions to shake even the outermost fringe of the hem of our religious faith; for the Scripture notion of revelation is a union of three elements —faith in the world of phenomena; God-given ideas in the world of thought; and a verifying faculty bestowed on the divinely-touched soul.[2]

6. And if we have arrived at such conclusions about the composite books of Scripture, it is our duty not to conceal them.   'There is a duty to speak the truth as well as to

---

[1] Also, on p. 262 of his book, Mr. Gladstone says that detriment ensues when we erect into dogmatic truth such propositions as: '1. That the material volume of the Holy Scriptures, . . . with every fact and sentiment it contains, must be received under the same materialised conception as that under which Mahometans are supposed to believe the Koran, and held absolutely true.   2. That there is no progression or distinction in the inspiration to which it is to be referred.'

[2] Rev. E. White, *Inspiration, a Clerical Symposium*, p. 149.

withhold it.   The voice of a majority of clergy throughout the world, the half-sceptical, half-conservative instinct of many laymen, perhaps also individual interest, are in favour of the latter course; while a higher expediency pleads that honesty is the best policy, and that truth alone makes free.'[1]

7. Upon the Higher Criticism is naturally based a principle of modern exegesis which may now be regarded as established—namely, that we must interpret the words of every Scriptural writer according to the language, tone of thought, and literary habits of the times in which he lived. This principle is more than two thousand years old.   Even the Rabbis, woodenly literal as was much of their exegesis, and slavish as were their theories of inspiration, yet laid down the wise rule that 'the law speaks in the tongue of the sons of men.'

'The Holy Spirit inspires and guides,' says an American professor,[2] 'but does not destroy or diminish personal peculiarities, not always even personal ignorance.'

8. But once more I must state with the utmost earnestness that by interpreting the Scriptures on such principles we do not touch one single truth of the Christian creed; nay, by removing enormous difficulties from the path of sound belief, we help to establish the eternal verities of our religion upon a surer foundation.

9. There is, however, one consideration which inspires most alarm into the minds of humble and earnest Christians.   They fear lest any discoveries respecting the origin and characteristics of the Old Testament books should in the smallest degree collide with the authority, or the recorded utterances, of our blessed Lord.   I have already touched on this subject, and it has been so clearly treated

<hr>

[1] Dr. Jowett.

[2] Professor Lemuel S. Potern.

by some recent writers that I cannot do better than quote
the words of Professor Driver respecting this important
question also.

'That our Lord appealed to the Old Testament as the
record of a revelation in the past and as pointing forward
to Himself is undoubted; but these aspects of the Old
Testament are perfectly consistent with a critical view of
its structure and growth. That our Lord in so appealing
to it designed to pronounce a verdict on the authorship
and age of its different parts, and to foreclose all future
inquiry into these subjects, is an assumption for which no
sufficient ground can be found. . . . He accepted as the
basis of His teaching the opinions respecting the Old
Testament current around Him; He assumed, in His allusions to it, the premises which His opponents recognised,
and which could not have been questioned (even had it
been necessary to question them) without raising issues for
which the time was not yet ripe, and which, had they been
raised, would have interfered seriously with the paramount
purpose of His life.'

Further, it should not be overlooked that by the very
fact of taking our nature upon Him Christ voluntarily
submitted Himself to human limitations. To become a
man 'He emptied Himself of His glory,' and this exinani-
tion involved the necessity for speaking as a man to men.
As far back as the second century, St. Irenæus, taking this
into account, and the saying of Christ that as man there
was something which even 'the Son' did not know, admitted that there was such a thing as the quiescence (τὸ
ἡσυχάζειν) of the Divine Word.[1]

10. All that our Lord said about the Prophets has been
abundantly verified. There was in them an intensity of

<hr>

[1] Iren. *c. Hær.* iii. 19. 3; Sanday, *Oracles of God*, xiv.

confidence, a buoyancy of hope, a depth of penitence, which have made them the most natural and fitting interpreters of the spiritual emotions of the godliest souls in all ages; but there is also 'a tone as of imperfect music, a looking forward and a longing for the fuller revelation of the purposes of God, a yearning for the time when a life should be lived upon earth in complete accord with His will.' Their convictions of the divine future fulfilment of this their hope centre in their inspired prophecy of Him who should hereafter be 'a light to lighten the Gentiles, and the glory of God's people Israel.' The great Messianic hope and prediction, in one form or another, runs through them all; and 'those who have felt this will not need any limping logic or illusory indications to prove to them the inspiration of the book which records it.'

Let us, then, bear in mind the warning of Hooker, that 'Whatsoever is spoken of God, or things appertaining to God, otherwise than the truth is, though it seem an honour, it is an injury.' And of three things the reader may be sure—namely, that

i. Nothing can prevent the acceptance of the general principles of criticism, because nothing can finally retard the linear progress of truth and knowledge.

ii. The things which cannot be shaken will remain.

iii. It is a dishonourable and faithless position to be the last defenders of traditional prejudices which have been disproved by thorough and fearless investigation.

I would add but one further warning. The wisest observers are aware that there is a tendency in advancing years to arrest our progress and stereotype our opinions. It does not follow that special theological views are true because they are separable accretions to a general system of the truth of which we are convinced. How wise was the resolution of Jonathan Edwards! 'Old men,' he said, 'have seldom any advantage of new discoveries, because they are beside a way of thinking they have been long used to. Resolved therefore, if ever I live to years, that I will be impartial to hear the reasons of all pretended discoveries, and receive them, if rational, how long soever I have been used to another way of thinking.'

Nothing will be more likely to shake the faith of the rising generation than that we should mingle our religious teaching with views which the progress of knowledge—itself a part of the slow revelation of God—has rendered untenable. 'You must teach your children truth in part,' said the late Bishop Phillips Brooks, 'but the partial truth you teach them must be true, and so have in it the essential completeness of all truth, or else they will outgrow it and cast it off, as hundreds of growing children do leave behind the whole well-meant but narrowly conceived religion of their nurseries, as they pass out of the nursery door into the world.'

I know that it will not be easy for some readers to abandon their former views on these subjects. Let them, however, be watchful against the subtle arrogance which may, as a result of the immobility of their own convictions, tempt them to bring 'railing accusations' against their brethren. Let them take to heart the warning of Scripture that 'a sluggard' may 'be wiser in his own conceit than seven men who can render a reason.' 'O merciful God,' exclaims Hooker, 'what man's wit is there able to sound the depths of those dangerous and fearful evils, whereinto our weak and impotent nature is inclinable to sink itself, rather than to show an acknowledgment of error in that which we have unadvisedly taken upon us to defend, against the stream as it were of a contrary public resolution.'[1]

---

[1] Hooker, *Eccl. Pol.* Pref. ix. 1.

CHAPTER X

THE BIBLE CONTAINS THE WORD OF GOD.

'Scriptura sacra continet omnia quæ ad salutem sunt necessaria.'
—Art. VI.

THE Bible as a whole may be spoken of as the word of God, because it contains words and messages of God to the human soul; but it is not in its whole extent, and throughout, identical with the Word of God.

In the 'Treatise of the Christian Religion,' by the Puritan scholar Thomas Cartwright (1616), occurs the question:

'How may these books be discerned to bee the word of God?' The answer is:

'By these considerations following—

'First, they are perfectly holy in themselves and by themselves: whereas all other writings are prophane, further than they draw holinesse from these, which is yet never such but that their holinesse is imperfect and defective.

'Secondly, they are perfectly profitable in themselves to instruct unto salvation. . . .

'Thirdly, there is a perfect concord and harmony in all their books. . . .

'Fourthly, there is an admirable force in them to incline men's hearts from vice to virtue. . . .

'Fifthly, in great plainness and easiness of style there shineth a great majesty and authority.

'Sixthly, there is such a gracious simplicity in the writers of these books that they neither spare themselves nor their friends.

'Lastly, God's own spirit, working in the hearts of His children, doth assure them that these Scriptures are the word of God.'

One or two of these propositions are true in part; but others are irrelevant; others exaggerated; others contrary to fact; and others tainted by a fallacy of impossible extension—in other words, while they apply to the Scriptures as a whole, they do *not* apply to their entire contents. It is not true that there is a perfect harmony and concord in all books of Scripture, for as we have seen they present wide differences of standpoint. It is not true that their style is invariably plain and easy; if it were, they would not have given room for such enormous divergencies of interpretation. It is not true that every passage of Scripture is perfectly holy in and by itself; still less true that all other writings are in any derogatory sense 'prophane.' It is historically false to say that all other books 'draw their holiness from them,' and spiritually false to assert that the holiness of all other books is imperfect and defective. All truth is sacred, and all truth comes from God. The heathen were not left destitute of the grace of God. To assert that they were is to contradict not only Solomon, St. Peter, and St. Paul, but even Christ Himself. Christ found in the Gentile centurion and the Syro-Phœnician mother a faith which He had not found in Israel. St. Peter was untaught his old narrow particularism, and learnt that 'God is no respecter of persons: but *in every nation* he that feareth God, and worketh righteousness, is accepted of Him.'[1]   St. Paul constantly testifies that the heathen knew God, and the judgment of God, because that which is known of God is manifest to them, for God showed it unto them.[2]   He told the heathen Athenians that God is not far from every one of us, and he quoted and endorsed the opinion of the pagan poet Aratus that 'We are also His offspring.' St. Augustine was first stirred to nobler efforts by reading the Hortensius of Cicero, and when heathen writers express the same truths which we find in Scripture it cannot be said that, so far, what is holy in them is always imperfect and defective.

> All knowledge is not couched in Moses' law . . .
> The Gentiles also know and write, and teach
> To admiration, led by Nature's light.[3]

Cartwright's other reasons express the glory and divine value of that revelation which the Bible *contains*, but are quite inadequate to support the proposition that the Bible *is* in every verse the word of God. God's Holy Spirit, working in the hearts of His children, does indeed bear witness to the voice of that Spirit; but the appeal to this subjective witness has all the effect of 'horrible irony' when it is used, as Cartwright himself used it, to support what is false and evil. For instance, he defended, as the Church of Rome still defends, the execrable doctrine that it is lawful to torture and murder people because of their religious opinions; and he adds that if this be regarded as 'extreame and bloodie' he is 'glad to be so with the Holy Ghost'! Thus, as we see again and again, 'the attempt

---

[1] Acts x. 35.   Compare Is. lvii. 19; Mal. ii. 10.

[2] Acts xiv. 17, xvii. 26–28; Rom. i. 19, 20, ii. 10, 11, x. 12, 13; 1 Cor. xii. 13; Gal. iii. 28.

[3] *Paradise Regained*, iv.

to attach a name of supernatural sanctity to the entire contents of the Bible ends in the degradation of that name itself.'[1]

If anybody is shocked by the plain statement that every word of Scripture is *not* the word of God, it can only be out of ignorance. For that statement is in exact accordance with the teaching both of Scripture and of the Church.

i. This view accords with the teaching of Scripture itself. Everywhere the style of the writers, and even the defects and infirmities of the style; everywhere the individuality of the writers, and often even the human weakness which their individuality betrays—in many places the marks of human passion and infirmity, and the consciousness that they are present—show that, though these holy men of old spake, indeed, as they were moved by the Holy Ghost, yet at the same time they remain liable to human limitations. Of many passages we may truly say, with Gregory of Nyssa, that 'if the corporeal veil of speech be removed, that which remains is Lord, and life, and Spirit.'[2] But always the corporeal veil of speech is there; and if human speech be but an *asymptote* to human thought—if it resemble that mathematical line which continually approaches towards the edge of the curve, but though infinitely produced yet never touches it—how can human speech be a perfect vehicle of the Divine thought? That may be one of the reasons why (as already pointed out) *not once throughout the New Testament is the Old Testament called 'the Word of God;' not once throughout all Scripture is the Bible called 'the Word of God,' though the phrase itself occurs between 300 and 400 times.* In the Old Testament 'the word of Jehovah' is always applied to some particular prophetic

---

[1] Rev. A. Mackennal.   [2] Greg. Nyss. *c. Eunom.* vii.

10

message or messages, which in their collective form may
be called (by way of figure, as John Damascene says)
'oracles of God,' because they contain such oracles.[1]   In
the New Testament the facts and oral preaching of the
Gospel are called 'the word,'[2] 'the word of hearing,'[3] 'of
truth,'[4] 'of salvation,'[5] 'of reconciliation,'[6] 'of grace,'[7] 'of
the kingdom,'[8] and are therefore rightly regarded as a
word or message of God, and about God; but in all these
instances the reference is *not to written books* at all, still less
to the entire contents of sixty-six written books, out of
which some twelve or more were only with hesitation
admitted as Deutero-canonical.   Even as applied to the
Gospel message the phrase is used in a secondary sense.
In its true and supreme sense the title 'the Word of God'
is applicable to Christ and to Christ alone.   Luther
pointed out long ago that 'God does not reveal grammatical vocables, but essential things.   Thus sun and
moon, Peter and Paul, thou and I, are nothing but words
of God.'   And we may, with Hartley Coleridge,

> Believe that every bird that sings,
> And every flower that stars the elastic sod,
> And every breath the radiant summer brings
> To the pure spirit, is a word of God.

But Christ alone is '*the* Word of God.'

ii.   And with this teaching of Scripture agrees the teaching of the Universal Church.   The formal identification of
the Bible in its whole contents with the very Word of God

---

[1] Hos. i. 1; Mic. i. 1; Joel i. 1; Rom. iii. 2.
[2] Luke i. 2; Acts viii. 4.   [3] 1 Thess. ii. 13; Heb. iv. 2.
[4] Eph. i. 13.   [5] Acts xiii. 26.   [6] 2 Cor. v. 19.
[7] Acts xx. 32.   [8] Matt. xiii. 19.

is neither ancient nor catholic. It may sometimes seem to be implied in the looser rhetoric of the Fathers, but is contrary to their deliberate method of handling Scripture, and is in fact an error of yesterday.

Perhaps the first writer who rigorously identified Scripture throughout its whole extent with the Word of God was George Major in his book, 'De origine et auctoritate verbi Dei,' 1550; but, as Diestel says, 'Luther never fell into the error. He gives to "the word of God" a narrower and a wider sense than the Scriptures. It is to him the expression of the Divine Will, especially on its religious side.'

As far back as the eighth century the eminently orthodox Father, John of Damascus, had laid down the rule that 'We apply not to the written word of Scripture the title due to the Incarnate Son of God.'

The doctrine of the Church in general is, and always has been, the doctrine of the Church of England, that 'Scripture *contains* the word of God.'   It was only to men like Calov that the testimony of the Holy Spirit became mainly an inward assurance that their own private opinions are irrefragably right! The work of the Holy Spirit was degraded into a recalling to memory of proof-texts; and Scripture was declared to be a sort of oracular teraph, a self-efficacious organism endowed with the inherent power of radiating infallible theology! The repeated comments of Luther and Calvin, in spite of their occasional laxity of popular declamation, show that they would have repudiated such views. 'It was,' it has been said, 'an after-thought of less original and courageous minds to make no distinction between different parts of the Bible, to regard it all with the same dull and superstitious reverence, and to force the most reluctant facts into the mould of their belief.' Nor were these extravagant assertions of Calov and others allowed to pass without protest. 'The external word,' said Schwenkenfeld, 'is the human voice, in which there is included no divine virtue.' 'If thou sayest among the inexperienced,' says Weigel, 'that the letter is God's word, thou art . . . a deceiver.' 'The Scripture is not called divine because everything contained in it should be imputed to a special revelation,' said the learned Georg Calixt (1656); and this view was also maintained by divines of such eminent learning and holiness both within and without the English Church as Baxter, South, and Doddridge.

To assert that the phrase 'Scripture containeth' (*complectitur*) instead of 'is' (*est*) the Word of God is only *an accident* in the formularies of the English Church, is the reverse of fact; for we find it three times over.

In the Sixth Article we have:

'Holy Scripture *containeth* all things necessary to salvation.'

In the Homilies:

'Unto a Christian man there can be nothing more necessary or profitable than the knowledge of Holy Scripture, forasmuch as *in it is contained* God's true word.'

And in the services for the ordering of priests and bishops we have the question:

'Are you persuaded that the Holy Scriptures *contain* sufficiently all doctrine required of necessity for eternal salvation through faith in Jesus Christ?'[1]

---

[1] The older confessions of the Reformed Churches deliberately used the same word, *Conf. Gal.* art. 5, '*Complectens* . . . quicquid requiratur;' *Conf. Belg.* art. 7, "Credimus Scripturas . . . omnem Dei voluntatem *complecti.*' The 'Formula Consensus Helvetici' (drawn up by F. Turretin in 1675) did indeed say 'Scriptura *est*

And so in the Shorter Catechism we read 'the word of God which is *contained* in the Scriptures of the Old and New Testament, is the only rule to direct us how we may enjoy and glorify Him.'

Whether then by providential superintendency or by reasonable knowledge, the Church of England has never pledged her children to maintain that every word of Scripture is infallible and inerrant, as though it came immediately from God Himself.

verbum Dei,' but by 1729 it was already rejected and forgotten. The words of the Helvetic Confession were 'Hebraicus Vet. Test. codex, tum quoad consonas tum quoad vocalia sive puncta ipsa, seu punctorum saltem potestatem, et tum quoad res, tum quoad verba, θεόπνευστος.'

CHAPTER XI

BIBLICAL INFALLIBILITY.

'Spiritus Domini replevit orbem terrarum.'—Wisd. i. 7.

'Lumen supernum nunquam descendit sine indumento.'—Kabbalah.

THE Bible is amply sufficient for our instruction in all those truths which are *necessary to salvation*. Its final teaching is our surest guide to all holiness. We hear the voice of God breathing through it; we see the hand of God at work in its preservation for the human race. The Bible contains the historic revelation of the Eternal Christ. And in the Old as well as in the New Testament we may and do find the promise of a Redeemer, and of His good will towards us. *In everything which is requisite for man's salvation*, the lessons contained in Scripture—*with the co-ordinate help of that Spirit by whom its writers were moved* to aid us in our discrimination—are an infallible guide to us in things necessary. This we hold with all our hearts, and for this we thank God continually. But this is wholly different from the assertion that the Bible is throughout and in all respects infallible or inerrant.

Man is always demanding an infallible authority on all subjects; and he cannot have it. God has granted to him a lamp unto his feet and a light unto his path, bright enough to guide him to eternal blessedness. He has caused a pillar of fire to shed its gleam through the midnight which surrounds him and to lead him through the wilderness. But as regards all else except the guidance of his journey to the promised land the pillar of fire avails not. The darkness is still darkness, and the wilderness is still the wilderness. Every Christian may learn from the Bible the sole knowledge which is infinitely needful. This is vouchsafed to him from above. For all other knowledge he is left to the exercise of his own intellect; nor has God ever supernaturally revealed any truth to which man could naturally attain.

The 'infallibility' then of the records of Divine revelation is rigidly circumscribed by the immediate purpose for which that revelation was intended.

And as though to indicate how unimportant is any such collateral infallibility, *there are scarcely any two great branches of the Christian Church which are even agreed as to what constitutes the Bible.* They are agreed neither as to the constituent books; nor as to the authoritative text; nor as to the correct interpretation; nor as to the question whether any supplemental authority is necessary; nor, if so, where the true supplement is to be found.

i. They are not agreed as to the books which constitute the Bible.

To the Church of the first century for many years the Bible was all but exclusively the Old Testament.

To the Church of the second and third centuries the New Testament was an indeterminate number of Christian writings.

To the Church of the fifth century—and to all the Western Church, especially since the Council of Trent— the Apocrypha was also a part of the Bible.[1]

---

[1] Conc. Trid. Sess. iv. 'Sacrosancta Synodus . . . omnes libros pari pietatis affectu et reverentia suscipit.'

The Syrian Canon only recognised three of the Catholic Epistles (James, 1 Peter, 1 John); and it rejected the Apocalypse, as do the lists of Chrysostom and Theodore.[1]

The ancient Jewish Church held that the Old Testament was insufficient without the addition of the oral Law.

The modern Jewish Church takes the Old Testament in connection with the oral Law, the *Torah Shebeal Peh*, now embodied in the Talmud—Mishna and Gemara.

In some of the Reformed Churches certain books of the Old and New Testaments are still considered to be of dubious authenticity and only secondary authority.

ii. Nor are the different Churches agreed as to the authoritative text.

To the Eastern Church the Old Testament is represented by the Greek translation.

To the Western Church the Bible means the Latin translation of Jerome (the Vulgate) with the Apocrypha.

To the English Churches the Bible means ultimately the Hebrew and Greek originals, exclusive of the Apocrypha.[2]

iii. Nor, again, are the Churches agreed as to any rule of interpretation.

In the Romish Church, interpretation must be consonant with the opinion of the Fathers, Councils, Popes, and 'tradition' generally. It appeals to an *unanimis consensus patrum* which has no existence, and to 'unwritten traditions,' of which many are mere sacerdotal inventions.[3]

---

[1] On the Syrian Canon see Bishop Westcott, *The Bible in the Church*, 231 ff.

[2] 'Divine authority cannot be claimed for anything which is not *a correct translation of an exact copy* of an originally authorised utterance and writing.'—Professor Olver.

[3] At the Council of Trent Bishop Nachianti, of Chiozza, maintained that Scripture was the only final authority, 'because in the Gospel everything was written which was necessary to salvation;'

The Reformed Churches maintain the right of private judgment, with no necessary reference to any such external authorities.

The Greek Church only lays down the vague rule that interpretation must be consonant with her own authority.

Thus, even if there be an infallible rule as to any truths outside the Catholic creeds, there is no agreement in the Churches of Christendom as to what the infallible rule is. 'The Bible' means one text, and one translation, and one set of books, and one line of interpretation to the Greek Church; another text, another translation, another set of books, and another line of interpretation to the Latin; and another to the Churches of the Reformation.

It is true that when Luther dethroned the Pope from his position of pretended infallibility, the narrow and greatly inferior divines of the succeeding century endeavoured to derive *from the Bible* the same infallible decision on all the subjects of human knowledge. It was assumed that this assertion of Biblical infallibility would secure unity in the views and uniformity in the practices of Christendom. And certainly if, on the whole breadth of subjects respecting which Christians differ, God had intended that there should be an infallible guide, we should have looked for some approach to unity, if not to uniformity, in the beliefs of Christendom. But an infallible guide would be obviously useless without infallible decisions as to what the guide is and what it says. We do find in Christian thought a general unity of creed; we find no unity whatever in opinions, in organisation, or in ceremonial. When the doctrine of Scriptural infallibility

but he was enormously outvoted, and it was decided that 'unwritten traditions' were to be accepted with the same veneration as the Holy Scriptures (Ranke, i. 203).

was proclaimed with the utmost fierceness of inflexible dogmatism, Werenfels—looking round him at the bitter opinionativeness which was raging in antagonistic sects —wrote, with a sigh, the celebrated epigram—

> Hic liber est in quo quærit *sua dogmata* quisque,
> Invenit et pariter dogmata quisque—*sua.*
>
> *His own opinions* here by each are sought,
> And here to each *his own opinions* taught.

Clearly, then, the infallibility of the letter, in all its details, even if it existed, and even if all were agreed as to what the letter is, would be useless without some further infallible guide as to what the letter *was intended to mean;* so that for all practical purposes the dogma is infinitely sterile and leads to no results.

The plain teachings of Christ are the sole infallible guide; and they deal with the essential faith, and that only. What do the wide differences of Christians mean, except that they practically refuse to accept Scripture alone as their guide, or are unwilling or unable to understand Scripture in the sense which it conveys to other Christians?

Divines of the most opposite schools—Popes and Reformers—have insisted on the absolute 'lucidity' of Scripture. It is true that in its simplest elements of Gospel morality—in all that is essential to human saintliness and human salvation—the meaning of the Bible is so transparent that he who runs may read, and that the wayfaring man, yea, and even fools, need not err therein; but when we proceed to the minutiæ of theology and ecclesiasticism the existing state of Christendom is alone a sufficient proof either that Scripture is *not* easy to be understood, or that Christians of all schools have gone out of the way to create the most immense difficulties for themselves.   What some Christians, even in the same Church, regard as dogmas and practices of consummate sacredness, others, quite as able and quite as sincere, despise as specimens of crude materialism and unworthy fetish-worship.

Whence comes the separation of antagonistic Churches and the multiplicity of dissident sects?   'The Romanist' (if I may adopt with some modification the words of another) 'reads the Bible, and he finds in it the primacy of Peter, the supremacy of the Church, and the direction to "do penance" for the forgiveness of sins.   The Protestant reads it, and he discovers that Rome is the "mystic Babylon," the "mother of harlots," the "abomination of desolation."   The Sacerdotalist reads it, and he sees priestly supremacy, eucharistic sacrifice, and sacramental salvation. The Protestant cannot find in it the faintest trace of Sacerdotalism, nor any connection whatever between offering and actual sacrifice and the holy memorial of the Supper of the Lord.   The Congregationalist reads it, and regards Sacerdotalism as an enormous apostasy from the meaning and spirit of the Gospel, and comes away convinced that every believer is his own all-sufficient priest. The Baptist looks into it, and thinks that in baptism true believers must go under the water as adults; most other Christians think that infants should be baptised and that sprinkling is sufficient.   Cromwell and his Roundheads read it, and saw everywhere the Lord of Hosts leading on His followers to battle.   The Quaker reads it, finds only the Prince of Peace, and declares, "He that takes the sword shall perish with the sword."   The Anglican Churchman was long persuaded that it taught the doctrine of passive obedience, and

The right divine of kings to govern wrong.

The Puritan dwelt on "binding their kings in chains and their nobles with links of iron." The Calvinist sees the dreadful image of wrath flaming over all its pages, and says to his enemies, "Our God is a consuming fire." The Universalist only sees the loving heavenly Father, and explains the most awful forebodings as Oriental tropes and pictorial rhetoric. The Mormon picks out phrases to bolster up his polygamy; the Monogamist cries out even against divorce; the Shaker and his congeners in all ages forbid or disparage all wedded unions whatever. The American of the Northern States loaded his gun with texts and went out to fight for freedom; the Southerner quoted the curse of Ham, and the Epistle to Philemon, declared that slavery was a divine institution, and that it was impious unbelief to regard it as a crime.'

'In the mirror of the Bible, each partisan will practically see nothing but his own face. Each declares, more or less emphatically, "All good and honest people see it as I do;" and many add, "a different opinion means wilful blindness and a bad heart." Each sect is tempted to treat its own enemies as the Lord's enemies; and when any one sect or branch of the Church is absolutely dominant, as was the Church of Rome in the Dark Ages, it has usually given its opponents a terrific foretaste of "uncovenanted mercies" by burning them alive in this world, and handing them over to endless torments in the next.'

Even as to the most obvious and elementary conceptions of how we may obtain salvation there are—though there ought *not* to be—the most striking differences. One man is convinced that faith alone saves us, and that 'works are deadly;' another can quote passages from Genesis to Revelation to show that the only way to please God is to do the thing that is right. One man attaches a notion of saintliness to exaggerated asceticism; another looks upon it as a faithless will-worship, a sin against the body, due to false and semi-Manichean conceptions of the God of love, and tending only to destroy the body and daze the soul.

Truly, if over the whole extent of what we call 'religion' men have an infallible guide, they have—and that to all appearance inevitably—rendered it worse than useless by fallible expositions. Of seven great systems of interpretation which have been dominant since there ever was a collected Bible, the bare rules and *à priori* conceptions on which six were based have been definitely abandoned, and have been, in their applications at any rate, demonstrably wrong.[1]

Whole libraries are filled with commentaries on the Bible, in all languages, which are now regarded as entirely obsolete. Yet they were laborious and honest attempts on the part of their authors to explain the true meaning of the Holy Scriptures. They were only vitiated by partial knowledge, false religious systems, or *à priori* prejudices which failed to see the significance of Scripture because they looked at it through blinding mists of traditional misconception.

[1] See the writer's Bampton Lectures on the History of Interpretation, p. 12. Who can say that the Rabbinic, the Kabbalistic, the Alexandrian, the Allegorical, the Mystic, the Inferential, the Scholastic system of Exegesis are not, as systems, dead and buried? Any commentary which adopted these methods would in these days be laughed out of court, or flung aside as obsolete, and almost as an insult to the understanding.

CHAPTER XII

DANGEROUS RESULTS OF THE SUPERNATURAL DICTATION THEORY.

'Ecclesia non facit Verbum, sed fit Verbo.'—LUTHER.

'Having waste ground enough,
Shall we desire to raze the sanctuary
And plant our evils there?'—WHITTIER.

DOCTRINES may be tested and disproved not only by demonstrating the falsity of the assumptions on which they profess to be founded, but also by showing the pernicious or dangerous character of their invariable results. This method is sanctioned by Christ Himself. 'By their fruits,' He said, 'ye shall know them. Do men gather grapes of thorns, or figs of thistles?'

What have been the fruits of this doctrine of Biblical infallibility?

Let us begin by testing it in one domain only—the domain of science.

It is now generally recognised, except among the half-educated, that on scientific subjects the Bible neither is, nor professes to be, nor in accordance with the whole economy of God's dealing with the human race ever *could* have been, any authority at all on subjects which do not fall under its proper object. 'The Scriptures,' said Archbishop Sumner, 'have never revealed a single scientific truth.' They do not concern themselves with the problems of which the solution belongs to experimental investigation. The knowledge of the writers of Scripture on the subject of exact science was simply the human and individual knowledge of those writers, and that was the knowledge, or rather the ignorance, of the most unscientific of all nations in the most unscientific of all ages. To the Hebrews by whom the greater part of the Bible was written science was unknown; their immemorial habits of thought were wholly alien from the scientific spirit.

Men cling so obstinately to religious hypotheses long exploded and originally without foundation, that some perhaps may regard these statements as heterodox novelties, whereas they were orthodox truisms long before anything that could be called science was established. They are practically admitted even by St. Augustine in the fourth century, and distinctly laid down by the famous schoolman Peter Lombard, 'the Master of the Sentences.' [1] No one has expressed them more clearly than Galileo, who was persecuted and forced to recant because he had dispelled an infallible ignorance and discovered some of the most splendid certainties which had yet been made known to the race of man. 'I believe,' he says, 'that the intention of Holy Writ was to persuade men of the truths necessary to salvation, such as neither science nor other means could render credible, but only the voice of the Holy Spirit. But I do not think it necessary to believe that the same God who gave us our senses, our speech, our intellect, would have put aside the use of these to teach us instead such things as with their help we could find out for ourselves, particularly in the case of those

---

[1] *Sentent.* ii. dist. 23.

sciences of which there is not the smallest mention in Scripture.'

There is scarcely a modern science which has not been brought into deplorable conflict with the Bible by theologians who misunderstood its scope and misapplied its expressions. The history of most modern sciences has been as follows. Their discoverers have been proscribed, anathematised, and, in every possible instance, silenced or persecuted; yet before a generation has passed, the champions of a spurious orthodoxy have had to confess that their interpretations were erroneous; and—for the most part without an apology and without a blush—have complacently invented some new line of exposition by which the phrases of Scripture can be squared into semblable accordance with the now acknowledged facts.

Mr. J. S. Mill was right in his keen analysis when he said that the reception accorded to each new truth passed through three phases. First it was declared to be dangerous and false; next it was acknowledged that there was something to be said for it; and, lastly, men turn round and declare, 'We said so all along.'[2] So, with reference to each new scientific discovery, religious teachers begin by saying, 'It is blasphemous and contrary to Scripture;' they soon maintain 'there is nothing in Scripture which absolutely contradicts it;' and they generally end by declaring that it is distinctly revealed in Scripture itself. Men build the tombs of the prophets whom their fathers slew, and in every way possible to them continue to

---

[1] Letter to Castelli, 1613. Compare the remarks made by Columbus at Salamanca in 1486.

[2] 'Lorsque Colomb avait promis un nouvel hémisphère, on lui avait soutenu que cet hémisphère ne pouvait exister; et quand il l'eut découvert, qu'il avait été connu depuis longtemps.'—Voltaire.

slay the prophets whom their own generation brings forth.[1]

The only question to be asked about any new datum of science is whether it is proven or not. If it be true, it is a revelation of God in the sphere of nature and cannot possibly contradict any other revelation. A new scientific discovery may very well contradict some incidental phrase in a book which is not concerned with physical inquiries; and it may collide still more absolutely with the ignorant misinterpretations and unwarrantable inferences of inquisitors and popes. The history of exegesis is, in great measure, a history of errors. But Nature is a book which contains a revelation of God in one sphere, and Scripture a book which contains a revelation of Him in another. Both books have often been misread, but no *truth* revealed in the one can be irreconcilable with any truth revealed in the other. Nothing has done deadlier injury to the majesty of Scripture in its own proper sphere than the pride which has led its incompetent interpreters to assume that they could utter infallible oracles respecting every branch of human knowledge and wield the thunderbolts of God with the puny impotence of man.

It is argued by writers like Gaussen that the Bible is a perfect authority in scientific matters. If that were so, how useless has such an anticipation of the scientific toil of years proved itself to be! If that be so, how comes it that all the leaders of science and discoverers of new truths have found their bitterest critics among religious teachers? and how comes it that the cosmogonies which were asserted to be based exclusively on Scriptural data have been so glaringly ludicrous? Will anybody accept

[1] See Dr. Andrew D. White, *New Chapters in the Warfare of Science* (New York, 1888).

11

in these days the tissue of absurdities professedly deduced
from Scripture by Pfeiffer in his 'Pansophia Mosaica'? or
the 'Lithographiæ Specimen' of Professor Beringer? or
the 'Topographia Christiana' of the Monk Cosmas In-
dicopleustes (about A.D. 540)? or 'The New Theory of the
Earth from its Original to the Consummation of all
Things,' by the Rev. William Whiston (1696)? or the
'Telluris Theoria Sacra' of Thomas Burnet? Such books
furnish the clearest *reductio ad absurdum* of the Biblical
theories from which they sprang. Their infallible science
is beneath criticism. 'Whiston,' said Hallam, 'opposed
Burnet's theory, but with one not less unfounded, nor with
less ignorance of all that is required to be known.'[1]

i. What has become of Lactantius's denial, on the authority of Scripture, that the world is round? What has
become of the confident assertion of Ambrose, and so many
of the Fathers, that the sky is a solid vault, because in
Genesis it is called in the Hebrew *raqiang*, and in the
Greek version στερέωμα? What has become of the assertion
of Augustine that there could be no Antipodes, because
such a belief would be contradictory to Scripture?[2] What
has become of the arguments of bigoted Spanish priests

---

[1] Hallam, *Lit. Hist. of Eur.* iii. 594. Calixt was called an impious
heretic for denying that heaven was a solid vault; and another theologian, in the sixteenth century, argued that God 'left the vault
swinging there until three days later he put the earth under it.' On
the whole subject see especially Zöckler, *Gesch. d. Beziehungen
zwischen Theologie u. Naturwissenschaft*; Lyell's *Geology* (Introduction); and the book of Dr. Andrew Dickson White, late President of
Cornell University, on the *Warfare of Science*. He points out the
three phases of this warfare—first, the hurling of Scripture texts at
the new scientific truth; then the pitting against it of some theological doctrine; thirdly, 'reconciliations' and 'harmonies.'

[2] Aug. *De Civ. Dei*, xvi. 9. Similarly Pope Zacharias, Ep. x. *ad
Bonifac.*, where the belief in the Antipodes is called '*perversa* et
iniqua doctrina.'

who tried on Biblical grounds to argue the impossibility that Columbus could discover another hemisphere? Did not even Calvin protest against the heliocentric system because it seemed to him inconsistent with 'He hath made the round world *so fast that it cannot be moved*'? 'Who,' he asked, 'will venture to place the authority of Copernicus above that of the Holy Spirit?' And did not even John Wesley reject the system of Copernicus because he declared it to be incompatible with Scripture? The learned Puritan John Owen had already done the same. 'Newton's discoveries,' he said, 'are against evident testimonies of Scripture.' Even Kepler had to suffer for years from the attacks and opposition of ecclesiastical ignorance.

'I challenge these divines and their adherents,' says Coleridge, 'to establish the compatibility of a belief in modern astronomy and natural philosophy with their doctrine respecting the inspired Scriptures, without reducing the doctrine itself to a plaything of wax—or rather a half-inflated bladder, which, when the contents are rarefied in the heat of rhetorical generalities, swells out round and without a crease or wrinkle.'

ii. In Roger Bacon (b. 1214) God gave to the world the keenest and noblest intellect which appeared for twelve centuries. Had he been left in peace to pursue the bent of his heaven-bestowed genius, he might have antedated by generations not a few of the most beneficent and beautiful of scientific discoveries. Unfortunately, however, he was a Franciscan, placed by his circumstances under the tyranny of friars. He was treated as a magician, ignorantly scorned, ignorantly thwarted, calumniated, tortured, for ten years confined to a dungeon.[1] And it is said that before he died he so felt the boundless stupidity and

---

[1] He says (*Opus Tertium*) that he was starved and treated 'ineffabili violentia.'

ingratitude displayed towards him in the world and by the Church as to declare that men were not worth serving and working for.

iii. God kindled another radiant light in the soul of Galileo (b. 1564). While still quite young the gifted boy, watching, if the story be true, the swinging of the great bronze lamp in the cathedral of Pisa, and measuring its oscillations by the beat of his pulse, discovered the 'isochronism of the vibrations of the pendulum.' He was still young when, by experimenting with metal balls from the Leaning Tower of Pisa, he discovered the law of the velocity of falling bodies. He invented the thermometer, and by his telescope discovered the phases of Venus and the satellites of Jupiter, and resolved into separate stars the Nebulæ of the Galaxy. In 1616 Pope Paul V. summoned him to Rome, and forbade him to teach the true theory of the universe. But in 1632 his famous dialogue on the Ptolemaic and Copernican systems raised an outcry at Rome; and Galileo, then sixty-eight, was summoned before the Inquisition, confined to prison, and forced to abjure on his knees the true doctrine of the motion of the earth. *E pur si muove!* The 'Holy Office' placed the 'De Orbium Cœlestium Revolutionibus' of Copernicus, and Kepler's abridgment of it, on the index of prohibited books.

In 1616 the theologians of the 'Holy Office' denounced the heliocentric theory as 'absurd in philosophy and formally heretical, because expressly contrary to Holy Scriptures,'[1] and the discovered rotation of the earth as 'open to the same censure in philosophy, and at least erroneous as to faith.'

iv. Similarly as late as the middle of the eighteenth

---

[1] The reference was to Josh. x. 12!

century the illustrious Buffon was assailed by the theological faculty of the Sorbonne, and forced to recant the
simple geological truths which he had stated. This
humiliating document reminds us painfully of that forced
upon Galileo. It runs, 'I abandon everything in my book
respecting the formation of the earth, and generally all
which may be contrary to the narrative of Moses.' The
line now taken by apologists is very different from that
of previous centuries, and less honest. It declares that
Genesis and geology are in exact accord. It no longer
refuses to believe the facts of nature, but instead of this
it boldly sophisticates the facts of Scripture.

v. We eulogise the martyrs of science, and declare that
we should not have been so foolish and so cruel if we had
lived in the days of our fathers. Yet we have learnt no
wisdom. When God gave the world the priceless boon of
anæsthetics, one of the most blessed and gracious gifts to
a worn and weary generation, there were many who declared that to use anæsthetics in the commonest cases of
anguish was to fly in the face of Providence by trying to
escape the curse which God had pronounced on the daughters of Eve! In these days no one ventures to reject the
results of modern geology; but when geologists began to
decipher the records carved by God's finger on the stone
tablets of the world, and were driven by the force of facts
to maintain that the world could not have been made in
six literal days, and must have lasted for indefinite æons
longer than six thousand years, they were met with floods
of furious anathema and declared to be blasphemers and
atheists deserving of everlasting perdition.[1] But 'such

---

[1] Thus, forgotten clergymen, the Reverend J. Mellor Brown and
the Reverend H. Cole, called men like Professor Sedgwick 'infidels,'
'impugners of the sacred record,' 'assailants of the volume of God,'

methods were like Chinese gongs and dragon lanterns against rifled cannon.'[1]

But what has now become of the notion of some that fossil remains were due to Noah's flood? What of Scheuchzer's *Homo diluvii testis* (1726), which turned out to be not a drowned giant, but a harmless fossil lizard? Where are all the scores of triumphant refutations of the wicked geologists?

In all such conflicts a self-styled theology, intruding into regions of which it is profoundly nescient, exhibits nothing but its own impotence and rage. No sight is more distressing than that of religious teachers who, knowing little of anything, and nothing of science, and not exhibiting the smallest sign of moral elevation over others, but often very much the reverse, assume oracular airs of superiority over the patient students of God's works. Nothing but rout has ever followed such attempted usurpations. Whatever inferences may have been drawn from the misapplication of the narrative of creation, there is no sane person who now believes that the world was made in six solar days; or that the trees and plants were created before there was any sunlight; or that all the stars were created after the earth was covered with vegetation; or that all the fishes and birds were created previ-

&c. See Lecky, *England in the Eighteenth Century*, ch. ix.; Lyell, Introduction to *Principles of Geology*.

[1] 'The favourite weapon of the "orthodox" party was the charge that the geologists were "attacking the truth of God." They denounced geology as "a dark art," "dangerous and disreputable," "infernal artillery," "an awful evasion of the testimony of Revelation." This attempt to scare men from the science having failed . . . it is humiliating to human nature to remember the annoyances, and even trials, to which the pettiest and narrowest of men subjected such scholars as Silliman, Hitchcock, and Louis Agassiz.'—Dr. White.

ously to all quadrupeds and reptiles; or a multitude of other details which have been inferred from regarding the first chapter of Genesis as a scientific document instead of regarding it as a religious revelation. It is now understood by competent inquirers that geology is God's revelation to us of one set of truths, and Genesis of quite another.

vi. Again, which of us does not remember the burst of scorn and hatred with which the theory of evolution was first received? Mr. Darwin endured the fury of pulpits and Church Congresses with quiet dignity. Not one angry or contemptuous word escaped him. The high example of patient magnanimity and Christian forbearance was set by *him;* the savage denunciations and fierce insolence came from those who should have set a better example. What has happened since then? The hypothesis of evolution, taken in its whole extent, is still an hypothesis only. Proofs final and decisive are confessedly wanting. On the admission of its supporters links are still missing from the evidence in its favour. Yet before Mr. Darwin's life was over two things had happened. On the one hand his hypothesis had been accepted as a luminous guide to inquiry by the large majority of the leading scientists of Europe and America; and even those who reject its extreme inferences fully admit that it rests on a wide induction and furnishes an explanation for many phenomena. That there is such a law as that of natural selection in the struggle for existence all are now agreed. Further, the theory of evolution has now been admitted as a possible explanation of the phenomena of life by leading theologians, and we have been told on all sides that, if it should prove to be true, there is nothing in it which is contrary to the creeds of the Catholic faith. Not a voice was raised in opposition when Mr. Darwin was laid with a nation's approval in his honoured grave in Westminster Abbey; and—seeing how noble was his example, how gentle and pure his character, how simple his devotion to truth, how deep his studies, how memorable his discoveries, even apart from the view which is mainly associated with his name— I regarded it as an honour that I was asked to be one of the bearers of his pall, and to preach his funeral sermon in the nave of 'the great temple of silence and reconciliation.'

vii. The dim and furious battle between science and that which was mistaken for religion has been chiefly waged over the first chapter of Genesis.   That chapter is of transcendent value, and in a few lines corrected the Idolatry, the Polytheism, the Atheism, the Pantheism, the Ditheism, the Agnosticism, the Pessimism of millions of mankind. No science has ever collided with, or can ever modify its true and deep object, which was to set right an erring world in the supremely important knowledge that there was one God and Father of us all, the Creator of heaven and earth, a God who saw all things which He has made, and pronounced them to be very good.   It was written to substitute simplicity for monstrous complications, and peace for wild terrors, and hope for blank despair.

It is not worth while to expose again the absurdities distorted out of this great chapter by its professed commentators.   I have shown in my Bampton Lectures the masses of folly educed from it by the systematised and fatal art of Jewish and Christian misinterpretation.[1] They who will may there read the trivialities, heresies, and forced inferences, for which the very first verse of it was made responsible by the Talmudists, by Philo, by the

---

[1] *History of Interpretation* (Bampton Lectures, 1885), pp. 36–41.

Fathers, by the Kabbalists, by Pico of Mirandola, and many more. St. Augustine, far wiser in some of his general remarks than in the minutiæ of his detailed explanations, truly says that 'the *Sense* of Scripture *is* Scripture;' but 'by giving it a wrong sense,' says Bishop Wordsworth, 'men make God's word become their own word, or even the Tempter's word, and then Scripture is used for our destruction, instead of making us wise unto salvation.'[1]

[1] *Miscellanies,* ii. 17.

CHAPTER XIII

THE BIBLE NOT THE ONLY SOURCE FROM WHICH WE CAN LEARN OF GOD.

'The fulness of Him who filleth all in all.'—Eph. i. 23.

'God hath filled all things, and hath penetrated all things, and hath left nothing empty or void of Himself.'—PHILO, *De Legg. Allegg.* iii. 2.

> 'One accent of the Holy Ghost
> The heedless world has never lost.'—EMERSON.

> 'Three volumes he assiduously perused,
> Which heavenly wisdom and delight infused,
> God's works, his conscience, and the Book inspired.'
> BISHOP KEN, *Hymnotheo.*

IT was the once widely current saying of Chillingworth that 'the Bible and the Bible only is the religion of Protestants.'

The phrase was far from accurate; for how can a book *be* a religion?

Many definitions of religion have been attempted. It has been called 'a likeness to God according to our ability' (Plato); 'reverence to the moral law as a divine command' (Kant); 'the union of the Finite with the Infinite' (Schelling); 'the whole duty of man' (Jeremy Taylor); 'submission with homage' (Holbeach). The essence of it has been said to consist 'in the sense of an open secret which man cannot penetrate' (Huxley) and 'the seeing in nature a somewhat transcending nature' (Renan). Fleck, after careful examination, defines it as 'a binding back, a restraining of men, an arrest of their natural impulses and desires.'[1] Whichcote admirably says, 'Religion is a good mind and a good life.' 'Religion,' says the Bishop of Durham, 'in its completeness is the harmony of Philosophy, Ethics, and Art, blended into one by a spiritual force, by a consecration at once personal and absolute.'[2]

In which of all these senses can the Bible *be* a religion? 'The letter,' said Lessing, 'is not the Spirit, and the Bible is not religion—the religion was there before a Bible existed.'

Chillingworth might have expressed what was no doubt his real meaning in many forms which would have been both true and unobjectionable. He might have said that the Bible sufficiently *contains* the religion of Protestants; or that Protestants refer to the Bible as their sole ultimate authority; or that the Bible, without any addition, will teach a Christian all that he ought to know for his soul's salvation.

But besides the slovenly laxity of calling the Bible 'a religion,' an entirely false conception may be conveyed by saying that 'the Bible *only* is the religion of Protestants.'

For this would seem to exclude all other sources of Divine instruction. God has provided us with other means of knowing Him, and it is not piety, but ingratitude and

---

[1] *Dogmatik*, 1–10. See Parker, *Disc. of Rel.* p. 27; Griffith, *Fundamentals*, p. 252. Fleck quotes A. Gellius, 'Religiosus pro casto atque observante, cohibenteque sese certis legibus finibusque dici est coeptus;' and Servius, 'Religio, *i.e.* Metus ab eo quod mentem religet;' Arnobius, 'Religio saepissime est horror, qui objectus nobis ab aliquo signo, coercet nos et quasi religatos tenet.'

[2] Westcott, *Rel. Thought in the West*, p. 344.

neglect, to close and repudiate the other works of God for the undue glorification of one among them.

Scripture is not God's *only* revelation to mankind. On the contrary, one of the priceless blessings which Scripture bestows upon our race is that it constantly refers us to other sources of revelation, and gives us our best help towards their interpretation. 'In the deepest meaning of the essential and only truth,' says Stier, 'all things in the world are only variously embodied words of the Creator, inasmuch as by His mighty word alone they are upheld in being. Hence the Hebrew *Dabhar* and the Greek *Rhema* signify in Scripture both "word" and "thing."' 'God does not speak grammatical vocables,' says Luther, 'but true essential things. Thus sun and moon, Peter and Paul, thou and I, are nothing but words of God.' 'Facts,' it has been said, 'are God's words, and to be disloyal to God's facts is to dethrone Him from the world.'

1. For instance, God is revealed to us in History. With God the facts of history are lessons. Amid the wildest tumults of national confusion His voice is heard. Amid the most intricate perplexities of human aims, His hand is still laid upon the wheelwork of human destiny. His Spirit is in the wheels, and unless the Spirit moves, the wheels move not. No man can study the authentic history of any nation without hearing a great voice rolling across the centuries which proclaims a law older and more majestic than any human legislation. Such Psalms as the 105th, the 106th, the 135th, the 136th; such swift summaries of the Jewish annals as are found in Deuteronomy i.–iii., in Joshua xxiv., in 2 Kings xvii. 6–23; such luminous expositions of

> What makes a nation happy and keeps it so,
> What ruins kingdoms and lays cities flat,

as are found in the Hebrew prophets, with their pæans of
promise and their burdens of woe—are all but comments
on the one Divine truth that 'He is the Lord our God; His
judgments are in all the earth.'   The Scriptures set forth
the one real philosophy of history, that 'Righteousness
exalteth a nation, and sin is the reproach of any people.'[1]
They constitute, in fact, that Divine interpretation of
Jewish history which reveals the eternal principle on which
all history may be judged and understood.   Vico said that
history is 'a civil theology of Divine Providence,' and that
is a truth which we learn from the Bible in its earliest pages.

Orosius began his history, which is practically a summary and illustration of St. Augustine's book 'On the City
of God,' with the famous words, 'The world and humanity
are under the guidance of a Divine Providence'—'Divina
Providentia agitur mundus et homo.'   Other histories—as
for instance the famous 'Discours sur l'Histoire univer-
selle' (1681) of Bossuet—were written to illustrate the
same great thesis.

'The history of the world is not intelligible apart from
the government of the world,' said Wilhelm von Hum-
boldt.   'Every step in advance in history,' said Fichte,
'every mental act which introduces into its chain of occur-
rences something absolutely new, is an inflowing of God.
God alone makes history, but He does this by the agency
of man.'[2]   'Die Weltgeschichte,' sang Schiller, 'ist das
Weltgericht.'   'Great men,' said Carlyle, 'are the inspired
texts of that Divine book of Revelations, whereof a chapter is completed from epoch to epoch, and is by some
named History.'[3]   St. Paul expressed this truth when to
the Stoics and Epicureans on the Areopagus he said, 'God

---

[1] Prov. xiv. 34.   [2] Fichte, *Spec. Theol.* p. 651.
[3] *Sartor Resartus*, p. 108.

made of one every nation of men, . . . having determined their appointed seasons . . . that they should seek God, if haply they might feel after Him and find Him, though He is not far from each one of us; for in Him we live, and move, and have our being, as certain even of your own poets have said, "For we are also His offspring."'

2. History, then, is a book of God in which we are able to read at large the lessons which are written on a smaller scale in the lives of individual men. In the book of biography we learn how God deals with separate souls; in the book of history how He deals with nations of men. In both books He reveals to us His will, and both are books of God. God never ceases to teach us; never ceases to be with us. Biography records the unending lessons of human experience, and

> All experience is an arch wherethrough
> Gleams the untravelled world, whose margin fades
> For ever and for ever as we move.

The wisely and truly recorded lives of men are beacon-lights of warning or of hope to future generations.

3. Again, Scripture frequently refers us to Nature, as a revelation of God to man. Now by Nature we do not mean some mysterious entity endowed by the imagination with independent power, but the sum total of those laws by which God governs the material universe. 'Duo sunt,' says St. Augustine, 'quæ in cognitionem Dei ducunt, creatio et Scriptura.' Such glorious Psalms as the 104th and the 107th, together with the whole concluding section of the Book of Job, lead us to see in Nature God's declaration of His omnipotence, His unchangeableness, His infinite majesty, the awfulness of His judgments, the tenderness of His love. We are taught indeed that this was the main

and, as far as it went, the adequate revelation of God to the heathen world. It was hereby that 'He left not Himself without witness, in that He did good, and gave us rain from heaven and fruitful seasons, filling our hearts with food and gladness.'[1] It was herein that men might 'seek the Lord, if haply they might feel after Him and find Him.'[2] It was herewith that God made manifest to them what may be known of Him,[3] 'for the *invisible* things of Him from the creation of the world are *clearly seen*, being understood by the things that are made, even His everlasting power and divinity.'

'Dei est Scriptura,' says Tertullian, 'Dei est natura, Dei est disciplina; quicquid contrarium est istis, Dei non est.'[4]

Men have been terribly the losers by neglecting the revelation of God in Nature. The co-ordination of the lessons taught to us by the visible creation with the lessons taught to us in Scripture would have helped to make the world more holy and more wise. For the moral lessons taught us by Nature and by Science are absolutely accordant with the moral lessons of Holy Writ.

i. How clearly, for instance, does Nature coincide with Scripture in teaching us that 'the soul that sinneth, it shall die.' Nature teaches us that punishment is no arbitrary infliction, but that it is due to the working of beneficent and inevitable laws. It enables us more clearly to understand the relation of our mortal bodies to the surrounding universe. It shows us that man's heaven-born spirit can triumph over the influence of its mortal environment, and by obeying law can make every power of law subservient to its own blessing.

---

[1] Acts xiv. 17.   [2] Acts xvii. 27.   [3] Rom. i. 19, 20.

[4] *De Virg. Vel.* 16.   He continues, 'Si Scriptura incerta est, natura certa est.'

ii. Or take but one further illustration of the truths which Nature reveals. 'By the greatness and beauty of the creatures,' says the writer of the Book of Wisdom, 'proportionably the Maker of them is seen.'[1] More overwhelmingly even than the Scriptures do 'the starry heavens above' make manifest to us the magnificence of the Creator. If those 'innumerable passionless eyes' have power to 'burn his nothingness into man,' they at the same time reveal to him his greatness, for they evince the love of the Father in heaven. The sense of the infinitude in which our own world is but an atom, and in the midst of which the life of man, apart from God, would be but

A trouble of ants in a million million of suns,

need not by any means crush the soul of man into abjectness. The heavens uplift us by their majesty and soothe us with their peace. They show us that He who implanted in the human soul the *sense* of beauty has gratified that sacred instinct abundantly with the *gift* of beauty, and has thus everywhere imparted to us a boon, superfluous to the working of His creative laws, yet infinitely precious, for our perpetual gratification. No portions of the Sermon on the Mount are more impressive than those in which the Saviour points to the lessons of the lilies and the sparrows; and no chapters of the Old Testament are more full of beauty and eloquence than those in which God answers Job out of the whirlwind and points him to the waters, and the heavens, and the storms, and the dew and frost; to the speed of the ostrich, the flight of the hawk, the lustre of the peacock's plumes, the war-horse with the terrible glory of his nostrils, 'Behemoth trampling the forests, and Leviathan tempesting the seas'!

[1] Wisdom xiii. 5. Compare Job xxxvii.-xli.

4. And there is yet another book of God. It is the *Conscience* of man—which an old divine calls 'the Private Secretary of God within us.' It is Conscience which makes us listen to Duty, that 'stern daughter of the voice of God.'

And St. Paul points to Conscience no less than to Nature as the Bibles of the Gentiles. 'For,' he says, 'when Gentiles which have no law do by nature the things of the law, these, having no law, are a law unto themselves; in that they show the work of the law written in their hearts, their conscience bearing witness therewith, and their thoughts one with another accusing or else excusing them; in the day when God shall judge the secrets of men.'[1]

Thus God's methods of revealing Himself are manifold:

> Not by one portal or one path alone
> His awful messages to men are known.

From History, and Experience, and Nature, and Conscience, and from other sources also, the Gentiles, by the aid of His Spirit, realised many of the same truths which are brought home to us by the witness of those Scriptures which they did not possess. The millions of the heathen were not unloved by their God and Father. He did not leave them to grope helplessly in the midst of a darkness which might be felt. In every age and in every land

> God, stooping, showed sufficient of His light
> For those in the dark to walk by.

We feel no misgiving when we are told that there is scarcely a single moral precept of Christianity which may not be paralleled from heathen sources. Those truths were revealed to the Gentiles by the same light which

---

[1] Rom. ii. 14, 15.

shines on us. The consummate superiority of the Scripture over the other Bibles of humanity lies in the fact that it sets forth to us the Gospel of the Eternal Christ. We should rejoice to know that the Divine glory, which shines like the noonday in our present dispensation, shot many a gleam of enlightenment upon distant countries and ancient times. And from these analogous revelations of History, Nature, and Conscience we may learn the law which characterises that fuller, freer, deeper, more explicit revelation which we learn from Holy Writ. There is inspiration whenever the Spirit of God makes itself heard in the heart of man. Enlightenment is not final, but progressive. It is not granted once and again and then withdrawn for ever. It does not come in one blaze of unbroken splendour, but in scattered rays shining amid interspaces of cloud and midnight. It does not come with shocks of overwhelming possession, but with the gradual increase of the dawn shining more and more unto the perfect day. After all that God has taught us respecting Himself, it still remains as true that 'clouds and darkness are round about Him,' as that 'righteousness and judgment are the foundation of His throne.' And even of those who as yet know not Christ, we are told that at last the nations shall come to His light and kings to the brightness of His rising.

Although the Bible has been to mankind a boon immeasurably precious, and though it contains the revelation of the Son of God, yet God has not *confined* His messages to its writers. 'Inspiration is the eternal act by which God, imparting Himself, so to speak, to men, manifests Himself to their divine nature;' and God can do this and has done it, and that for ages, without any aid from the written word.

Was it not so among pagan nations? To them, too,

virtue was possible, because they were faithful to the best
they knew. In Bishop Ken's 'Hymnarium,' Thought is
led by Lazarus through the unseen world, and

> 'Know,' Socrates reply'd,
> 'I for the one true God a martyr dy'd;
> I knew great God by native Light,
> And Conscience told me what was right.'

We do not, indeed, hold 'that every man shall be saved by
the law or sect which he professeth, so that he be diligent
to frame his life according to that law and the light of
nature.' For 'Holy Scripture doth set out unto us only
the name of Jesus Christ, whereby men must be saved.'[1]
But we do hold that by the name of Christ multitudes of
the heathen are saved though they know Him not. He is
found of them that sought Him not. Such is the truth
which the saintly Bishop puts into the mouth of the
Athenian sage,

> My soul with *miserere* left my clay,
> And, as I rov'd to find the happy way,
>   An Angel brought me to the judgment seat;
>   And prostrate at God's feet
> Taught me the virtue of the promised Seed
> With humble confidence to plead.
>   No Gentiles to this region ever came
>   But pardon gained by that and by no other name.[2]

Consider the history of Religion. The faith which is
the assurance of things hoped for, the test of things not
seen, existed for ages without any Scriptures. Abel,
Enoch, Noah, Abraham, Isaac, Jacob, Moses, Gideon,
Barak, the judges and heroes of Israel—what Bible had

---

[1] Art. xviii.

[2] Ken's *Hymnarium*, p. 131; Dean Plumptre's *Life of Ken*, ii. 247.

they? Many of them none at all. And what Bible had David and Solomon and the early kings and prophets, and the thousands who in their days never bowed the knee to Baal? Yet all these, having served God in their generation, fell on sleep. And was their religious life less deep than that of the Scribes and Pharisees, hypocrites who, in that long and dreary interval in which the living voice of prophecy had ceased, had access to the sacred literature which Ezra and his successors had edited? But they used it mainly to crush the essentials of mercy, justice, and truth, and glorify the ritualistic trivialities of phylactery and fringe, till their religionism brought forth its natural empoisoned fruit in the spiritual atrophy which led them to murder the Lord of Glory.

And if the religion of the Hebrews existed anterior to and independently of the Old Testament, so did Christianity exist anterior to and independently of the New. The early Christians—those in the first century, whose glow of enthusiasm and love gave the first impulse to the evangelisation of the world—had no Gospels and no Epistles. Their exultation and exceeding joy in the midst of poverty and persecution were maintained, not by written records, but by the constant sense of Christ's living Presence. Even in the second century, when the whole New Testament existed, years elapsed before it was placed on the same level as the Old Testament, and before it was finally dissevered—as being *sui generis*—from other Christian literature. For many a century the religious life was maintained with but indirect support from the *written* word. The Bible was hid and buried in dead languages not understanded of the people, from whom it was jealously kept by those to whose pretensions its simplicity was fatal. When they did possess it, but few could read it; and there is abundant evidence that even to the generality of the clergy alike its spirit and its letter were unknown. Great indeed was their loss, and glorious the awakenment at the renascence, when 'Greece rose from the dead with the New Testament in her hand;' but their loss was not such as wholly to cripple the religious life.

So that, to quote from a sermon by John Wallis, one of the clerks of the Westminster Assembly, and part-author of the Shorter Catechism, 'The Scriptures in themselves are rather a Lanthorn than a Light; they shine indeed, but it is *alieno lumine;* it is not their own but a borrowed light. It is God which is the true light, that shines to us in the Scriptures; and they have no other light in them, but as they represent to us something of God, and as they exhibit and hold forth God to us, Who is the true light that "enlighteneth every man that comes into the world." It is a light then, as it represents God unto us, who is the original light. It transmits some rays, some beams of the Divine nature; but they are refracted, or else we should not be able to behold them. They lose much of their original lustre by passing through this medium, and appear not so glorious to us as they are in themselves. They represent God's simplicity obliquated and refracted by reason of many inadequate conceptions; God condescending to the weakness of our capacity to speak to us in our own dialect.'[1]

The Bible, when our spirits bear witness to its divinest teachings, is our chief guide to the truths of which religion is composed; but to speak of it as being itself 'a religion' is a loose form of speech, and to say that it is 'the *only* religion' of any body of Christians is not true in any intelligible sense.

[1] Quoted by Briggs, *The Bible, the Church, and Reason.*

CHAPTER XIV

MISINTERPRETATION OF SCRIPTURE.

'He that is spiritual judgeth all things, and he himself is judged of no man.'—1 Cor. ii. 15.

'Lacte gypsum male miscetur.'—IRENÆUS.

'It is the province of reason to judge of the morality of Scripture.'—BUTLER, *Analogy*, II. iii. 26.

'Legimus scripturam omnem *ædificationi habilem* divinitus inspirari.'—TERT. *De Cult. Fem.* ii. 3.

NOTHING but blessing has ever sprung from the *right use and true understanding* of the Bible; nothing but disaster from those superstitious and perverted uses of it which spring from false methods of regarding it.

Let us take a few instances, of which neither can the truth be denied nor the significance overlooked by any fair-minded inquirer.

1. I have already alluded to the wars of extermination enjoined upon the Israelites by Moses, by Joshua, by Samuel, and by other great Prophets; and the principle which underlies them is recognised in the Psalms, the Book of Jeremiah, the Book of Esther, and other passages of the Old Testament.[1]

---

[1] See *ante*, p. 82. Deut. xx. 16: 'Thou shalt save nothing alive that breatheth.' 1 Sam. xv. 3: 'Slay both man and woman, infant and suckling, ox and sheep, camel and ass.'

Yet the unsophisticated conscience of mankind revolts with horror from the cold-blooded massacre of innocent men and women and children—the sick, the aged, the harmless, and the miserable—which a war of extermination involves.[1] The Israelites never thoroughly obeyed these commands; the instances were very few in which they even attempted to do so. So far were the Canaanites from being exterminated that they long continued to be the recognised traders of Palestine, so that 'Canaanite' became the equivalent of 'merchant.' The Canaanites even possessed a recognised mercantile quarter of their own in Jerusalem itself, known as *Maktesh* or 'the Mortar.'[2] The sense of pity is deeply implanted by God in human nature. Any king or general who should act in these days as we are told that Moses and Samuel ordered the Israelites to act in the name of God, would be overwhelmed by the execration of mankind.

i. But it has been urged that the moral standard of the Jews was so low as not to be shocked by commands to commit savage deeds, and that the aborigines of Canaan were so abnormally wicked that their extermination was morally necessary. Is there any proof that they were more wicked than multitudes of nations have been—even nations professedly Christian, and even in modern times?

[1] 'We should feel it impossible that God would really command us to do such acts now, whatever commands He may have given in former ages' (Mozley, *Lectures on the Old Testament*, p. 85). 'The acts to which we refer are not only contrary to the law of love, but also to our idea of justice' (*Id.* p. 85).

[2] See Hos. xii. 7; Zeph. i. 11 (Heb.); Job xli. 6; Prov. xxxi. 24.

[3] This sophistry is found in St. Augustine. 'Digni ergo erant *et* isti quibus talia juberentur et illi qui talia paterentur' (Aug. c. *Faust.* xxii. 72). It is thus that Dante defends his faithlessness to Friar Alberigo. '*E cortesia fu lui esser villano*' (*Inf.* xxxiii. 150).

Were they in any appreciable sense more wicked or even (circumstances considered) so wicked as Rome was for centuries together in the days of the mediæval Papacy, or London amid the orgies of the Restoration?

I have always been astonished that the masculine intelligence of such a man as Dr. Arnold should have been deluded by this untenable pretence. 'The Israelites' sword,' he says, 'in the bloodiest executions wrought a work of mercy for all the countries of the earth to the very end of the world. They preserved unhurt the seed of eternal life.'[1] The statement is hardly true to fact; but in any case are we justified in doing evil that good may come?

ii. Again, men have urged the sophistic plea that as God might have employed the whirlwind or the famine to destroy idolaters, so He might have seen fit to order their destruction by human agency.

But man in no way resembles those vast, dull, inanimate forces, 'stern as fate, inexorable as tyranny, merciless as death, which have no ear to hear, no heart for pity, no arm to save.' The agencies of nature are irresponsible and mechanical; the whirlwind and the pestilence have no conscience; but God Himself has created in the soul of man the sense of pity and love, which are likest Himself of all the elements which He has implanted. Dead agencies cannot be a model or exemplar to man. Man could not, without inconceivable wickedness, take upon him to imitate the destruction wrought by the hurricane, or excuse himself for deeds of ravin and brutality by pleading that they might have been accomplished by the tiger or the ape.

In what sense, then, can God ever have *commanded* men

1 Arnold, *Sermons,* ii. 390.

to commit acts which the human conscience, expressly because it is illuminated by the Holy Spirit of God, justly brands as revolting and horrible?

It is no answer to say that this is a mystery beyond our ken; that we must not be wise above what is written. It is true that whatever answer we give must touch upon a mystery. 'All things,' said the old aphorism of theology. 'end in a mystery,' and that mystery is the existence of evil. We are not, however, peering into mysteries, but are seeking for practical guidance as to the eternal and unchangeable will of God.

Can God—Who is of purer eyes than to behold iniquity, and with Whom is no variableness—ever have commanded man to commit crimes which are hateful to the enlightened conscience, and which we now know to be abhorrent from His own nature?[1]   Are we to regard the laws of right and wrong as Eternal Facts or as arbitrary mandates? Or at the best only as flexible rules which, like the leaden measure of Lesbos, can be bent and unbent at will?

Have we not reached a point of moral elevation as high as even Plato had reached nearly two millenniums and a half ago? The poems of Homer were the Bible of the Greeks, yet Plato said that 'God is simple and true both in word and deed, neither is He changed Himself, nor does He deceive others, neither by visions nor discourses nor the pomp of signs. Therefore,' he continues, 'when any

---

[1] Canon Mozley pleads that 'these commands had no resistance from the moral sense; they did not look unnatural to the ancient Jew,' &c. (*l.c.* p. 63). Neither did they to the Thugs, who likewise regarded it as a religious duty to commit murder. But does this account for a positive command? God may condescend to man's imperfections, but can we conceive of Him as *ordering* immoral acts?

one alleges such things about the gods we must show disapproval.'[1]

Bishop Butler says, 'If it were commanded to cultivate the principles and act from the spirit of treachery, ingratitude, cruelty: the command would not alter the nature of the case, or the action, in any of these instances. But it is quite otherwise in precepts which require only the doing of an external action.'[2] Can any one be content with this? Armenian atrocities are only external actions. Are they right because fanatical Turks may think them right?

Can anything be said but this—which is practically the answer given by Canon Mozley in his 'Ruling Ideas in the Early Ages'—that the Israelites knew no better; that they and their rulers, in thus butchering even the women and infants of their enemies, *thought* ignorantly that they did God service? It required but the softening influence of time and civilisation to obliterate in the best minds those fierce misconceptions. When the King of Israel saw the deluded Syrians safely in his power in his own capital, he eagerly exclaimed to the Prophet Elisha, 'My father, shall I smite them? Shall I smite them?' What was the Prophet's answer? Was it a rebuke to him for even hesitating to slay the enemies of the Lord and of his people? On the contrary, Elisha said, 'Thou shalt not smite them: wouldest thou smite those whom thou hast taken captive with thy sword and with thy bow? set bread and water before them, that they may eat and drink, and go to their master.'[3]

Beyond that we are not able to go. The difficulty which

---

[1] Plato, *Republic*, ii. *ad finem*. He is specially objecting to duplicity being predicated of the gods.

[2] *Analogy*, II. iii. 27.   [3] 2 Kings vi. 21, 22.

remains unsolved is not that such commands should be attributed to God on the page of Scripture—which is no difficulty if parts of those ancient records only reflect a moral knowledge which Christ Himself has taught us to have been ignorance, and a spirit which He has told us was alien from His spirit—but that a people whom God had partially enlightened should have supposed that such deeds could be in accordance with His will, and that they could most acceptably pray to Him with hands red-wet with the blood of innocents.

'If a difficulty meets thee which thou canst not solve,' said Luther, 'so let it go.' And he said also, 'I cannot prevent the birds of the air from flying about my head, but I can prevent them from building their nests in my hair.'

We must not, however, let such *passages* blind us to the general fact that, as a rule, in the Old Testament, as in the New, love is the fulfilling of the law. In spite of imperfections due to rude times and hard hearts, there is a singular tenderness in many parts of the Mosaic code. There is tenderness to slaves, whom in some ways it sheltered from oppression;[1] to the accidental homicide, for whom it provided the cities of refuge;[2] to the poor, whom it protected from cruel usury;[3] to the depressed toilers, whose lands it restored in the Sabbatic year;[4] to the destitute, in whose interest it forbade the hard stripping of the fields, the mean exhaustion of the gleaned vineyards, or the niggardly beating of the topmost olive boughs.[5] There is tenderness to the dumb animals. To show that God cared even for the falling sparrow and the

---

[1] Deut. v. 14, 15, xii. 19, &c.   [2] Num. xxxv. 13, 15.
[3] Deut. xxiii. 19, xxiv. 6, &c.   [4] Levit. xxv. 4, &c.
[5] Deut. xxiv. 20.

dumb cattle, the great legislator was bidden to lay down a rule that the heedless boy should not take the mother-bird when he took from the nest her callow young;[1] that the oxen were not to be muzzled when they trod out the corn;[2] and that the ox and ass were not to be yoked together at the plow, lest the burden should fall on the smaller and weaker beast.[3]   Even the thrice-repeated rule, 'Thou shalt not seethe the kid in its mother's milk,'[4] besides the deep warning which it conveys of the horrible sin of destroying human beings by means of their best affections, was rightly interpreted as a reprobation of unfeeling cruelty, because it looks like a hard mockery, an offence against the mercifulness of nature, to seethe the youngling in the very milk which nature had designed for its sustenance; for 'God's tender mercies are over all His works.'[5]

One fact ought to be plain, which is, that if the eternal laws of morality and love are to be regarded as flexible and accidental things; if any human being could ever be blessed for taking innocent little children—children differing in no respect from those whom Jesus loved and took in His arms and blessed—and dashing them against the stones;—if indeed such commands and sentiments were ever, in any sense, a word of God to those savage tribes, they are in no sense a rule for us.   We judge of them precisely as we believe that Christ would have judged of them, and as He has taught us to do by the Spirit which He has given us.   Whatsoever things are real, whatsoever things are lawful, whatsoever things are pure, lovely, and of good report—whatsoever things are truly excellent and

---

[1] Deut. xxii. 6.   [2] Deut. xxv. 4.   [3] Deut. xxii. 10.
[4] Ex. xxiii. 19, xxxiv. 26; Deut. xiv. 21.
[5] Ps. cxlv. 9; compare Lev. xxii. 28.

stand in harmony with our best reason and minister to our highest development—those alone, and not the things which bring forth evil fruit, are the word of God to us.

In such things the Bible abounds; they glisten and shine forth in myriads as the sand-grains on the seashore when the sunbeam strikes them; and no advance in mental culture, no deepening and broadening of the natural sciences, no expansion of the human mind can ever go beyond, or can ever supersede them![1] 'They,' said Kant, 'are always in the service of God whose actions are moral.'

2. And if we form this judgment respecting the Law of Mercy, we come to a similar conclusion respecting the Law of Truthfulness.

We hold that God is a God of Truth; that He desires truth in the inward parts; that whatever view we may choose to take of the unreprehended deceitfulness of Abraham, Isaac, Jacob, Samuel, David, and other characters in the Old Testament, and however we may choose to interpret the fact that they may seem to represent God in some cases as having commanded any form of dissimulation, we can only read such passages historically, and no sanction of apparent unveracity, or Jesuitical tampering with truth, can ever be a word of God to us. Here again the unsophisticated conscience of mankind says even in the days of Homer,

> Who dares think one thing and another tell,
> My soul detests him as the gates of hell.

In the New Testament at any rate the law of truthfulness is laid down undeviatingly and absolutely, and to quote

[1] See Goethe, *Conversations*, March 11, 1832.

any passage in the Bible as an excuse for falseness is a gross misinterpretation if not of this or that passage, yet of the Bible as a whole.

Now turn to the history of the Albigensian Crusades and let us realise the frightful mischief of putting the Bible to wrong uses, as we consider the deep damnation of deeds of deceit and sanguinary ferocity committed in the name of Holy Writ. When Innocent III. was giving to Arnold, Abbot of Cîteaux, his infamous advice to entrap the Count of Toulouse to his ruin, he appealed to Scriptural authority both for his falsity and his ruthlessness. 'We advise you,' he said, 'to use cunning in your dealings with the Count of Toulouse, *treating him with a wise dissimulation that the other heretics may be more easily destroyed.*'[1] 'Slay them all,' said Arnold of Cîteaux to the brutal Albigensian Crusaders; 'God will discriminate His own.' We look on the Crusades in the light of poetry and romance; we admire the meekness of Godfrey of Bouillon in refusing to wear a crown of gold where his Saviour had worn a crown of thorns. But how did the Crusaders behave on their journey in the brutal massacre of defenceless and unoffending Jews? And how did they behave in Jerusalem itself? Happy the innocent women and children whose heads they swept off with one stroke of the sword, or whom they stabbed to the heart at a single blow! But besides these murders they snatched infants from their mothers' arms and hurled them on the stones, or with horrid mutilation dashed their heads against sharp angles; and they made men and boys marks for their

---

[1] Ep. 232. 'According to the canons, faith was not to be kept with him who keeps not faith with God' (*Regesta*, xi. 26; Lea, *Hist. of the Inquisition*, i. 228). On the systematic deceit used to extort confessions see *id.* p. 416.

archers, shooting at them till they leapt down the precipice; and others they tortured inconceivably; and others they burnt alive at slow fires. And what was the plea for the commission of these and other execrable atrocities? The savage commands to exterminate said to have been given by Moses to the rude serfs who had fled from Egypt into the wilderness! Priests also found an imaginary consecration of dishonesty in their own ignorant misuse of some fragments of Scripture! And these were manipulated to supersede the plain unexceptional rule of the Gospel: 'Wherefore, putting away lying, let every man speak truth to his neighbour.'

When we read of such crimes and horrors and find religious teachers giving their sanction to them on grounds of Holy Writ, we can only deplore so gross a confusion of the voices of cruel bigotry and usurping ambition with the voice of God. But

> The devil can cite Scripture for his purpose.
> An evil soul producing holy witness
> Is like a villain with a smiling cheek,
> A goodly apple rotten at the heart.

In some of their deadliest sins against the human race corrupted and cruel Churches have ever been most lavish in their appeals to Scripture. But no sophistry can alter our conviction that the laws of mercy and truth are unchangeable and eternal; and even a heathen poet could say,

> οὐ γάρ τι νῦν γε κἀχθὲς, ἀλλ' ἀεί ποτε
> ζῇ ταῦτα κοὐδεὶς οἶδεν ἐξ ὅτου φάνη.

3. Take, again, the case of witchcraft.

We find in Ex. xxii. 18 the verse, 'Thou shalt not suffer a witch to live.'[1]

---

[1] Compare Lev. xix. 31, xx. 27; Deut. xviii. 10, 11; 2 Kings xvii. 17; Is. ii. 6; Mic. v. 12.

It may be said with truth that the meaning of the Hebrew word rendered 'witch' is of uncertain significance,[1] and 'sorcerers' and 'witches' may merely be regarded by the Mosaic Law as 'impious and nefarious impostors.' If this had been understood 'the history of the Christian Church would not have been disgraced by the fatal absurdities of witch trials.'

Yet it is plain that in the days of Moses, and for thousands of years afterwards, it was universally believed that human beings might by unlawful means have intercourse with fiends and demons, and use the supernatural power so acquired for the injury of their fellows.

The belief is now all but universally abandoned. All pretensions to witchcraft, and all belief in it, are treated as proofs of ignorant superstition. There is not a court in any civilised and Protestant country which would not cover itself with execration if it executed a woman on the ground of her being a witch.

Yet how frightful has been the injustice, how terrible the agony caused to hundreds of thousands of hapless human beings, by so entirely mistaking the true nature and objects of the Bible as to treat that verse of Exodus as though it involved the revelation of a fact and the inculcation of a present duty!

The law as a Jewish law may have been justifiable, or at the lowest excusable. Even if it had its roots in ignorance and superstition, the *attempt* to consult demons, and the malefic practices connected with such an attempt, may, in the more ruthless system of rude days, have deserved death.

---

[1] מכשפה. The LXX render it by φαρμακός, and the Vulgate *maleficus*, in Ex. vii. 11. See Kalisch, *Exodus*, p. 427. This text was 'the war-cry of the clergy against myriads of aged and defenceless women.'

But to assume that this dubious fragment of old legislation proved the existence of witches as understood in the middle ages, and that God commanded the infliction of death on all the poor wretches who under the agonies of torture confessed to being witches, was, again, a gross misuse of the Bible, a gross misinterpretation of the purposes for which it was intended.

In 1437 Pope Eugenius IV. stirred up inquisitors against witches, especially such as raised storms, and a similar edict was issued in 1465.

In 1484 Pope Innocent VIII. sent a Dominican monk as commissioner to extirpate witchcraft. His name was Sprenger, and he was the author of a frightful book on sorcery, which has gained him the name of *Malleus Maleficarum*.[1] This bull of Pope Innocent VIII.—*Summis desiderantes* (1484)—has the melancholy pre-eminence (except that which commanded the crusades to exterminate the pious Albigenses) of having cost more torrents of innocent blood than any other. Thousands of women, young and old, were terrified and tortured into preposterous confessions, and as they writhed on the rack were prepared to avouch anything. The Jesuits were specially active in these horrible proceedings. Remigius, in his *Dæmonolatreia* (1595), boasted that he had sent 900 to death

---

[1] He gives a specimen of his learning by his derivation of Diabolus from 'dia,' two, and 'bolus,' a pill, because the devil makes but one pill of soul and body! or the name may mean (for Sprenger is liberal of his etymologies) *clausus ergastulo*, or *defluens*, because he fell from heaven! He derives *maleficiendo* from *male de fide sentiendo*—so that all heretics are potential sorcerers, and should be burnt! See Michelet, *Renaissance*, p. 128; Lea, *Hist. of the Inquisition*, ii. 421, iii. 443. Dr. A. D. White (*Warfare of Science*) refers to Soldan's *Gesch. d. Hexenprozessen* and Roskoff's *Gesch. d. Teufels.*

for storm-raising by witchcraft in fifteen years.[1] Seven thousand so-called 'witches' are said to have been burnt at Trèves; 1,000 in a single year at Como; 800 at Würzburg.

The growth of knowledge has made it certain that not one of these miserable victims can have been guilty of the crimes laid to their charge by blundering terror and deadly superstition.

Sir Matthew Hale in 1665 said to an English jury who condemned two poor wretches to be burnt, 'that there were such things as witches he made no doubt at all, for first the Scriptures had affirmed so much.'[2]

Wesley said that to give up witchcraft was to give up the Bible.[3] The belief in witchcraft is absolutely dead, and yet to Christian hearts the Bible is as infinitely dear as it ever was. We disbelieve in witches, but can still say of the Bible, with Sir Matthew Hale, ' It is a book full of light and wisdom, and will make you wise to eternal life,' and with Wesley that therein God teaches us the way to heaven.

4. Again, take the case of religious persecution.

The days are not far distant when it was regarded as a positive duty to put men to death for their religious opin-

---

[1] See Dr. A. D. White, 'Meteorology' (*Popular Science Monthly*, July, August, 1887, New York).

[2] He went on to say that 'the wisdom of all nations had provided laws against such persons, which is an argument of their confidence of such a crime.' No doubt; but (1) their 'confidence of such a crime' was a baseless error, and (2) in most cases they founded it on the misuse of Scripture.

[3] Wesley, *Journals*, pp. 602, 713. Parr's *Works*, iv. 18; Buckle, *Hist. of Civilisation*, i. 334; Michelet, *La Sorcière*, p. 425; Lecky, *Hist. of Rationalism*, i. 1–150: 'So late as 1716 a woman and her daughter of nine years old were hanged at Huntingdon for raising storms by witchcraft. In Germany no fewer than 100,000 women and children are said to have suffered a cruel death under the stupid and ferocious persecution of witches.

ions, and this horrible offence against the free conscience of humanity, this 'storming of the very citadel of heaven,' was defended by the Old Testament examples of Elijah and others, in spite of our Lord's distinct teaching that the Elijah-spirit was far different from the Spirit of the Christ. It is true that one or two 'texts' of the New Testament were impressed into the same odious service. Scraps of texts and shreds of metaphor—parabolical, irrelevant, entirely wrenched from their context and real significance—were constantly on the lips of men like Torquemada and Innocent IV. and Alexander VI. The two favourite ones were 'Constrain them to come in'[1] and 'Gather up the tares in bundles and burn them.' The first was made responsible for the use of violence to compel men to confess what they held to be lies, and to worship what they regarded as idols; the second was considered as a sufficient justification for the torture used against the innocent by the familiars of the Inquisition. By virtue of texts like these such enemies of the human race as Fulk of Toulouse were enabled to combine the garb and language of priests with 'the temper and trade of executioners.' But, as Shakespeare complained so bitterly,

> In religion
> What damned error but some sober brow
> Will bless it and approve it with a text,
> Hiding the grossness with fair ornament?

[1] Augustine seems responsible for the first gross misuse of this fragmentary clause from a parable, *Ep.* xciii. 16 (see my *Lives of the Fathers*, ii. 400). His earlier and truer opinion was in favour of toleration. See *Opp.* viii. 151*a*. 'With shame and sorrow we hear from Augustine himself that fatal axiom which impiously arrayed cruelty in the garb of Christian charity' (Milman, *Lat. Christ.* i. 127). See *Opp.* ii. 230; iii. 382.

This sanction of cruelty to enforce current opinion was
entirely alien from true Christianity. When the fiery
disciples said to Christ that 'they had seen one casting out
devils in His name and they forbade him because he fol-
loweth not after us,' Christ said at once, 'Forbid him not,'
and 'He that is not against us is with us.' The principle
on which the early Christians acted was expressed in the
motto '*Force is hateful to God.*' Lactantius, Tertullian,
and other early Christian writers had emphatically stated
the principle that religion was not a thing which could be
coerced. 'It is no part of religion,' said Tertullian, 'to
compel religion.'[1]

The first blood of Christians ever shed by Christians
on the ground of religion was that of the learned and
pious Priscillian, Bishop of Avila, and of his followers.
The execution was ordered by the usurper Maximus, whose
hands were red with the blood of the innocent and charm-
ing Gratian; but the instigators of the crime were the
two Spanish bishops, Ithacius and Idacius.   Yet no sooner
was the crime consummated than the two saintliest prelates
of the day, St. Ambrose of Milan and St. Martin of Tours,
raised their voices in indignant reprobation of the crime.
They refused to communicate with Maximus or his epis-
copal advisers, and their sentiments were confirmed by
every Christian bishop to whom the dark deed became
known. But in these days the Inquisition—that execrable invasion of the indefeasible rights of mankind
—is toasted by Madrid professors, openly eulogised by
Dominicans in the pulpit of Notre-Dame, and is still de-

---

[1] Tert. *ad Scap.* 2: 'Humani juris et naturalis potestatis est uni-
cuique quod putaverit colere, nec alii obest aut prodest alterius
religio. Sed nec religionis est cogere religionem, quæ sponte sus-
cipi debeat, non vi.'

fended in the controversial writings of the Romish hier-archy![1]

From Augustine's days down to those of Luther scarcely one voice was raised in favour, I will not say of *tolerance*, but even of abstaining from fire and bloodshed in support of enforced uniformity. But Luther boldly proclaimed that 'thoughts are toll-free.' 'Heresy,' he said, 'is a spiritual thing which cannot be hewn with any axe, or burned with any fire, or drowned with any water.' Augustine's views involved a fatal retrogression. Origen and Athanasius had shown themselves incomparably more wise. 'Nothing,' says Athanasius, 'more forcibly marks the weakness of a bad cause than persecution.'[2] The best early Christian writers shuddered at those who were 'in name priests, but in reality executioners.' Tertullian, Gregory of Nazianzus, Lactantius, Martin of Tours, Chry-sostom, Augustine himself in his earlier and better days, had expressed the same views.[3] 'Summo supplicio et

[1] A Dominican wrote *Lob und Ehrenrede auf die heilige Inquisition* (Wien, 1782), in which he argues that 'fire is the peculiar delight of God to extirpate heresy,' and quotes Deut. xiii. 6–10 'as almost lite-rally the law of the Holy Inquisition' (Lea, i. 228). 'The Catholic Church,' says Cardinal Vaughan, '*has never spared the knife, when necessary*, to cut off rebels against her faith or authority.'

[2] *Hist. Arian.* iv. 7. 'The devil, when he has no truth on his side, attacks,' &c., *id.* iv. 7. 'Force is an evil thing,' *id.* v. 4. 'It is the part of true godliness not to compel, but to persuade,' *id.* viii. 4. Song of Solomon v. 2. See Milman's Gibbon, v. 114.

[3] Tert. *ad Scap.* 2; *Apol.* 24; Lact. *Instt.* v. 9, 20; *Epit.* 24; Chry-sostom, *Orat. in Babyl.*: 'Christians are not to destroy error by force and violence, but should work the salvation of men by per-suasion, instruction, and love.' Sulpicius Severus (*Hist. Sacra*, ii. 50) and St. Martin of Tours alike condemn the wretched sophism that the Church does not put to death, but only hands over to the secular arm, and call it '*inauditum nefas, ut causam Ecclesiæ judex sæculi judicaret.*'

inexpiabili poena jubemus affligi' was a law as indefensible when Theodosius aimed it at the Manichees as when Nero and Diocletian had aimed it at the Christians.

Yet when Alva was carrying out with massacre and conflagrations the behests of popes and 'most Christian' emperors—massacres in which we are told by Grotius that from 75,000 to 100,000 persons were put to death for their religion in the Netherlands alone—this ruthless butcher received from Pope Pius V. a jewelled sword with the inscription *Accipe sanctum gladium munus a Deo!*

But alas!

> Crime was ne'er so black
> As ghostly cheer and pious thanks to lack.
> Satan is modest.   At Heaven's door he lays
> His evil offspring, and in Scripture phrase
> And saintly posture gives to God the praise
> And honour of his monstrous progeny!

Charles IX. of France, the author of the Massacre of St. Bartholomew, is one of the most wretched figures whom history presents to our indignant pity and contempt, and the only sign of grace in him is the agonising remorse which haunted the rest of his miserable life.

After a crime so monstrous as the predetermined and treacherous murder of 50,000 of his subjects,[1] we should have imagined that the voice of Christian execration would have rung through Europe with a horror which none could have mistaken.   If St. Ambrose and St. Martin were shocked by the legal execution, after long trials, of five hated and persecuted heretics, what would have been

---

[1] See Ranke on the Massacre of St. Bartholomew, in *Hist.-polit. Zeitschrift*, ii. 111.   Sansorio, Cardinal of San Severino, in his diary, speaks of 'Carlo IX, *di gloriosa memoria, in quel celebre giorno di S. Bartolommeo, lietissimo a' cattolici*' (Ranke, *Popes*, ii. 235).

their sense of heartrending astonishment to hear that a Christian king had ordered the midnight murder of thousands of his innocent and peaceful subjects? But alas! a fearful change had come over the spirit of Christianity. Instead of horror there was festivity; instead of execration there were pæans! Pope Gregory XIII. struck a triumphant medal in honour of the massacre, ordered Vasari to paint a picture of it for the Vatican, and went in procession with his priests and bishops to sing an ecstatic Te Deum to express the joy of the Papacy at so many atrocious murders! The cannon thundered from the Castle of St. Angelo, bonfires illuminated the streets of Rome, and the Cardinal of Lorraine gave a thousand gold scudi as a reward to the courier who brought the horrid news. Cardinal Orsino 'sought out the leader of the butchery at Lyons, and gave him his blessing and his absolution.'[1]

'The history of Europe for a hundred years was the history of the efforts of the Church, with open force or secret conspiracy, with all the energy, base or noble, which passion or passionate enthusiasm could inspire to crush and annihilate its foes.[2] No means came amiss to it, sword or stake, torture-chamber or assassin's dagger. The effects of the Church's working were seen in ruined nations and smoking cities, in human beings tearing one another to pieces like raging maniacs, and the honour of the Creator of the world befouled by the hideous crimes committed in His Name. All this is forgotten now, forgotten or even

---

[1] Froude, *Council of Trent*. On Louis XIV. and the horrors which accompanied his faithless Revocation of the Edict of Nantes, see Michelet.

[2] Lecky, *Rationalism*, ii. 35. 'The Church of Rome has shed more innocent blood than any other institution that has ever existed among mankind. All this is very horrible, but it is only a small part of the misery which the persecuting spirit of Rome has produced.'

audaciously denied.'　The popes should have learnt St. Jerome's lesson : 'Non ob Sardorum mastrucam tantum Christum mortuum esse.'　Christ died as little for the Popish usurpation only, as for the skincloth of Sardinian sectaries.[1]

Nor must it be supposed that the persecuting spirit has ceased to exist, or that even in these days intolerance has ceased to justify its burning hatred by Scripture quotations. It has lost its power, not its virulence ; its effectiveness, not its fury.

> Fagot and stake were desperately sincere ;
> Our cooler martyrdoms are done in type.

5. It is strange that Scripture should have been exclusively relied on to defend two things so opposite to each other, yet alike so deadly to the happiness of mankind, as (i) passive obedience on the one hand, and (ii) on the other the assassination of kings.　Yet such is the case!　The majority of the English clergy in the reigns of James I. and of Charles I. and after the Restoration of Charles II. habitually preached the duty of passive obedience, which they wrongly deduced from Scripture.[2]　Fortunately a doctrine resting on such false inferences breaks down the moment it is tested.　The Stuart Kings learnt by experience that, however much the clergy might maintain the theory, they would resist and rebel against kings the

---

[1] I have never yet found any Roman controversialist who will condemn the 'Holy (!) Office' of the Inquisition and its cruel horrors. So far from it, in the oath taken by Roman bishops (*Rom. Pontificale*, p. 63, ed. Rom. 1818) may be seen the passage : 'Hæreticos omnes, schismaticos et rebelles [and therefore all the Protestants of England] eidem Domino nostro [the Pope] et ejus successoribus, pro posse persequar et impugnabo.'

[2] Hallam, *Hist. of Eng.* ii. 459.

moment their own rights were invaded or their own interests touched.

'The Church of England,' says Macaulay, 'continued to be for more than a hundred and fifty years the servile handmaid of monarchy, the steady enemy of public liberty. The divine right of kings and the duty of passively obeying all their commands were her favourite tenets. She held those tenets firmly through times of oppression, persecution, and licentiousness, while law was trampled down, while judgment was perverted, while the people were eaten as though they were bread.'[1] 'Anglicanism,' says Mr. Lecky, 'was from the beginning at once the most servile and the most efficient agent of tyranny.' In the reign of Charles I. she showed deadly hostility to the champions of liberty. In the vile reign of Charles II. she had few or no rebukers for the hideous corruption of the Court, but was busy with repression of dissenters, and Test Acts, and Five Mile Acts, and was preaching assiduously that 'Kings are above all, inferior to none, to no man, to no multitude of men, to no angels, to no order of angels; their power is not only human, but superhuman. It is participating in God's own omnipotence.'[2] In the reign of James II. they were not roused by the infamous atrocities of Kirke and Jeffreys and Claverhouse, but only began to fling their theories to the winds when the feeble and cruel despot began to tamper with ecclesiastical monopolies. In the reign of George III. they were 'astonishingly warm'[3] in favour of the American War, and 'flashed in the faces of

---

[1] *Essays*, i. 132. See Lecky, *Rationalism*, ii. 178; Hallam, *Hist. of Eur. Lit.* ii. 39–46; Oxenham, *Ethical Studies*, pp. 406, 413. Mariana (*De Rege*, 1599), Keller (*Tyrannicidium*), and Suarez justify regicide.

[2] Dr. Mainwaring (see Perry, *Hist. of the Church*, pp. 358–366).

[3] Burke.

the Americans the old rusty but refurbished weapons of passive obedience and non-resistance.'

6. And if Protestant clergymen have preached passive obedience, Romish emissaries have misused Scripture to justify the assassination of kings. The murder of Henry III. by the monk Jacques Clément was publicly applauded by Pope Sixtus V.[1] The murder of Henry IV. by Ravaillac, the murder of William of Orange by Balthasar Gérard,[2] the nefarious Gunpowder Plot, received the sanction of Romanist divines. 'Mariana pronounced a eulogy full of pathetic declamation on Jacques Clément, who *first took counsel of divines*, assassinated his king, and made himself a great name.' 'It is only to the hand of the Almighty Himself,' wrote Mendoza to Philip, 'that this fortunate event is to be assigned.'[3]

'It was impossible to deny,' says Macaulay, 'that Roman Catholic casuists of eminence had written in defence of equivocation, of mental reservation, of perjury, and even of assassination. It was alleged that every one of these crimes had been prompted or applauded by Roman Catholic divines. The letters which Everard Digby wrote in lemon juice from the Tower to his wife had recently been published, and were often quoted. He was a scholar and a gentleman, upright in all ordinary dealings, and strongly impressed with a sense of duty to God. Yet he had been deeply concerned in the plot for blowing up King, Lords, and Commons, and has, on the brink of eternity, declared that *it was incomprehensible to him how any Roman Catholic should think such a design sinful*'! Even the attempt to murder the Emperor of Germany in 1884 was defended

---

[1] De Thou, liv., xcvi. 'In many churches the image of the murderer was placed for reverence upon the altar of God' (Lecky, *Rationalism*, ii. 177). Ranke, Bk. v. § 13.

[2] Ranke, ii. 111.   [3] See Ranke, ii. 177, 199.

by the murderers and those who abetted them, by the examples of Ehud and Jael!

7. The spirit which was guilty of these opposite and equally shameful misapplications of the Bible is not dead. To this day the Mormons defend polygamy out of the Old Testament. In the Civil War of America the pulpits of the South rang with incessant Scriptural defences of slavery. 'From its inherent nature,' said a South American Bishop, 'slavery has been a curse and a blight wherever it exists; yet it is warranted by the Bible. Therefore, as slavery is recognised by the Bible, every man has a right to own slaves, provided they are not treated with unnecessary cruelty'! Was there ever a stranger utterance on the lips of a Christian bishop? Could there be a more certain way of distorting the Bible into purposes the very opposite from those for which it was intended, than to make it the sole authority for maintaining an institution which was confessed to be, 'by its inherent nature, a curse and a blight'? [1]

'Of crude morality,' says the Rev. Professor A. B. Bruce, 'there are numerous instances in the Old Testament, and no one can use it as a perfect guide who does not understand this.'

'If we find even in the Bible,' says a Scotch divine, 'anything which confuses our senses of right and wrong, which seems to us less exalted and pure than the character of God would be; if after the most patient thought and prayerful pondering it still retains this aspect, then we are not to bow down to it as God's revelation to us, since it does not meet the need of the earlier and more sacred revelation He has given us in our own spirit and conscience which testify of Him.'

---

[1] 'The craft of the devil is so great that he introduces his deadly doctrines by adding to or taking from, by distorting or changing, the written words.'—St. Chrys. *Opp.* vi. 162.

CHAPTER XV

FURTHER MISINTERPRETATION OF THE BIBLE.

τοὺς ἐντυγχάνοντας τοῖς ἱεροῖς γράμμασιν οὐ δεῖ συλλαβομαχεῖν, ἀλλὰ πρὸ τῶν ὀνομάτων καὶ ῥημάτων τὴν διάνοιαν σκοτεῖν.—PHILO, *Fragm.* (ed. Mangey, ii. p. 656).

'The aim of all Scripture is the reformation of mankind.'

St. Chrys. Opp. vi. 314.

'Alia quae absque auctoritate et testimoniis Scripturarum quasi traditione Apostolica sponte referunt atque confingunt, percutit gladius Dei.'—Jer. *in Hagg.* i. 11.

'Nostra damus, cum falsa damus, nam fallere nostrum est;
Et cum falsa damus, nil nisi nostra damus.'

THE facts at which we have glanced are surely full of warning! By the superstitious misapplication of the mere phrases of Scripture, the Bible has been quoted against Copernicus, and Kepler, and Galileo, and Columbus; on the perversion of 'Honour the King' was built the ruinous opposition to national freedom and the slavish theory of 'passive obedience;' on the *super hanc petram* the colossal usurpations of Papal tyranny; on 'Cursed be Canaan' the shameful infamies of the slave trade; on 'Constrain them to come in' the hideous crimes of the Inquisition; on 'Thou shalt not suffer a witch to live' the deplorable butcheries of Sprenger; on 'Being crafty I caught them with guile' (St. Paul's ironic reference to a gross calumny) the disgraceful advice to entrap and ruin heretics by ecclesiastical treachery. Even Philo, profound as was his reverence for Scripture, corrected such servile tendencies nearly two millenniums ago. He bade us not to fight about words and syllables, but to discover the essential meaning.

That the evils on which I have dwelt have sprung chiefly from misuse of the Bible cannot be denied; but it is absurd to charge them upon the Bible itself, because the Bible, taken as a whole, and in its full and final teaching, constitutes their most emphatic condemnation. The blame of them belongs not to the Book, but to those who abase it to the lowest depths under pretence of exalting it; and to those who nullify its essential purpose by professing to adore its separate words and letters. Through the narrow chink of perhaps some single text—and that usually misinterpreted and torn from its context—they let in the flood-tide of errors which every genuine wall, bastion, and foundation of the Book was intended to keep out for ever.

It is no more an argument against the Bible that it is misused than it is against the vine that so much of its clustered fruit is made the instrument of drunkenness. If it be true, as an American writer says, that 'we have drawn from it the power to save men and to slay them; to establish peace and to mass artillery; to be Christians of the noblest type and bigots of the direst'—that is because we wholly misunderstand its nature. If we choose to wrest or 'torture' Scripture, as St. Peter expresses it, we may always find in it this power for evil as well as for good, 'the inspiration of life unto life or of death unto death, the light of heaven or the smoke of hell. It is as wings to the spirit of one man and as lead to another; it brings sight or begets blindness, makes melody or creates discord.' But why is this? It is because men go to it as though it were one, and homogeneous. It is because men go to it not for what they find in it as a whole, but for what they can wrench out of its isolated utterances; and, worse than this, because they go to it not for what they really find there as its final teaching, but for what they *want* to find there in support of their own interests and opinions. They illustrate the sarcasm of Kant: 'Go to the Bible, but mind, you must not find there anything *we* do not find there; anything except what *I* find; because if you do you are wrong.'

Those who would make the Bible itself responsible for this abuse of its isolated, imperfect, or misused passages, should further remember two facts:

1. First, they are using it in a manner to which it lends no sanction, but to which it has been perverted by theories of human invention; secondly, the crimes and errors which were sometimes defended on its supposed authority were mainly confined to ages in which it was least known, or which inherited the errors which had become the stereotyped result of that previous ignorance.

If the defence of polygamy, of slavery, of witch-burning, of religious persecution, of exterminating wars really resulted from any *right* use of the Sacred Book, how came it that these wrongs, each and all, were distinctly repudiated by the earlier generations of Christians, who as yet possessed no New Testament whereby to correct any errors which might have sprung from a mistaken application of the Old?

From the first, among the early Christians—poor and ignorant as most of them were—polygamy was unknown; slavery was partly ameliorated into brotherhood, and partly discouraged or suppressed; religious persecution was regarded with horror; witches were practically unheard of. So far from approving of exterminating warfare, Ulfilas, the great apostle of the Goths in the fourth century, would not even translate into Gothic the more warlike books of the Old Testament, lest they should furnish any incentive or excuse to the wild passions of his converts. The Christians of those days understood at least thus much—that to support on Biblical authority anything which was alien from the Spirit of Christ was not to use but to misuse the Bible. If it involved no misinterpretation of the particular passages referred to, it involved a fundamental misinterpretation of everything which the Bible was meant to be. Whether practices or institutions which we now regard as execrable were once *relatively* excusable is at the best a speculative question. Whatever may be said about them in the earlier books of the Bible, they are now, at any rate, absolutely and for ever wrong.

2. And it is the Bible itself which has at length delivered mankind from the curses which arose from its abuse.

The horrors on which I have touched belong mainly to the dark ages, or were part of the worst legacy which they bequeathed. But in the dark ages less was known of the real meaning of the Bible than at any other period. To the mass of Christians under the Papal tyranny it was a sealed book. They could form no sort of judgment respecting it, except such as they derived from men whose policy it has always been to keep it out of their hands, who ruled over their consciences with a rod of iron, and who abused its perverted texts to establish their own tyranny.

Take for instance the entire system of priestly penances. How could Christians know that it was wholly without

Scriptural authority when, ignorant of the original Greek, and dependent on the faulty Vulgate, they read in Acts ii. 38 '*pœnitentiam agite*,' which was explained to mean 'do penance' ?[1] Can we wonder at the intense flash of illumination which thrilled through Luther's soul, when, having held this view for many years of his life, he suddenly discovered that μετανοήσατε ('repent ye') had no shadow of such a meaning, and had no connection whatever with the system which the Church of Rome had elevated into a spurious sacrament?

'What meanings the monks had got out of the Vulgate, Erasmus illustrates by a hundred instances. He was present once when some of them were arguing whether it was right to put heretics to death. A learned friar quoted from St. Paul, "Hæreticum devita!" He had conceived that by "devita" St. Paul had meant an order *de vita tollere*.'[2]

It may be proved with certainty that the ignorance of the Bible was absolute, as it still is in South America and most Romish countries. There was extreme hostility against every attempt to make it better known, and this hostility was due in great measure to the fear lest a better knowledge of it should entirely overthrow the sacerdotal

---

[1] Pope Gregory I. said rightly 'Pœnitentiam agere est et *perpetrata mala plangere* et *plangenda non perpetrare.*'

[2] Froude, *Lectures on the Council of Trent*, p. 59. The ignorant error is by no means isolated. We are told of many Catholics who understood Ps. xxxiv. to mean, not 'thou hast founded it upon the floods' (*super maria*), but 'upon Mary' (*super Mariâ*); and of Calvinists who denied the necessity of repentance to the elect, because the calling of God is 'without repentance ;' and of an English archbishop before the Reformation, who argued the supremacy of the Roman Church, because, he said, every one knows that 'kephas' means 'a head.'

despotism which professed to be based upon its inspired authority. 'The encroachments of the Papacy had absorbed all subordinate authority, and from the Papacy the poison of simony and profligacy had gone through every vein and artery of the Catholic Communion.' If those are the words of a Protestant writer, they are no whit more strong than passages which might be cited from popes and saints as to what kind of men were many of the priests who lorded it with awful spiritual autocracy over the free consciences of men. 'The corruption of the people,' said Pope Innocent III. in his opening address to the great Lateran Council, 'has its chief source in the clergy. From this arise the evils of Christendom; faith perishes; religion is defaced; liberty is restricted; justice is trodden under foot.' Pope Adrian VI. spoke quite as strongly, and pointed to the Roman *curia* as the very source and fount of the universal depravity.

As to the general ignorance, the 'Epistolæ Obscurorum Virorum' illustrates the conviction among free and thinking men that the struggle between the Reformers and the Papacy was the struggle of knowledge against obscurantism, of light against darkness, of morality against corruption, of freedom against a servility which was intolerable and degrading to the awakening conscience of mankind. There was a story current, far from impossible, of a priest who thought that Greek and the New Testament were two recent heresies! Luther tells us that he had attained the age of twenty-six before he had read a complete Bible. Hebrew was stupidly denounced by Dominicans and inquisitors as 'an accursed tongue.' When Reuchlin lectured on Hebrew at Heidelberg he had to do so secretly, and he was perpetually worried by suspicious ignorance.

14

> At last Erasmus, that great injured name,
> The glory of the priesthood and the shame,
> Stemmed the wild torrent of a barbarous age
> And drove the holy Vandals off the stage.

He complained that 'men and women chattered like parrots the Psalms and prayers which they did not understand.' 'The Italians say,' complains Melanchthon, 'he is a good grammarian; therefore he is a heretic.' There were thousands even of theologians who did not know whether the Apostles wrote in Greek, in Hebrew, or in Latin. A professor of the Sorbonne, in a public lecture aimed against the new Scriptural studies, exclaimed : 'By heavens! I was more than fifty years old before I knew what the New Testament was.' The learned and able Carlstadt says that he had been a Doctor of Divinity for eight years before he had read the whole of the New Testament. The current systems of belief in many points were drawn, says Robert Stephens, 'not from the oracles of God, but from Peter Lombard, the Sophist Aristotle, and the Mahometan Averroes.'[1] They were, in fact, dependent for most Christians upon the bald dicta of priests, and were to a great extent false. Even had they been true, yet, as Milton says, 'if a man believes things only because his pastor says so, or the assembly so determines, without knowing other reason, though his belief be true, yet the very truth he holds becomes his heresy.'

I have already quoted some of the passages of Holy

---

[1] See the authorities referred to in *History of Interpretation*, pp. 316-323. In 1199 Innocent III. ordered Arnold of Cîteaux to suppress Bible-reading at Metz, on the plea that the Bible was 'far beyond the grasp of the simple and illiterate.' The present Pope says in his Encyclical on the Bible, 'Incorruptum Sacr. Litterarum sensum *extra Ecclesiam* neutiquam reperiri.'

Writ which require us to exercise the right of private judgment, the light of reason and conscience in judging of every truth which is presented to us (Prov. xx. 27, 1 John iv. 1, 1 Thess. v. 21, 1 Cor. ii. 11, 15, Luke xii. 57, &c.); and our greatest divines and thinkers have not failed to learn the lesson. 'For men to be tied and led by authority,' says Hooker, 'as it were by a kind of captivity of judgment, and though there be reason to the contrary not to listen to it, but to follow like beasts the first in the herd, this were brutish.'[1]

'Reason,' says Culverwell, 'is the daughter of Eternity, and before Antiquity, which is the daughter of Time.'[2] 'Reason,' says Bishop Butler, 'can and ought to judge not only of the meaning, *but also of the morality and evidence of revelation.*'[3] 'No apology can be required,' says Bishop Herbert Marsh, 'for applying to the Bible the principles of reason and learning; for if the Bible could not stand these tests it could not be what it is—a work of Divine wisdom. The Bible therefore must be examined by the same laws of criticism which are applied to other writings of antiquity.'

The determination with which the priests and monks of those days endeavoured to keep the Bible from the hands of the people is equally clear.[4] When Wycliffe gave the English a Bible from which they could for the first time judge for themselves, Archbishop Arundel, writing to the Pope, described him as 'that pestilent wretch, John Wy-

---

[1] *Eccl. Pol.* ii. 7, § 6.   [2] *Duct. Dubit.* I. ii. § 64.
[3] *Analogy*, II. iii. 26.

[4] On the first Index Expurgatorius, published by Pope Paul IV. in 1559, he placed all Bibles in modern languages, enumerating forty-eight editions, chiefly printed in Roman Catholic countries (Hallam, *Lit. of Europe*, ii. 265, and authorities there quoted).

cliffe, the son of the old Serpent, the forerunner of Antichrist, who has completed his iniquity by inventing a new translation of the Scriptures.' When Tyndale completed his inestimable version, the priests and bishops burnt it by thousands at the old cross of St. Paul's, as '*a burnt offering most pleasing to Almighty God;*' and to crown his glorious labours he was finally strangled and burnt. For many centuries in many countries it was death to possess and excommunication to read a translation of the Bible. Charles V. and Philip II. passed a decree which inflicted the punishment of death by burning on any in the Netherlands who presumed to read the Bible in any language which they could understand.[1]

In proportion as the Bible has become known, in that proportion has it dispelled the atrocities and tyrannies which were based upon its misuse.

'Truth,' says Milton, 'is compared in Scripture to a streaming fountain; if her waters flow not in a perpetual progression, they sicken into a muddy pool of conformity and tradition.'

As late as 1816 Pope Pius VII. declared in a bull that 'it is evident by experience that when the Holy Scriptures are circulated in the vulgar tongue, through the temerity of men more harm than benefit results.'[2]

We are not therefore surprised to know that Pius IX. spoke of Bible Societies as 'pests' on the same level with

[1] Motley's *Rise of the Dutch Republic*, i. 73, 228.

[2] 'Plus inde detrimenti quam utilitatis oriri.' It is not thought good *to let every curious busybody of the baser sort* read and examine the Bible in their common language.'—HARDING. The Bull *Unigenitus* of Clement XI. in 1703 condemned Quesnel's propositions, one of which was that 'to prohibit the reading of the Scripture . . . is to deny the use of light to the children of light' (Sixtus of Amana, *Antibarb. Bibl.* ii. 7). See the remarkable preface to the Bible of the

Communistic Societies; or that Leo XIII. spoke of vernacular Bibles as 'poisonous pastures.'

The Council of Trent decreed that 'he who shall presume to read, or to have a Bible without a license, may not receive absolution until he has surrendered the Bible.' The Romish theologians professed to base their system upon the traditions of men, and they knew that a thorough knowledge of the Bible by the multitude would emancipate them from the yoke of those hard doctrines. 'The Bible is in its essence the most essential book of freedom and equal brotherhood before God. The complaints against its dissemination came from those who would fain have kept men's souls in docility to their own bondage.' Erasmus said that he should prefer to hear young maidens talking about Christ, than some who in the opinion of the vulgar are consummate Rabbis; but Cochlæus made it a ground for complaint, as Theodoret had done of exultation,[1] that now even cobblers and women knew the New

Translators of 1611, where they call the supposed free permission of Rome to let the Bible be used as a δῶρον ἄδωρον, because Romanists 'must first get a license in writing before they may use them, and to get that they must approve themselves to their confessor—that is, to be such as are, if not frozen in the dregs, yet soured in the leaven of their superstition.' They go on to mention that Clement VIII. withdrew the license to read the Bible in the vulgar tongue granted by Pius IV. (*Index Prohib. libr.* p. 15, vs. 5). 'So much are they afraid of the light of the Scriptures (*Lucifugæ Scripturarum*, as Tertullian speaketh) that they will not trust the people with it—no, not as it is set forth by their own sworn men; no, not with the license of their own bishops and inquisitors. Yea, so unworthy are they to communicate the Scriptures to the people's understanding in any sort, that they are not ashamed to confess that we forced them to translate it into English against their wills. This seemeth to argue a bad cause, or a bad conscience, or both.'

[1] Περὶ φύσεως ἀνθρώπου.

Testament by heart.   Wycliffe made it the effort of his life
to place the Bible in the hands of the multitude, but the
chronicler Knighton angrily curses him for having made
it 'common and more open to laymen and to women than
it was wont to be to clerks well learned and of good understanding, so that the *pearl of the Gospel is trodden under foot
of swine.'*

We see, then, that in the Romish Church there has been
an extreme reluctance to allow to the people the free use
of the Bible in tongues which they understand.   Pius IV.
granted such a license, but Clement VIII. withdrew it.

Unstudied, unthought of, except by a few, lay the sacred
writings where alone the truth was to be found which
men were now demanding.   It was the free and open Bible
which secured to us the blessings of 'the bright and blissful Reformation.'   'The *translated Bible*,' Cardinal Newman
says with reluctant admiration, ' is *the stronghold of heresy.*'[1]
'Lately,' says a Roman Catholic writer in the 'Contemporary Review,' 'I asked of a parish priest, "Do you allow
your flock to read the Bible at all?"   "No, sir, I do not,"
he replied.   "You forget that I am a spiritual physician,
not a poisoner of souls."'[2]

Tyndale, in answer to the profane remark, that ' we had
better be without God's laws than the Pope's,' uttered the
noble boast, 'If God spare my life, ere many years I will
cause the boy that driveth the plough to know more of
Scripture than thou dost;' but as a consequence of his
labours, Bishop Nikke complained to the Archbishop, 'It
passeth my power, or that of any spiritual man, to hinder
it now, and if *this continue much longer it will undo us all.*'

The perversions of Scripture by ignorance, pride, and

---

[1] Froude, *Lectures on the Council of Trent*, p. 59.
[2] See too Lasserre, *Pref.* ii.

self-interest become a thousandfold more perilous when it is kept as a whole from the hands of Christians and its fragments are only manipulated by those who would fain lock the doors of knowledge.

It has been said that 'there is no folly, no God-dishonouring theology, no iniquity, no sacerdotal puerility, for which chapter and verse may not be cited *by an enslaved intelligence*. And under these circumstances *it is impossible to express in adequate terms the importance of a correct estimate and exposition of the Bible.*'[1]

That correct estimate depends most of all on our rejecting every false theory respecting it; and in judging each book and part of it in accordance with the purest light of the reason and the conscience enlightened by the teaching of Christ.

When we do this, we shall see that as a whole it uplifts to the nations a loftier standard of righteousness and freedom, a purer ideal of Eternal Life, than all the other literature of all the world, including all the most sacred books of the nations. For when we do this we shall see that in it we may find the power of God unto salvation through Jesus Christ. Theories of plenary inspiration and supernatural infallibility in every part; theories that the sacred writers were all and always not only the penmen but the inanimate pens of the Holy Ghost; theories that the Bible in every verse not merely *contains* but *is* the word of God—these and similar theories snatched up in defiance of all the phenomena, and supported by a casuistry which revolts the healthy conscience and common sense of mankind—have been, in age after age, prolific of terrible disasters. Yet even in despite of such errors the essential teaching of Scripture has been an inestimable blessing to

[1] The Rev. E. White.

generation after generation; and when once it has been
disencumbered of pernicious falsities, and judged for what
it is—the fragmentary yet sufficient record of a progressive
revelation; the most precious outward contribution to the
slow, manifold, partial, and gradual education of the human race in the will of God—then the Bible has been and
will for ever be the source of blessings which no arithmetic
can number and no eloquence express. One who was at
least a most keen and able critic says with truth, 'Taking
the Old Testament as Israel's sublime establishment of the
theme "*Righteousness is salvation;*" taking the New as an
incomparable elucidation by Jesus of what righteousness
is and how salvation is won, I do not fear comparing the
power, over the soul and imagination, of the Bible, taken
in this sense—a sense which is at the same time solid—
with the like power in the old materialistic and miraculous
sense for the Bible, which is not.'[1]

It is an entire mistake to imagine that the cause of God
and of religion has gained in *any* way from that mechanical theory of inspiration which has been the taproot of so
many crimes against humanity. On the contrary, it has
lost unspeakably. 'The natural result of a man like Calov
was a man like Voltaire.' Of Voltaire it has been said
that 'He saw only a besotted people led in chains by a
crafty priesthood. Men spoke to him of the mild beams
of Christian charity, and where they pointed he saw only
the yellow glare of the stake; they talked of the gentle
solace of Christian faith, and he heard only the shrieks of
the thousands and tens of thousands whom Christian persecutors had racked, strangled, gibbeted, burnt, broken on
the wheel. Through the steam of innocent blood which
Christians for the honour of their belief had spilt in every

---

[1] Matthew Arnold, *God and the Bible*, Pref. p. xxv.

quarter of the known world—the blood of Jews, Moors, Indians, and all the vast holocausts of heretical sects and people in eastern and western Europe—he saw only dismal tracts of intellectual darkness, and heard only the humming of the doctors as they served forth to congregations of poor men hungering for spiritual sustenance the draff of theological superstition.'[1] When we are shocked at the ribaldries and blasphemies of Voltaire, let us not forget that he identified the spirit of Christianity with deeds so horrid as the execrable cruelty inflicted by an unworthy Church on Jean Calas, the Servins, and the young De la Barre; and that these deeds were sanctioned and defended by shreds and scraps of Scripture texts.

The confession of Richard III. might have been made by many:

> 'And thus I clothe my naked villany
> With odd old ends stolen forth of Holy Writ,
> And seem a saint when most I play the devil.'[2]

And when we meditate on all the unmingled blessings which the Bible, rightly used and understood, would have brought to mankind, and on the many curses for which its misuse has been made responsible, we can find no words more suitable than those of the fervid Quaker poet:

> Foul scorn and shame be on ye all,
>   Who turn the good to evil;
> Who steal the Bible from the Lord
>   And give it to the devil.

> Than garbled text and parchment law
>   I own a statute higher;
> And God is true—were every book
>   And every man a liar.

---

[1] J. Morley, *Voltaire*, p. 236.   [2] *Rich. III.* Act i. Sc. 3.

CHAPTER XVI

THE WRESTING OF TEXTS.

'Every word of God is pure. Add not thou unto His words, lest
He reprove thee, and thou be found a liar.'—Prov. xxx. 5, 6.

'Ἀτόπως δρῶσιν ὅσοι ἐκ μέρους τινὸς κρίνουσι τὸ ὅλον, ἀλλὰ τοὐναντίον ἐκ τοῦ
ὅλου τὸ μέρος.—PHILO, *Ex. qu. in Gen. Fragm.* (ed. Mangey, ii. 657).

Μὴ βιαζόμενοι τὰ ὑπὸ τοῦ Θεοῦ δεδομένα.—HIPPOLYTUS, *C. Noetum*, 9.

'In iis quae aperte in Scripturis posita sunt inveniuntur illa omnia
quae continent fidem moresque vivendi, *spem scilicet et caritatem.—*
AUG., *De Doctr. Christ.* ii. 9.

'The Scripture stands, not *in cortice verborum*, but *in medullâ sensus.*'
—VINES, Commons Sermon, 1646.

'The interpretations of the Scriptures are of two sorts—methodical
and solute or at large. For this divine water . . . either is first
forced up into a cistern, and from thence fetched and derived for use,
or else it is drawn and received in buckets and vessels immediately
where it springeth. The former sort whereof, though it seem to be
the more ready, yet in my judgment is more subject to corrupt.'—
BACON, *Advancement of Learning*, Book II.

'The mere first-impression reader is always liable to misapprehend. The number of texts generally misapplied, the character and
amount of that misapplication, are perfectly astonishing.'—DEAN
ALFORD.

ONE great source of the misinterpretation of the Bible,
and the consequent wrongs inflicted upon it, has been the
habit of treating it as though it were a congeries of isolated

texts. This may sound like the merest truism, but the merest truisms often need to be repeated, because they tend to become the most neglected truths. 'There are,' says Coleridge, 'some truths so true that they lie in the lumber room of the memory, side by side with the most exploded errors.'

To act thus is to 'rend the Urim and Thummim from the breastplate of judgment, and to frame oracles by private divination from each letter of each disjointed gem . . . deserted by the Spirit which shines in the parts only as it pervades and irradiates the whole.' We may apply to these strange mosaics—made up of accommodated phrases, incidental allusions, fancies, traditions, apologues, and *argumenta ad hominem*—the remark of St. Irenæus, that, by the same method, you might break up the mosaic of a king, and alter its constituent pieces into the semblance of a dog or of a fox. And this is practically done when rhetoric is turned into logic; the fluid words of poetry into the rigid metaphysics of dogma; the *obiter dicta auctoris aliud agentis* into supernatural decisions of tremendous problems; the popular allusions of past millenniums into barriers against the mighty tide of scientific progress; and warnings of temporal calamity into menaces of everlasting torment. *Corruptio optimi pessima.* Men betray the Bible with a kiss.

Any collection of books treated as the Bible has been treated—snipped into phrases and fragments—dissevered from their context, and from their primary historic sense, and all regarded as equipollent—may be abused to prove anything. When it is thus mishandled, the Bible may be quoted in support of any number of propositions, however self-contradictory, however intrinsically absurd, however entirely alien from its own general spirit. 'To understand that the language of the Bible is fluid and literary, not rigid, fixed, and scientific,' is, as Matthew Arnold truly said, 'the first step to a right understanding of the Bible.'[1]

Still more false and futile may be the conclusions built upon a book of varied contents, when, as is the case with the Bible, whole systems of theology are read between the lines of it; and colossal superstructures built upon the narrow base of some separate phrase. The Bible has been known for thousands of years through imperfect translations. It has been elaborated into enormous institutions, encumbered with alien traditions, explained by unnatural methods. It has been adopted by nations who have been entirely ignorant of the modes of thought and modes of expression current in the ages and countries in which it originated. Its heterogeneous elements, divided from each other by centuries of progress and difference, have been dealt with as though they were one homogeneous and supernatural whole. Can we wonder that many of the inferences which professed to be deduced from the Bible have been contradictory, perilous, and full of error?

It is the doctrine of the supernatural infallibility of every book and sentence of Scripture—'notwithstanding the repugnancy of the doctrine in its unqualified sense to Scripture, reason, and common sense theoretically, while to all particulars it is intractable, unmalleable, and altogether unprofitable'—which so utterly ruined for centuries the sanity and honesty of Biblical exegesis. 'On what other ground,' asks Coleridge, 'can I account for the whimsical *subintelligiturs* of our numerous harmonists— for the curiously inferred facts, the inventive circumstantial detail, the complemental and supplemental history, which, in the utter silence of all historians and absence of

---

[1] *Literature and Dogma*, p. xii.

all historical documents, they bring to light by mere force of logic? Allow me to create chasms *ad libitum*, and *ad libitum* to fill them up with imagined facts and incidents, and I would almost undertake to harmonise Falstaff's account of the rogues in buckram into a coherent and consistent narrative.'

There are probably thousands of uneducated persons who think that the Bible was originally written in that atomistic form—in those separate sentences and scraps of sentences—which we call 'texts.' The printing of the Revised Version in paragraphs instead of texts will gradually help to dissipate this delusion, and will contribute in this way, as in many others, to restore truer conceptions of what the Bible is and means. Even those who know that the Bible was written, like all other books, in paragraphs, are unaware how late was the origin of its separation—and sometimes very unintelligent separation—into chapters and texts. Among the Jews, for the convenience of public reading in the synagogue, the MSS. of the Law were marked into sections (*Parashoth*), 290 in number, marked with a ס (p); and into smaller paragraphs (*Sedarim*) marked with a ס (s), 379 in number. Similarly the *Haphtaroth*, or lessons from the Prophets, were divided into fifty-four.[1] Our division of the Bible into chapters originated, not (as is often said) with Hugo de Sancto Caro († 1263), but with our great Archbishop Stephen Langton († 1228).

The habit of adducing shreds of Scripture phrases as 'proof texts' for all sorts of minute and inferential doctrines has been the source of unnumbered errors. Those

---

[1] There are fifty-four larger Parashoth which marked the Sunday lessons. See Wildeboer, *Origin of the Old Testament Canon* (E.T.), p. 8. There were 23,203 texts in the Hebrew Massorah.

errors have been multiplied and rendered more pernicious
(1) by mistranslations; (2) by attempts to allegorise and
spiritualise plain passages into irrelevant exhortations and
dogmas; (3) by enormous and unwarrantable inferences;
(4) by reading modern and Western ideas into ancient and
Eastern modes of thought; and (5) by a total divorce of separate passages from their original and contextual meaning.

'Twenty doctors,' says William Tyndale, 'expound one
text twenty ways, and with an anti-theme of half an inch
some of them draw a thread of nine days long.'[1]

I will give one or two instances of this perverse citation
and use of texts—instances which might be indefinitely
multiplied. They will be sufficient to put us on our guard
against that wresting of the Scriptures which had begun
in the days of the Apostles and has never ceased since
then.[2] They will serve to show the absurdity of attacks
on Scripture which have nothing to do with Scripture.
They will protect us against sweeping peremptory interpretations, which do not explain but explain away. They
will emancipate us from dogmas which reproduce the
words but travesty the meaning of the sacred writers.
When we are told that 'the Bible says' this or that, they
will enable us to reply at once that 'the Bible,' as a whole,
says nothing of the sort, but perhaps the very reverse; and,
very often, that the 'text' specifically quoted means something entirely different.

1. I recently read a contemptuous attack on the wisdom
and morality of the Bible on the ground that it adopts a
Manichean disparagement of the human body. The 'text'
quoted in proof of the charge was Phil. iii. 21—'Who shall
change our *vile body*.'

<hr>

[1] Tyndale, *Obedience of a Christian Man.*

[2] 2 Pet. iii. 16. στρεβλοῖσιν. So ancient was the crime of stretching Scripture on the rack!

When Archbishop Whately lay on his deathbed his
chaplain quoted this phrase. 'The Bible does not say that,'
said the Archbishop. 'Surely it does,' replied the chaplain,
turning to this verse. 'Read it in the Greek,' said
Whately. The chaplain read: ὃς μετασχηματίσει τὸ σῶμα
τῆς ταπεινώσεως ἡμῶν. 'Ah!' said the Archbishop, 'the
words are not "our *vile body*," but "*the body of our humiliation :*" *that* is something very different.'

And so it stands corrected in the Revised Version.
There is not the least ground for charging St. Paul with
any ascetic or neo-Platonic contempt for this our mortal
frame, which is so fearfully or wonderfully made. So far
from resembling the philosopher Plotinus, who blushed
that he had a body, St. Paul knew and taught that man's
mortal body is the Temple of the Holy Ghost.

2. Of the allegorical misuses of Scripture I gave one or
two instances in a previous chapter. It has always been
the fashion among a certain school of thinkers to represent that method as a badge of orthodoxy.[1] Yet as an
historical fact, it is in origin pagan and Jewish, and in
practical use it first flourished even more among the heretics than among the Catholics. Irenæus complains that
it was universal among the Gnostics.

---

[1] Thus Cardinal Newman says that 'heresy and the rejection of the
allegorical interpretation have always gone together.' But no more
damaging condemnation of 'orthodoxy' could be pronounced than
the false assertion that it depends on an arbitrary and pagan method
of distorting plain words into impossible meanings. Further than
this, Father after Father and Schoolman after Schoolman practically
declares that the method of allegorising is quite useless and superfluous, for they all lay it down as a rule that nothing is taught 'allegorically' in Scripture which is not also taught plainly and literally
in other passages ; so that by their own admission 'the mystic sense'
only supplies us with more uncertain and more enigmatic repetitions
of doctrines independently set forth.

St. Augustine gives an amusing specimen of the way in which this 'mystical interpretation' can be made to prove anything or everything. The Manichees taught that Christ did not retain His mortal body in heaven, but left it in the sun: and to demonstrate this dogma they quoted Ps. xix. 4, 'In them hath He set a tabernacle for the sun.' In the old Latin versions this ran *Posuit tabernaculum suum in sole* ('He hath placed His tabernacle in the sun'). Now 'tabernacle' or 'tent,' said the Manichees, means 'the body,' as in John i. 14, 'the Word tabernacled ($\dot{\epsilon}\sigma\kappa\dot{\eta}\nu\omega\sigma\epsilon\nu$) among us.' The meaning therefore is that Christ when He ascended left His mortal body behind Him in the sun!

3. Another instance may be quoted. In the middle ages it was common to appeal to St. Peter's reply to Christ, 'Lord, here are two swords,' in proof that the Pope possessed both the spiritual and the temporal power. This was specially relied upon by Boniface VIII., who also deduced from 'Feed My lambs' the inference that popes might trample on the decrees of kings! Innocent III. claimed superiority over the Emperor because God had made 'the greater light' (which he declared to represent the Pope) to rule the day, and only 'the lesser light' (the Emperor) to rule the night. Such preposterous perversions are endless, and they are immeasurably beneath contempt. Luther might well exclaim with respect to them, 'O reckless impudence and wicked ambition!'[1]

---

[1] What masses of false religion have been built on allegorical misinterpretations of 'We have an altar;' on 'Knowing therefore the terror of the Lord;' on wrong interpretations like 'Take no thought for the morrow;' on 'He found no place for repentance;' on 'Sell all that thou hast;' on 'This is my body;' on 'The whole head is sick, and the whole heart is faint;' on 'Where the tree falleth there shall it lie;' or, again, on wrong renderings like 'We are saved by faith only,' and '*If* they shall fall away.'

4. Perhaps the worst injury that has been inflicted on Scripture by the perversion of texts is the manner in which they have been used as pin-points on which to build inverted pyramids of theological system, and that despotism which has usually proved itself to be so deep a curse to every nation which has been pusillanimous enough to submit to it.

The scanty, sensuous, passionate, pictorial character of Hebrew language and literature is least of all adapted for this torturing process.

Often the whole atmosphere of religious belief has been filled with smoke by what Coleridge calls 'the ever-widening spiral ergo from the narrow aperture of single texts.'

Round the interior of the vast dome of St. Peter's runs in colossal letters the inscription, 'Thou art Peter, and upon this rock will I build My Church.'[1] The *exact* significance of this text is all the more uncertain because we do not know whether our Lord was speaking in Syriac or in Greek, nor can we tell the exact shade of difference between *Petros* (Peter) and *Petra* ('rock'). Its general significance seems to be that Peter should be the first of the Apostles to admit the Gentiles into the Church; the first of the Apostles to lay the foundation of a wide conversion.[2]

It has always been a matter of uncertainty whether by 'this rock' our Lord meant Peter, as Roman Catholics aver; or Himself, as St. Augustine thought; or the faith of Peter's confession, which is the explanation of St. Chrysostom. But the immense majority of the Fathers—and to Romanists at any rate who profess to follow the *unanimis consensus patrum* this ought, on their own principles, to be decisive

---

[1] Matt. xvi. 18. 'Quid hæc ad *Romam ?*'—Bengel.
[2] Acts ii. 41, x. 44–48.

15

—combine to explain it—as do Pope Felix V. and the Council of Trent—*not of Peter personally, but of his confession.*[1]   And even if supremacy were given to Peter, there is not the most attenuated ghost of evidence, or shadow of argument, to show that he *could*, much less that he *did*, transmit it to his successors; or that those successors were the Bishops of Rome; or that his so-called supremacy bore the most infinitesimal resemblance to the enormous super-structure of fraud, tyranny, ruthlessness, and corruption which was reared upon this pretence.   That Christ's promise gave to St. Peter no supremacy, no infallibility, no recognised authority over the other Apostles, is proved again and again in the most decisive manner by the New Testament itself.   It is further a matter of historical certainty that St. Peter was *not* the founder of the Church of Rome; there is an absence of *decisive* proof that he ever visited Rome at all; if he ever did visit it—as is probable—there is not a trace of any evidence that he had anything more to do with it than that he was martyred there.   It is also as certain as anything can be that, for three centuries at least, the right of Rome to tyrannise over any other Church was decisively rejected, and that the full-blown usurpation of autocracy by the Bishop of Rome was not achieved till centuries afterwards—and then only in part because of accidental historic circumstances, and because the world in general, covered with the thickest darkness of ignorance, was deceived by the gross forgery of the Donation of Constantine, the Decretals of Isidore, and forged interpolations in the writings of the Greek Fathers, which even deceived St. Thomas Aquinas.   And yet on that text, and on that text almost alone until it was

---

[1] 'Super ista confessione ædificabo Ecclesiam meam.'—Pope Felix V., *Ep.* 5.

propped up by usurpation and fraud, was built a colossal
priestly tyranny which was sometimes placed in the hands
of men consummately wicked and worthless—of men like
Benedict IX., Alexander Borgia, or Innocent VIII.

5. But other errors, no less serious, have sprung from
an opposite blunder to that of exorbitant inferences—for
opposite blunders have been pressed with equal alacrity
and insistence into the service of false religion. That
opposite blunder is a literalism which insists on interpreting Eastern and ancient and metaphorical phraseology
into modern and alien notions which had not so much as
emerged above the horizon in the days of the ancient
Hebrews. Thus, to the injury of unnumbered souls, the
‘power of the keys,’ and the power to forgive sins, which
none can do save God only, have been arrogated by priests
on the ground of the promise in Matt. xvi. 19.[1] On this

---

[1] The metaphor of ‘binding’ and ‘loosing’ does not occur elsewhere in Scripture in this connection; but we learn from the Talmud
that, in the Jewish sense (compare Matt. xxiii. 4), it did *not mean to
remit or retain sin*, but to declare what was lawful and what was unlawful, as (*e.g.*) the Apostles did at the first Synod in Jerusalem (Acts
xv. 28, 29), and as St. Paul did as regards circumcision. Nor is John
xx. 21–23 applicable to the claim to confer absolution in the Romish
sense. None can forgive sin but God only, and the Apostles only
remitted or retained sins, even with their miraculous powers, *by the
ministry of the word* (Acts ii. 38, iv. 12, xiii. 38, 39, xvi. 31; John iii.
36; Rom. v. 1; 1 John ii. 1; Tert. *De Judic.* p. 21). ‘You who affect
to remit sin,’ says Dr. Burnett, ‘prove your possession of the miraculous power which accompanied such a gift.’ Further, the promise
was not to the Apostles only, but to ‘*all the disciples*’ who were present
(compare Luke xxiv. 33). It was a commission to the society, and
has been usurped by those who falsely pretended to be the only
Christian priests. Once more, the ‘remit,’ like the ‘retain,’ is referred not to individuals, but to classes (ἄν τινων . . . αὐτοῖς, see
Westcott, *ad loc.*); and, as even Peter Lombard teaches in his *Sen-*

text has been based the deadly system of auricular confession.

But of what avail can it be to quote this text as sufficient to support the system of the confessional, when we know that 'the keys' and 'binding' and 'loosing' were common Jewish metaphors which have not the smallest bearing on the pretensions which they have been adduced to maintain? which, even if they had, belong to all true Christians, and not in any sense peculiarly to 'priests;' and which have been branded in their evil results by the unanimous voice of history and of living experience in age after age. Scripture only teaches us to confess to God (Ps. xxxii. 5; Josh. vii. 19; Ezra x. 11; Dan. ix. 4), or 'to one another' (Jas. v. 16), not to 'priests,' since none can forgive sins but God only. 'Quid ergo mihi est cum hominibus,' asks St. Augustine, 'ut audiant confessiones meas, quasi ipsi sanaturi sunt omnes languores meos? *Curiosum genus ad inquirendam vitam alienam, desidiosum ad corrigendam suam;*' and even St. Cyprian quotes under this head '*Maledictus qui spem habet in homine.*'[1]

6. Again, when Luther, abandoning the modern Romish doctrine of transubstantiation, adopted that of consub-

---

tentiæ, is not a power *solvendi* and *ligandi*, but *ostendendi solutos rel ligatos* (lib. iv. dist. 14-20). The absolution, he says, is not judicial, but the *declaration* of God's decree; just as the Jewish priest did not *cleanse* lepers, but declared them clean. 'The sinner,' he says (quoting Cassiodorus), 'is forgiven by God as soon as he repents, and is not therefore liberated by the priest from God's anger, from which his repentance set him free.' See Dean Plumptre, *Confession and Absolution*, p. 4. There is not a trace of the form *Absolvo te* before the thirteenth century. The 'power of the keys' in Jewish metaphor simply means the right to teach (Luke xi. 52).

[1] Aug. *Conf.* x. 3. Cypr. *De Lapsis*, 17. Jer. *in Matt.* xvi. 19. *Quum* apud Deum *non sententia sacerdotum* sed reorum vita quæratur.

stantiation, which was rejected by Zwingli and the Swedish Reformers, he thought it sufficient to knock down all arguments by constantly repeating, and by constantly writing with his finger on the table, the words ' *This is My body.*'   Yet no argument could be more intrinsically feeble than the insistence on the material interpretation of the text, in spite of the proofs that it could have no such meaning.   There was no more reason to press the word ' *is*' literally than to press it in such cases as ' the seven good kine *are* seven years.'   Such a materialistic interpretation is pressed in defiance of our Lord's own explanation and warning : ' The flesh profiteth nothing : the *words* which I speak unto you, *they* are spirit and *they* are life ; ' as well as of the fact that when He spoke *His body and the bread were two separate and distinct things*, so that it would have been *impossible* for them to understand the words otherwise than symbolically.

Seeing that when our Lord spoke He had not yet been sacrificed there could be no excuse for maintaining that ' My body' could only mean the mortal flesh.   Seeing, further, that the metaphor of ' *eating*' was perfectly familiar to the Jews as implying ' close union with '—as for instance in Rabbinic phrase, ' to eat of the years of Shechinah,' and in the Book of Ecclesiasticus (xxiv. 21), ' They that eat me (Wisdom) shall yet be hungry '—it is clear that the reiteration of the ' text' had no real bearing on the view which it was quoted to support.

7. The neglect of the context has also been a constant source of the error of quoting as Scripture what is not Scripture at all.

It used to be common to see in schools the words ' *Touch not ; taste not ; handle not*' (Col. ii. 21).   The words in themselves were sufficiently senseless as a universal command; but besides this, as quoted by St. Paul, they are so far from representing any advice of *his* that they belong to the rules of that ascetic Gnosticism which he is rejecting, and which it was the main object of his Epistle to condemn. The passage from which they are borrowed used to be a stock argument in favour of fasting. It is in reality an emphatic declaration of the inefficacy of fasting. For the true meaning of the passage was for the first time made clear to many English readers by the Revised Version; and so far from recommending asceticism, it expressly lays down the rule that the precepts and doctrines of humanly invented externalism 'have indeed a show of wisdom in will-worship, and humility, and severity to the body; but *are not of any value against the indulgence of the flesh.*'

8. The doctrine of 'eternal torments' has been again and again 'proved' by Is. xxxiii. 14, '*Who among us shall dwell with the devouring fire? Who among us shall dwell with everlasting burnings?*' Even a moderate study of the context might have sufficed to show that the verse has not the most remote connection with that terrific dogma. No such doctrine, it may be confidently affirmed, was ever on the horizon of the Prophets, or other Scripture writers, before (at the earliest) the days of the Exile. The passages quoted in favour of it from the Old Testament are only relevant in erroneous versions; or when irrelevant connotations are read into them; or when they are pressed into impossible syllogisms. Isaiah is speaking mainly of *temporal* judgments (compare xxxi. 9); and the exclamation here referred to is simply the terrified complaint of the people, 'How can we possibly bear the ravaging and conflagration of the land by our enemies with which we are threatened?' If the text prove anything at all, it tends

to prove the exact reverse of the doctrine in support of
which it is quoted, for it shows that in the language of
Eastern hyperbole the word 'everlasting' and its equiva-
lents were constantly used of transitory and temporal
afflictions.

9. The phrases of the New Testament are interpreted
in the same bare and bald way, without any reference to
history, literature, and the common laws of Eastern language—just as though they had first appeared in some
book of yesterday. The words of Christ and of the
Apostles are habitually forced into senses accordant with
popular dogma, without any reference at all to the meaning of the Old Testament passages on which they are
founded.

Thus the fearful metaphors, to be 'cast into hell fire,'
and 'where their worm dieth not, and the fire is not
quenched' (which occurs in Mark ix. 48, but is interpolated
into verses 44 and 46), are part of a parabolic passage so
entirely built on Jewish metaphors and idioms that apart
from them it cannot be understood. It is quoted as a
decisive proof of 'endless torments.' Its bearing on such
a dogma evaporates to nothing when we examine it. In
the first place, 'hell' can only mean what the original
word 'Gehenna' means; and 'Gehenna' was the vaguest
and most metaphorical word of later Jewish theology. In
our Lord's time Gehenna was a pleasant valley outside Jerusalem; but five centuries earlier it had been first desecrated
by Moloch worship, then defiled with corpses, and lastly
purified from pestilence by huge fires. To have the dead
body thrown into Gehenna was a terrible indignity, and
became a metaphor for severest punishment; but the use
of the phrase in this proverbial way no more sanctions
the belief in the 'hell' of the middle ages than the use of

Tartarus in 2 Peter ii. 4 shows that the author intended to vouch for the stories of Ixion and the Danaides; or than Luke xvi. 22 proves that Abraham literally carries the millions of the blessed dead in his actual bosom. Further, our Lord is quoting almost verbally from Is. lxvi. 24; and Isaiah—or the later Prophet who wrote that chapter—is describing in highly metaphorical terms how men of various nations shall come to Jerusalem to see— *not the living torments, but the consumed and consuming carcases* of the rebels against God. On such isolated phrases we have no warrant for building up vast and terrific doctrines which run counter to many plain passages of Scripture; and to its representation of God's mercy; and to the moral sense of mankind—which is itself a source of the divinest revelation.

I have only given these few instances by way of illustration; but they are more than sufficient to prove to all men of open minds the truth of the rules that (i), as the wisest Rabbis said,

'The Scripture speaks in the tongue of the sons of men;' that (ii), as St. Augustine said,

'Only the real meaning of Scripture is Scripture;' and that (iii), as is said in the 'Imitatio Christi,'

'All Holy Scripture ought to be read in the spirit in which it was written.'

The perspicuity of Scripture is absolute as to every truth which is essential for salvation. 'Whatever is necessary,' said St. Chrysostom, 'is clear.' As to those truths which are *required* for man's guidance, whosoever walketh in the way, even fools, shall not err therein.[1] But when Scripture is quoted for controversial purposes, it is, in hundreds of instances, quoted to all intents as falsely

---

[1] Is. xxxv. 8.

as it was by the woman who, on her deathbed, told her clergyman that she was not called upon to repent, because 'the gifts and calling of God are without repentance.' The Bible does not say one tithe of the things which it has been asserted to say. The Bible as such does not, and cannot, say anything on points which were not even in the view of the majority of its writers. What is said by a particular text—even when we have convinced ourselves that the text is neither mistranslated, nor misinterpreted, nor metaphorical and symbolic, nor torn from the significance of its context, nor unduly pressed—may still need correction by, and co-ordination with, other texts, and may after all only express the isolated sentiment of an individual writer, not a final oracle of God.

Very wise on this subject are the remarks of John Wesley. When confronted with 'texts' which were adduced to prove the doctrine of reprobation to endless torments, he replied, 'Whatever that Scripture proves, it can never prove this. Whatever its true meaning, *this* cannot be its true meaning. Do you ask "What is its true meaning, then?" If I say "I know not," you have gained nothing, for there are many Scriptures, the true sense whereof neither you nor I shall know till death is swallowed up in victory. But this I know—*better it were to say it had no sense at all than to say it had such a sense as this.* Let it mean what it will, it cannot mean that the Judge of all the world is unjust. No Scripture can mean that God is not Love, or that His mercy is not over all His works.'

Christ only is the Eternal Truth. Christ only in the full and perfect sense is the Word of God.

And here, surely, the words of the late Dr. Thirlwall, Bishop of St. Davids, are very apposite. 'The Old Testament history,' he says, 'so far as it is a narrative of civil and political transactions, has no essential connection with any religious truth; and if it had been lost, though we should have been left in ignorance of much that we desired to know, our treasure of Christian doctrine would have remained unimpaired. The numbers, migrations, wars, battles, conquests, and reverses of Israel have nothing in common with the teachings of Christ, with the way of salvation, with the fruits of the Holy Spirit. They belong to a totally different order of subjects. They are not to be confounded with the spiritual revelation contained in the Old Testament, much less with the fulness of Grace and Truth which came by Jesus Christ.'

CHAPTER XVII

SCRIPTURE DIFFICULTIES.

'Hanc garrula anus, hanc delirus senex, hanc sophista verbosus, hanc universi praesumunt, lacerant, docent antequam discant.'—JER. Ep. liii. 7.

'Oh let Thy Scriptures be my pure delight; let me not be deceived in them, neither let me deceive by them.'—ST. AUGUSTINE.

'Wherein are some things hard to be understood, which the ignorant and unstedfast *wrest, as they do also the other Scriptures, unto their own destruction.*'—2 Pet. iii. 16.

THE knowledge of mankind advances continually, and the advance of knowledge is the result of continuous *revelation*. The new truths which God is ever making known to us in nature and history are of their very nature sacred; for they are *truths*, and they must all be considered in the great system of human belief respecting God, Man, and the Universe.

It is not, therefore, faith but cowardice, not piety but obscurantism, to ignore what God has taught us by science, and metaphysics, and literature, and historic criticism in all its branches. Scripture must be henceforth interpreted with reference to something besides the accretion of arbitrary fancies, which has been stereotyped in long obsolete commentaries. Rabbinism and scholasticism in exegesis are no longer possible to any reasonably educated or independent mind. They would never have been possible at all if men had judged of Scripture by its own claims and by its actual phenomena, instead of seeing it magnified and refracted through the dense fogs of ignorant tradition. To accept in these days the views of the Rabbis, the Fathers, the mediæval commentators, the Schoolmen, or the post-Reformation bibliolaters, without the largest modification, involves a treason against light and knowledge. Criticism and comparative religion are already sciences, and no competent interpreter can disregard their conclusions. What should we think of an historian of Rome who should attempt to relate the story of the kings with no reference to the researches of Niebuhr, Mommsen, and their successors?

In this chapter I propose to consider some of the narratives—both supernatural and moral—which constitute serious difficulties to many inquirers, and are made the topic for ridicule by sceptical critics. It will be my object to illustrate how little ground there is for such assaults, and how completely such difficulties vanish when the narratives are regarded in the light thrown upon them by unbiassed investigation.

It would not be possible, nor does it fall within my present scope, to deal with *all* the objections which have been urged against the propriety or truth of some of the Bible narratives. If I touch on one or two it may suffice to show how much less difficult they become when they are regarded from the right point of view.

I

The Bible is assailed on the ground that it contains coarse and unedifying stories.

Let us, then, take one or two instances and examine them.

1. The story of Lot, related in Gen. xix. 30–38, has always been a subject of difficulty. It greatly exercised the ingenuity of some of the Fathers to show any reason why such a tale should find a place on the page of sacred literature. Taken as a whole, the books of Scripture are incomparably more pure and free from stain than any of the other bibles of humanity. To what good end, then, was such a story admitted?[1]

It is often overlooked that ethnographical and other details, which have lost their interest for us, may yet have had an intense interest for the age and nation to which they were addressed. The fortunes of Israel were closely and fatally linked with those of the cognate tribes of Moab and Ammon. Any story of their origin would have had for the Hebrews no ordinary significance.

Now, what was the exact origin and intention of this story, it is impossible for us to affirm. We have no data to go upon. Nor does it much concern us in any way to decide whether it was at all *meant* for a narrative of fact, or whether it represents in a concrete form some ethnographic affinity, perhaps disguised and distorted by the bitterness of national hatred. But when the story is denounced as a blot on the sacred page, we have to remember two things:

i. The rigid external modesty and propriety of modern and English literature is disgusted and offended by statements which gave no such shock to ancient and Eastern readers. What may be said, and what may not be said, with plainness, depends greatly upon national custom; and what we call 'coarseness' is a thing so far relative that its offensive character is determined to a great extent by

---

[1] Celsus attacked it, and Origen defends it by giving it an allegorical sense.

the standard of the times. There are other passages of Scripture, happily disguised by the euphemism of translations, which, if their exact meaning were understood, could not be read without a blush. In old days, they would have raised no blush upon the purest cheek, because no habit of reticence upon such subjects had been fixed by the demands of national propriety. The keenness of modern English sensibility on such subjects has done much to preserve our literature from blemish; but it is of recent growth. Ladies in the days of the Tudors commonly used language which would seem grossly immodest now. The plain-spokenness of Orientals involved no necessary offence against abstract morality.

ii. Modern investigation makes it probable that this story about Lot is merely a symbolic way of illustrating certain tribal relations. It must be borne in mind that in early days, before the habits of literary expression were formed, and when the power of penning the simplest story was regarded as an astonishing accomplishment, language was of necessity pictorial. National affinities were described under physical symbols. It is at least possible that the three cases of gross immorality narrated in the Book of Genesis—namely, those of Reuben, Judah, and Lot—are thus figurative. 'The Hebrews,' say learned scholars, 'were undoubtedly accustomed to state facts as to relationships, and fusions of clans and communities under the figures of paternity and marriage; and this plan inevitably led in certain cases to the figurative supposition of very strange connections. The form of the figure was probably not repulsive when first adopted. Marriage with a stepmother is a Semitic practice of great antiquity, and at one time was known to the Israelites.' The story of Reuben therefore may allude to some obscure and now forgotten combination against the unity of Israel and the hegemony of Joseph. The story of Lot wears a very different complexion if we regard it as an exhibition of unknown traditions about the connection between the Israelites and the tribes of Moab and Ammon.[1]

2. Take, again, the pathetic story of Hosea as narrated in Hos. i. 1–3, iii. 1–3. It is not unnatural that such a story should have been subjected to hostile criticism, or that abundant casuistry should have been expended in its defence by those who understood it to mean that God commanded His Prophet to take in marriage a degraded and immoral woman. It is, to say the least, doubtful whether such is the true interpretation. Scholars who have profoundly studied Semitic methods of expression think that the opprobrious name given to Hosea's wife, Gomer-bath-Diblaim, is proleptic—*i.e.* that it applies to her subsequent shamelessness, not to her character when the Prophet took her to wife. It was the anguish caused by her infidelity that first woke Hosea to the sense of Israel's infidelity to Jehovah, whose relation to the Chosen People was repeatedly represented under the type of marriage. 'God speaks in the events of history and the experiences of human life. He spoke to Amos in the thundering march of the Assyrians, and He spoke to Hosea in the shame of his blighted home. The struggle of Hosea's affection with the burning sense of shame and grief when he found his wife unfaithful, is altogether in-

---

[1] See Robertson Smith, *Prophets of Israel*, p. 407; *Encycl. Britan.*, art. 'Judah;' *Journ. of Philol.* ix. 86, 94; *Old Testament in Jewish Church*, p. 438. In 1 Chron. ii. 24 the true translation, according to the Septuagint, is, 'And after Hezron was dead, Caleb went into Ephratah, wife of Hezron his father, and she bare him Ashur, the father (*i.e.* the chief) of Tekoah.'

conceivable unless his first love had been pure, and full
of trust in the purity of its object. In the midst of his
great unhappiness he learned to comprehend the secret of
Jehovah's heart in His dealings with faithless Israel, and
recognised the misery of his married life as no meaningless calamity, but the ordinance of Jehovah, who called
him to the work of a prophet. This he expresses by saying that it was in directing him to marry Gomer that
Jehovah first spoke to him.' In the agony of personal
experience he learnt the true spiritual meaning of the
marriage tie as a doctrine of holy love. He was taught to
understand that it should be separated from henceforth
from the carnal alloy which disgraced the crude nature-
worship of idolaters, and that it was an emblem of the
union between Jehovah and His people, as it signifies to
us the mystical union which is betwixt Christ and His
Church.

Read in this light of modern criticism, what is there in
the story of Hosea but what is in the highest degree pure
and noble?

II

Let us now turn to another quarter in which the Bible
is assailed.

It is constantly represented to the multitude as a book
which abounds in stupendous supernatural interferences
for inadequate ends; as a book which makes impossible
demands upon our credulity, and asks us to believe in the
most fabulous portents.

I am not here about to enter upon the whole question
of miracles. I am not one of those who feel any doubt
that God has, on due occasions and for adequate purposes,
in the days of the Old as well as in the days of the New

Dispensation, made Himself signally and supernaturally manifest in the affairs of men. The miracle of Creation —the miracle which first called light out of darkness and order out of chaos—the miracle which first thrilled the spark of life into inanimate matter and evolved from its dust the rich diversities of sentient existence—the miracle of the human nature of the Son of God—those two miracles of the Creation and the Incarnation involve and include to my mind the credibility of *all* other miracles. I withhold my credence from no occurrence—however much it may be called 'miraculous'—*which is adequately attested; which was wrought for adequate ends; and which is in accordance with the revealed laws of God's immediate dealings with man.* I may hold that some stories represented as miraculous may have borrowed from error or from metaphor their supernatural complexion. I may hold that the providential has sometimes been confused with the supernatural. I may attach to miracles less evidential value because, in many cases, I may regard the miracles not as the attestation of other truths, but as being themselves attested by those truths, which depend on deeper and more cogent evidence. I hold myself at perfect liberty to believe that some events once regarded as miraculous were due to the action of laws once unnoticed or ill-understood; and that others may be but poetic and symbolic descriptions, and may have been prosaically misinterpreted from incidents in a cycle of ancient and poetic legend. I therefore admit the right to consider each miraculous narrative with reference to the amount and credibility of the whole testimony on which it rests; and then it seems to me that to a mind which realises the myriadfold complexity of the miracles in the midst of which we live and move and have our being—to a mind

16

that grasps the truth that the word 'Nature' is absolutely
meaningless without the word 'God'—there would be a
greater abstract and *à priori* difficulty in denying that
miracles have ever happened than in asserting the reality
of their occurrence. About the miracles performed by
our Lord and Saviour Jesus Christ—about the Incarnation,
the Resurrection, and the Ascension, which are the most
stupendous of them all—I can still say with all my heart,
'*Manet immota fides.*'

But the Old Testament narratives which have been made
the main subject of attack are those which have in all
probability been most completely misunderstood.

I have already spoken of the narrative of the Six Days'
Creation, and the ends which it was meant to serve; I
will now say a word of the story of the Fall.

i. When infidels turn it into ridicule they ridicule one
of the profoundest and most instructive lessons which
was ever penned for the warning and instruction of mankind.

They are most certainly not called upon—nor is any
Christian called upon—to believe that there was an actual
garden, an actual talking serpent, actual trees of which
one bestowed the knowledge of good and evil and the
other an immortality of life. Such an interpretation was
rejected two thousand years ago by Philo, and it has been
rejected by many Christian interpreters since—and even
by English bishops like Warburton and Horsley. The
Bible is a book of Eastern origin, and can only be understood by the methods of Eastern literature. Now there
is no other Eastern book in the world which we should
have dreamed of understanding literally if it introduced
speaking serpents and magic trees. Even the Rabbis,
stupidly literal as were their frequent methods, were per-

fectly aware that the story of the Fall was a philosopheme —a vivid pictorial representation of the origin and growth of sin in the human heart. The inspired character of the narrative is to me evinced by the fact that all the literature of the world has failed to set forth for human warning any sketch of the course of temptation which is comparable in insight to this most ancient allegory. The effect of a prohibition in producing in man's free will a tendency to disobedience; the peril of tampering with temptation and lingering curiously in its vicinity; the promptings of concupiscence, reinforced by the whisperings of doubt; the genesis of sin, from the thought to the wish, from the wish to the purpose, from the purpose to the act, from the act to the repetition, to the habit, to the character, to the necessity, to the temptation of others; the thrilling intensity of reaction in the sense of fear, shame, and of an innocence lost for ever; the certain and natural incidence of retribution; the beginning of a new life of sorrow and humiliation; the workings of deathful consequence with all the inevitable certainty of a natural law—all this, and the awful truth that death is the wages of sin, and the fruit of sin, and that death *is* sin, has been set forth since then by all the loftiest literature of the world. Yet all the literature of the world, even when it speaks through the genius of a Dante and a Milton, has added, and can add, nothing essential to the primeval story of Genesis, which it can but illustrate and expand. What, then, does it show but our own ignorance if we ridicule the very symbols which were required by the Understanding as its literary form, and which have proved so incomparably vivid and appropriate for the preservation and conveyance of such necessary truths?

ii. Or take the story of Babel. Are we asked to believe

literally the anthropomorphic details with which it is invested?

Truly, if all this is to be taken *literally*, we should be inclined to say of it as St. Gregory of Nyssa does, that it is Ἰουδαϊκὴ φλυαρία καὶ ματαιότης ('Jewish nonsense and folly'); but if we take it as an ancient, Eastern, and symbolic way of expressing the truth that God breaks up into separate nationalities the tyrannous organisation of cruel despotisms, it ceases to be a childlike myth and becomes an indication of deep historic insight. To adopt such a view is no more to adopt the allegorising method than is the explanation of any other avowed parable. Any Eastern reader would at once understand as an apologue the story of a heaven-reaching tower, and God coming down to perplex the builders by making them speak different languages. Rightly understood, it teaches a permanently valuable lesson; but if it be understood as a literal account of the diversities of language, it is treated as it was never meant to be treated, and becomes an unintelligible tale.

III

The story of Balaam is another theme for ignorant ridicule. One would suppose that nothing was worth notice in that impassioned and most instructive story except the three verses about the ass, which narrate the merest incident in it.[1] To better instructed readers, those verses present no difficulty at all. They regard them as a mere symbol in the splendid narrative, which is rich in almost unrivalled elements of moral edification. It never occurs to them to suppose anything so needless as that the ass *really* spoke, or that the original narrator intended his

---

[1] Num. xxii. 28–30.

story to be so understood.[1]   Talking animals are common in Eastern and ancient literature, and no one would dream of supposing that they are anything more than a part of the literary form.   The general story about this great Mesopotamian sorcerer has every appearance of being a genuine and straightforward narrative in its main outlines, but set forth in the language of a warm imagination.   It would not have been easy for the narrator in that early phase of the human intellect to state in abstract terms the truth that those who will persist in blinding and sophisticating their own consciences by yielding to the impulse of a besetting sin must come, sooner or later, to a narrow path where it is not possible for them to turn aside : yet that, even at that crisis, the self-blinded soul may fail to see the confronting wrath of God, though it is manifest to all around, and though even dumb animals may show themselves conscious of the peril involved in an evil course. But what comes so tamely when it is expressed in generalities becomes vivid and forcible when it is set forth by living and familiar symbols.   Those symbols would not have seemed vulgar or ludicrous to an Eastern listener, and his realisation of their force would have better enabled him to understand the lesson, that

> In outlines dim and vast,
> Their fearful shadows cast
> The giant forms of empires on their way
> To ruin ; one by one
> They tower and they are gone,
> Yet in the Prophet's soul the dreams of avarice stay.[2]

---

[1] It is childish to quote the incidental allusion in 2 Pet. ii. 16 as though it were decisive as to the *literal* meaning of the passage.

[2] The moral significance of the narrative was dealt with more fully by the writer many years ago in the *Expositor*, first series, i. 366–379.

IV

Again, the lovers of Scripture are upbraided with the credulity which can possibly accept stupendous and disproportionate impossibilities.

If we take literally the tenth chapter of Joshua, it narrates a miracle so immense as to throw every other miracle into the shade. And the most amazing hypotheses have been deduced from it. I have for instance heard it deliberately suggested that to this suspension of the laws of the universe at the word of Joshua was due the upheaval of vast mountain-chains on the earth's surface!

Has it never occurred to such theorists how totally unlike the economy of God's dealings would be so immeasurable an interference for so trivial an end? All the laws of the planetary system intercepted and suspended in order to complete the petty victory of one small Semitic tribe over a few insignificant sheykhs! And this most transcendent display of the supernatural not once alluded to again in the whole history of the Chosen People!

The Israelites and Joshua believed, and had full right to believe, that God was with them, and to acknowledge His aid in the courage which enabled them to defeat their enemies. Further than this, it is doubtful whether there was the slightest intention to imply a miracle on the part of the poet to whom the quotation in the narrative is referred. Had the same poet been describing in Oriental method the battle of Mortimer's Cross, which induced Edward IV. to take as his cognisance 'the rose in the sun,' he might have used similar expressions. To a Jew the providential was indistinguishable from the miraculous.

The battle of Gibeon was practically won. The five

petty emirs had been routed and were flying headlong up the pass to Beth-horon the upper, and down the steep descent to Beth-horon the nether. Their total defeat had been precipitated by a storm of hail which burst upon them. There were two records of the battle which the Children of Israel regarded as so glorious and decisive. One was in prose, one in verse. The latter seems to have been a fine poem, enshrined among the national pæans of the Book of Jasher. The date of this poem is entirely unknown to us. It may have been written no earlier than the days of David.[1] The present form of the narrative in which it is embodied cannot be proved to be more ancient than many centuries after the event.

In the poem, Joshua was represented as standing on the heights of Beth-horon, uplifting his victorious spear, and uttering the fine poetic apostrophe:

> Sun, stand thou still[2] upon Gibeon!
> And thou, Moon, in the valley of Ajalon!
> Till the nation have avenged themselves upon their enemies;

which in plain prose was equivalent to a prayer that ere sunset the rout and massacre might be complete. The daylight lasted long enough for the purpose of decisive triumph. This was represented in the antistrophe of the ode by the words,

> And the Sun stood still[3]
> And the Moon stayed
> Till the nation had avenged themselves upon their enemies.

---

[1] See 2 Sam. i. 18.

[2] דֹּם. Lit. 'be silent.' The appeal is exactly analogous to that of Agamemnon in the *Iliad*, ii. 412 (compare xvii. 232; *Od.* xxii. 241).

[3] It is as needless to take it literally as to take literally 'the stars in their courses fought against Sisera;' or 'the hills melted like wax at the presence of the Lord;' or Ps. xviii. 8, 16.

To this poetic quotation the prose chronicler adds his comment: 'So the sun stood still in the midst of heaven, and hasted not to go down about a whole day.' It is mainly from this comment that the notion has been derived of a prodigy which would utterly throw into the shade the wildest dreams of Hindoo or Mahometan fancy.[1] We are to suppose on such evidence that the laws of the whole solar system were reversed, with all the millions of subordinate miracles which such an intervention would have rendered necessary, for no other purpose than to enable Joshua to destroy some Palestinian tribes, whose defeat, in accordance with the entire unbroken economy of God's dealing, could have been accomplished in such infinitely simpler ways!

That the words are founded on the old astronomic error which supposed that the world is stationary and that the sun moves round it, is admitted by everybody. The most stolid of literalists must therefore tamper with the words, and admit that neither the sun nor the moon *really* stood still; but that either (1) the earth ceased to rotate on its axis, and that the millionfold crash and catastrophe which would have resulted from such a staying of the wheel of being was prevented by a millionfold and most stupendous interference with natural laws; or (2) that there was a parhelion, or some form of refraction and semblance; or some other hypothesis almost too absurd to have occurred to any human mind not hopelessly distorted by a false theory.[2]

---

[1] The subsequent words (Josh. x. 14, 'And there was no day like that,' &c.) are quite consistent with the feeling of intense thanksgiving for a day of decisive success.

[2] Such as that the earth's orbit was affected by a shower of meteorites! or that lightning followed the hail; or that Joshua and the

But if such manipulations of the narrative be admissible, it is clear that no basis is left for any belief in the miracle in the form in which it is narrated. We are sure that by God's blessing Israel defeated five sheykhs in a long day's battle. The amount of evidence on which we are asked to accept the prodigy involved by an unimaginative interpretation of the poem is *nil*. An anonymous record in some fragmentary Jewish annals; the isolated quotation from a battle-ode in a lost book of poems of uncertain date —can any reasonable man regard this as sufficient evidence for the most overwhelmingly portentous event ever heard of in the annals of the world?

'The ground of credit,' said Hooker, 'is the credibility of things credited; and things are made credible either by the known conditions and quality of the utterer, or by the manifest likelihood of truth which they have in themselves.'[1] In this instance, in addition to the fact that we know nothing of the poem quoted, and that the event *literally* taken combines in itself every element of unlikelihood, we have the further consideration that the original lyrist in all probability did not dream that any reader would take literally what he sang poetically.

But it may be said the annalist understood the poem literally? Possibly he did; but we cannot be sure. The prose sentence in verse 13 may imply nothing more than that the Masoretic or other editor—so far from being the *stupidus ille Masoreticus* of one critic—had caught something of the magnificently imaginative spirit which

Israelites were so absorbed in massacre that they thought one day was two days! This is the device of Keil, with whom that archaic style of exegesis may be said to have finally expired, at any rate in learned Germany.

[1] Hooker, *Eccl. Pol.* bk. ii. ch. iv. p. 1.

breathed through the grand apostrophe placed by the poet in the mouth of the Hebrew leader. He may not have *intended* to imply that there was any further miracle than the superintending providence of the God of Battles.[1] Even if he did, the laws of literary criticism are sufficient to show us that *we* should not be bound by so servile a letter-worship. At any rate, while so many uncertainties surround every element of the narrative, it must be clear that the view taken is one with which essential religion can have no concern. He who chooses may believe that the most fundamental laws of the universe were arrested to enable Joshua to slaughter a few more hundred fugitives; and he who chooses may believe that nothing of the kind even entered into the mind of the narrator.

Let each man be fully persuaded in his own mind. No one is bound by the assertions of any one else on this subject.

V

It will be unnecessary to refer to more than one other narrative in proof that each question which arises must be considered on its own merits, and with reference to its own evidence and meaning.

The story of Jonah and the whale is perhaps the most frequent object of jeering allusion by those who hold up the Bible to ridicule, and of untenable defence by those who insist on false views of Biblical interpretation.

---

[1] In Ecclus. xlvi. 4 we read, 'Did not the sun go back by his means' (lit. 'in his hand'); but this is a blunder for 'stand still,' and some consider the verse an interpolation (compare Ecclus. xlviii. 23). Josephus, on the other hand (*Antt.* V. i. 17), only says, 'Moreover it happened that the day was lengthened'—a very mild allusion to an event which, if understood literally, was the most tremendous prodigy which had ever occurred in all human history!

The Book of Jonah is full of Divine and deeply needed wisdom. Derided by the sceptic now, as it was by the pagan in old days, a source of perplexity to many, of late and wholly uncertain date, of warmly disputed interpretation, it yet stands very high in moral insight and elevation, and towers above whole masses of Jewish literature in the breadth of its comprehensive tolerance.

The historic Jonah, the son of Amittai, was born at Gath-Hepher, a village of Zebulon. He flourished about eight centuries before Christ in the prosperous days of Jeroboam II. A Jewish legend identified him with the son of the widow of Sarepta whom Elijah restored to life, and with the youth whom Elisha sent to anoint Jehu King of Israel. We know nothing farther about him from the historic books, nor is it possible to tell whether this anonymous narrative of uncertain date was intended to represent fact or psychological fiction.[1] Dr. Wright, in his 'Biblical Essays' (pp. 34–98), points out many striking reasons for regarding it as an allegory of the fate of Israel founded on descriptions given in the Hebrew Prophets. The story briefly is that God bade Jonah leave his home in Israel and cry against Nineveh. He felt the task too terrible, and flying to Joppa embarked on a ship going to Tarshish. Summoned eastward to the capital of Assyria, he tried to escape along the whole Mediterranean to the farthest limit of Western civilisation, to hide himself, if possible, from the presence of the Lord.[2] He soon found that man cannot escape from God. 'The Lord sent out a great wind upon the sea,' and the Tartessian ship was

---

[1] Some Hebrew critics, judging from the language and style and tone of thought, assign the book to a century later than the return from the exile—about B.C. 400.

[2] Jonah means 'dove' (compare Ps. lv. 6–8).

nearly swamped. The sailors were terrified, but Jonah slept, as for a time his conscience also slept. The heathen mariners awake him and bid him call on his God; but the storm continues, and they become convinced that it has been sent because they have some guilty man on board. They cast lots to find the criminal; the lot falls on Jonah. He tells them who he is, and the heathen reprove the Hebrew. For a time they honestly endeavour to save him, but it is impossible. They rowed hard—they 'dug the sea'—but they could not reach the land. Then, with a prayer for mercy and pardon, they cast him overboard; the sea grows calm; they thank God and offer a sacrifice.

Two verses exhaust all that Scripture has to tell us about the method of his deliverance.[1] 'The Lord had prepared a great fish to swallow up Jonah. And Jonah was in the belly of the fish three days and three nights. . . . And the Lord spake unto the fish, and it vomited out Jonah upon the dry land.' Between these two verses comes the prayer which Jonah is supposed to have offered in the fish's belly. It consists of a cento of phrases from the Psalms. It is moreover but little appropriate to the supposed situation, for so far from being a *prayer* for deliverance from a position infinitely loathsome, it is a *thanksgiving* for deliverance; and it is a singular circumstance that this Prophet of the northern kingdom twice

[1] It is remarkable that in 2 Kings xiv. 25 not an allusion is made to any mission or adventure of the historic Jonah; nor is there the faintest trace of his mission or its result amid the masses of Assyrian inscriptions. 'Some devout but imaginative interpreters,' says Professor Elmslie, 'have endeavoured to reduce the difficulty of the miraculous by quoting parallel wonders from apocryphal bits of natural history; but from beginning to end the narrative is one continuous chain of surprises, providences, and marvels, **of a very unusual description'** (*Book by Book*, p. 288).

alludes to the Temple of Jerusalem.[1]   And surely it is but reasonable to ask whether we could ever have been supposed to understand *literally*, and not as a symbol or didactic fiction, 'a narrative in which a man is represented as composing a poetical prayer, surrounded with water, his head bound with seaweed, and drifting with marine currents, while inside a monster of the sea.'[2]   'It is very significant,' says Dr. Wright, 'that almost every sentence of the Song of Jonah is either directly borrowed from, or can be illustrated by the songs anticipative of the Captivity, or sung during the dark days of Israel's exile;' and the only sin alluded to (ver. 8) is not the grave sin of faithless disobedience of which Jonah *had* been guilty, but the sin of idolatry, of which he was entirely innocent.[3]

Now it is on the single portent of the 'great fish' that the attention of most readers has been concentrated. Those who accepted it as a *prodigy* have anathematised all who presumed to regard it as a moral figure, and called them wicked unbelievers.   Those who have interpreted it as a *symbol* have derided all who accepted it as a miracle, and called them ignorant blunderers.   It would have been better if both sets of critics had contented themselves with learning from this remarkable little story lessons of the love of God towards man, and of the tolerance due from men to one another.   The *last* purpose of the Book of Jonah was that all the most trivial and superficial readers should 'pore over the whale, and forget God.'

It ought not, however, to be systematically overlooked that, regarded as an allegory, *nothing was more natural than this metaphor of being swallowed alive by a monster; and that, in one form or another, it is applied to Israel several times in*

---

[1] Jon. ii. 4, 7.   [2] *What is the Bible?* p. 84 (Ladd).
[3] *Biblical Essays*, p. 61.

*the Prophets, who also image the enemies of Israel as a levi-
athan of the sea.*[1]

In spite of this great rescue, Jonah is represented to us
in the selfish and sinful littleness of his character. He
goes indeed to Nineveh, a city which is described as being
sixty miles in circumference. He passes through the city
a day's journey, delivering ever his monotonous message
of five Hebrew words, 'Yet forty days, Nineveh shall be
overthrown.' The king, the nobles, the whole city hear
the message, and are bidden by royal edict to fast, pray,
and repent. The very animals are included in the general
humiliation. This one Lent of penitence saves 600,000
souls. 'God repented of the evil which He had said that
He would do unto them; and He did it not.'[2]

What man of the most ordinary sensibility would not have
rejoiced at the success, so unparalleled, of a sermon so simple?

> Who with repentance is not satisfied
> Is not of heaven, or earth!

But the deliverance of Nineveh 'displeased Jonah exceedingly'! He wishes himself dead because God does not
burn up Nineveh as He burned up Sodom. He had
thanked God for his own preservation, but he is indignant
and miserable that these 600,000, with the 180,000 children
'and also much cattle,' should be spared!

---

[1] See Is. xxvii. 1, Ps. lxxiv. 13, Hos. vi. 1, 2, and especially Jer.
l. 17; li. 34, 44. 'Nebuchadrezzar hath devoured me, he hath crushed
me, he hath made me an empty vessel, *he hath swallowed me up like
the sea monster*, he hath filled his belly with my delicates, *he hath cast
me out*' (Wright, *l.c.* p. 53).

[2] For similar instances of what is technically called *anthropopathy*
—*i.e.* the description of God's nature under the analogy presented by
human passions—see 1 Kings xxi. 29 f., Jer., xviii. 8 f., Ezek. xxxiii.
7-16, Jer. xxvi. 18, 19.

Yet God is tenderly compassionate to this hard and infinitely pitiless Pharisee! In answer to his bitter complaint against God, his peevish and petulant prayer for death, his justification of his first flight on the ground that he knew God to be 'gracious and merciful, slow to anger, and of great kindness,' God only says to him, by the voice of conscience, 'Doest thou well to be angry?'

But Jonah, still retaining his frightful hope, went sullenly outside the city and made himself a booth, and sat under it, still desiring that the forgiven city, which glittered hatefully before his eyes, might be calcined or engulfed. 'Better the whole city perish than that *I* be proved in the wrong!' Jesus wept over lost Jerusalem; Jonah is 'very angry' because of Nineveh reprieved.

A few words end the story. God deals tenderly even with this petty and loveless nature. The sun was hot; God causes a quick-growing palm-christ to overshadow the Prophet with its broad green leaves. Jonah was exceedingly glad.[1] Next morning God prepares a worm which gnaws at the plant's root, and it withers; and as the simoon breathes its hot flames, and the sun beats on the fretful egotist, he once more wishes himself dead. Again the gentle question: 'Doest thou well to be angry for the palm-christ?' Again the petulant answer: 'I do well to be angry, even unto death.' Poor splenetic nature, with its fierce religionism and its personal pique; equally miserable over the saved city and the withered plant; little in its disappointments, and base in its aspirations! One may well hope that this is instructive fiction. We may

---

[1] 1 Kings xiv. 25. Ewald, Hitzig, and others think that the ancient fragment of prophecy in Is. xv., xvi., was a prophecy by the historic Jonah. (See Is. xvi. 13, where 'since that time' should be rendered 'in time past.')

well hope that the historic Jonah, whose name was utilised for the purposes of this Haggadah, was a nobler character than this![1]

Then the book ends with words of noblest significance: *'Thou hast had pity on the palm-christ, for the which thou hast not laboured, neither madest it grow; which came up in a night, and perished in a night: and should not I have pity on Nineveh, that great city; wherein are more than sixscore thousand persons that cannot discern between their right hand and their left hand; and also much cattle?'* In large-heartedness, in spirituality, in moral insight, the book is not only the noblest of its class, but in some respects pre-eminent in Jewish literature.

The raging spirit of national and religious hatred which finds such manifold expression in the later Jewish writings would have met with a wholesome corrective if the Jews had attained to the nobler standpoint of this little book. The lesson of the Book of Jonah is the lesson of the noblest passage in the Book of Wisdom. O God, 'the whole world before Thee is as a drop of the morning dew. But Thou hast mercy upon all. For Thou lovest all the things that are, and abhorrest nothing that Thou hast made. But Thou spare stall, for they are Thine, O Lord, Thou lover of souls!'

To the supernatural incidents, which only belong to the allegorical form of the story, the author attached no importance; they were but the machinery of the vehicle to which he entrusted his lofty and humane conceptions. To a Hebrew of that age the notion of the three days in the fish's belly presented nothing so extravagant as to prevent him from using that form of incident to point a moral. Even the less imaginative Greeks had their stories of sea

---

[1] Compare Lam. iv. 20.

monsters which destroyed, and dolphins which saved, human life; and in the hagiography we have the legend of St. Margaret swallowed by a dragon, which bursts asunder, and enables her to come forth uninjured when she makes the sign of the cross. Such stories are only intended to be the embodiment of an idea. The particular form of incident was (as we have seen) probably suggested by the Hebrew lyrics, which symbolised affliction by the picture of being swallowed up by the devouring sea, or its fierce leviathans, and visiting 'the monstrous bottoms of the world.'

But some readers will already have asked why I have not referred to the argument which they regard as a proof of the historicity of the narrative—namely, the allusions made to it by our Lord. These allusions occurred in His refusal to show 'a sign' to the jeering Pharisees, when He said that no sign should be given them but 'the sign of the Prophet Jonah;' and told them that the repentant Ninevites should rise in judgment against that generation and should condemn it (Matt. xii. 40, 41, xvi. 4; Luke xi. 30, 32).

Now in these passages—which refer to the same occasion—the allusion to Jonah being 'three days and three nights in the whale's belly' occurs in Matt. xii. 40 *alone*, and not in the parallel passage of St. Luke. The reference moreover involves several serious difficulties, which make it doubtful whether it may not represent a comment or marginal note by the Evangelist, or of some other Christian teacher. For not even by the Jewish mode of reckoning was our Lord *three days and three nights* in the heart of the earth, but only two nights and *one day*. This is nothing but a slight peculiarity of language. Had it stood alone it might have passed without notice; but when taken in connection with St. Luke's *omission* of so remarkable a reference, it has led many critics—and among them men

17

so eminent as Ewald, De Wette, Bleek, and Neander—to
suppose some misapprehension on the part of the disciples.
For the sign to which our Lord appeals, in *both* Evangelists, as is shown by the entire context, is *not* the miracle
of the fish, but the *repentance of the Ninevites at the Prophet's preaching.* But even if our Lord did allude to 'the
whale,' the question might still be fairly asked, whether
this incidental allusion to the allegoric *story* requires a
literal acceptance of the actual *fact.*

Certainly the mere reference to a story is no proof of
any belief that the story is literal history. St. Paul makes
didactic use of Rabbinic legends and Rabbinic reasoning:
no one supposes that he must necessarily be taken *au pied
de la lettre.*[1] St. Jude, and the author of St. Peter, allude
to strange Jewish myths, as to the Fall of the Angels and
the dispute between Michael and the devil about the body
of Moses: is any one expected on that account to accept
those wild legends as actual facts? In 2 Peter we find the
word ταρταρώσας, 'hurling to *Tartarus*' (ii. 4); yet no
human being supposes that the author meant thereby to
imply the truth of the Greek eschatology. St. Jude makes
an undoubted quotation from the spurious and fantastic
Book of Enoch; are we therefore compelled to maintain
that the Book of Enoch is genuine and true?[2]

---

[1] Dr. Otto Zöckler candidly admits that the literal truth of the story
cannot be grounded on Matt. xii. 39 (*Handbuch*, p. 149); so, too, Dean
Plumptre, *ad loc.* On the whole book see Kalisch, *Bible Studies;*
Nöldeke, *Alt-test. Litteratur;* Kleinert in Lange's *Bibelwerk;* Professor
Cheyne, *Jonah, a Study in Jewish Folklore,* &c.

[2] The late Archbishop Benson asked the pertinent question, '*May
not the Holy Spirit make use of myth and legend?*' Are the parables
of Christ less fraught with eternal instruction because they are imaginary stories? Any Haggadah may be most divinely true to fact,
though (like the *Pilgrim's Progress*) it adopts the vehicle of fiction.

Was not Goethe right when he said, 'Much debating goes on about the good and the harm done by free circulation of the Bible. To me this is clear: it will do harm, as it has done, if used dogmatically and fancifully; and do good, as it has done, if used didactically and feelingly'? And 'I am convinced that the Bible always becomes more beautiful the better it is understood, *i.e.* the better we see that every word has a specifically direct bearing on the *spiritual life* of the time in which it was written.'

CHAPTER XVIII

SUPREMACY OF THE BIBLE.

'Let Thy Scriptures be my pure delight; let me not be deceived in them, neither let me deceive by them.'—AUGUSTINE, *Confessions*, ii. 2.

'A worn-out Dogma died; around its bed
Its votaries wept as if all truth were dead.
But heaven-born Truth is an immortal thing;
Hark how its lieges give it welcoming:
"The King is dead—long live the King!"'
JOHN HOOKER.

'It is religion that has formed the Bible, not the Bible that has formed religion.'—R. D. C. LEVIN.

'For my part I am at an utter loss to conceive of a revelation from heaven that must not be trusted alone.'—ROBERT HALL.

WE have seen in the preceding pages how deep are the wounds with which the Bible has been wounded in the house of its friends; how grossly it has been misrepresented; by what foolish methods it has been interpreted; what crimes it has been adduced to sanction; to what deadly uses it has been applied; how complete has been the failure to catch the true meaning and spirit alike of separate passages and even of entire books of which it is composed. Men have misused Scripture just as they misuse light or food. And yet the Holy Scriptures continue to be—and even *increasingly* to be—the Supreme Bible of Humanity. There could be no more decisive proof of the unique transcendence of Holy Writ, and its essential message to mankind, than the fact that it has not only triumphed with ease over the assaults of its enemies, but has also continued to command the reverence, to guide the thoughts, to educate the souls, to kindle the moral aspirations of men through all the world. Were we to collect the impassioned eulogies which have been pronounced upon it by the saints and theologians of every age we should require a volume, and he must be indeed a cynic who could declare that testimonies so numerous and so fervent are due only to insincerity or custom. Yet if such expressions of gratitude and even of ecstasy be suspected, how can we possibly explain the fact that the most advanced critics—that literary men outside the sphere of Church influence—that men who would be denounced as heretics—nay, even that avowed sceptics, who have approached the Bible without a single trammel of doctrine or tradition—have yet spoken of it in terms of astonishment and admiration no less glowing than those which have been used by preachers and divines?

I will collect a few of these estimates of Scripture formed by men of independent minds and of the highest ability, and by men who have approached the Bible solely from its literary and humanitarian side. Their evidence will show that the ignorant contempt with which the Bible is often disparaged only proves the incapacity of its assailants to grasp its real significance. It is a literature which no age or nation can equal or supersede, 'though every library in the world had remained unravaged, and every teacher's truest words had been written down.' 'What problems do these books leave unexamined? what depths unfathomed? what height unscaled? what consolation unadministered? what conscience unreproved? what heart untouched?' How absurd it must be to scoff at a book which, through all the long centuries, thousands of great men have reverenced in proportion to their greatness; a book for which, in age after age, warriors have fought, philosophers laboured, and martyrs bled! The Lord Christ Himself did not disdain to quote from the Old Testament. Its literary splendour was acknowledged even by heathen critics like Longinus, who referred to the sublimity of Genesis and the impassioned force of St. Paul. It exercised the toil of Origen and Jerome; it fired the eloquence of Gregory and Chrysostom; it moulded the thoughts of Athanasius and Augustine; the 'Summa Theologiæ' of St. Thomas Aquinas was but a meditation upon its theology, and the 'Imitatio Christi' of St. Thomas à Kempis an attempt to express its spirituality. All that is best and greatest in the literature of two thousand years has been rooted in it and has sprung from it. It has inspired the career of all the best of men who 'raised strong arms to bring heaven a little nearer to our earth.' St. Vincent de Paul learnt from its pages his tenderness for the poor; and John Howard his love for the suffering; and William Wilberforce his compassion for the slaves; and Lord Shaftesbury the dedication of his life to the amelioration of the lot of his fellow-men. Has there been one of our foremost statesmen or our best philanthropists who has not confessed the force of its inspiration? It dilated and inspired the immortal song of Dante and of Milton. All the best and brightest English verse, from the poems of Chaucer to the plays of Shakespeare in their noblest parts, are echoes of its lessons; and from Cowper to Wordsworth, from Coleridge to Tennyson, the greatest of our poets have drawn from its pages their loftiest wisdom. It inspired the pictures of Fra Angelico and Raphael, the music of Handel and Mendelssohn. It kindled the intrepid genius of Luther, the bright imagination of Bunyan, the burning zeal of Whitfield. The hundred best books, the hundred best pictures, the hundred greatest strains of music are all in it and all derived from it. Augustine said long ago that in the great poets and philosophers of pagan antiquity he found many things that are noble and beautiful, but not among them all could he find 'Come unto Me, all ye that are weary and heavy laden, and I will give you rest.'

> We search the world for truth; we cull
> The good, the pure, the beautiful
> From graven stone and written scroll,
> From all old flower-fields of the soul;
> And, weary seekers of the best,
> We come back laden from our quest,
> To find that all the sages said
> Is in the Book our mothers read.[1]

I

Vast indeed is the cloud of witnesses to the glory and supremacy of the Holy Scriptures. 'Out of the mouth of two or three witnesses shall every word be established.' I will begin with a pleiad of witnesses, chosen first by way of specimen from all sorts and conditions of men, yet unanimous in their testimony to the eternal preciousness of Holy Writ. I will once more adduce the opinions of a Romish Cardinal; a Jewish *littérateur;* an American Unitarian; a German scholar; a French critic; an Englishman of science; and an Englishman of letters.[2] All of them

---

[1] J. G. Whittier, *Miriam.*

[2] I have quoted these seven in *The People's Bible History.*

differed; some of them disbelieved: yet they are all at one as to the unapproachable supremacy of the Holy Scriptures.

1. *John Henry Newman* was a Romish Cardinal of sincere goodness and refined genius. He said of the Bible, 'Its *light* is like the body of heaven in its clearness; its *vastness* like the bosom of the sea; its *variety* like scenes of nature.'

2. *Heinrich Heine* was a Jew, half German, half French; a man of flashing wit, a brilliant stylist, a confirmed doubter. After a Sunday of leaden ennui in Heligoland, he writes that he took up the Bible in desperation, and spent most of the day in reading it. Though he confesses himself a secret Hellene, he admits that he was not only well entertained but deeply edified. 'What a book!' he exclaimed. 'Vast and wide as the world! rooted in the abysses of creation, and towering up beyond the blue secrets of heaven! Sunrise and sunset, birth and death, promise and fulfilment, the whole drama of Humanity are all in this book!'

'It is the Book of Books—*Biblion*. The Jews may easily console themselves for having lost Jerusalem, and the Temple, and the Ark of the Covenant, and the golden vessels, and the precious things of Solomon. Such a loss is insignificant compared with the Bible, the imperishable treasure which they have rescued. If I do not err, it was Mahomet who named the Jews "the people of the Book" —a name which remained theirs to the present day, and is deeply characteristic. A book is their fatherland. They live within the boundaries of this Book. Here do they exercise their inalienable rights of citizenship. Here they can be neither persecuted nor despised. Absorbed in the study of this Book, they observed little of the changes which went on about them in the world. Nations arose and perished; States flourished and disappeared; revolutions stormed forth out of the ground, but they lay bent over their Book, and observed nothing of the wild tumult of the times that passed over their heads.'

Nor was this a mere passing spasm of admiration. When he was near his death, after years of agony on his mattress-coffin, when he had become a changed man, Heine wrote, 'I attribute my enlightenment entirely and simply to the reading of a book. Of a book? Yes! and it is an old homely book, modest as nature—a book which has a look modest as the sun which warms us, as the bread which nourishes us—a book as full of love and blessing as the old mother who reads in it with her dear trembling lips, and this book is *the* Book, the *Bible*. With right is it named the Holy Scriptures. He who has lost his God can find Him again in this book, and he who has never known Him is here struck by the breath of the Divine Word.'

3. *Theodore Parker* was a Unitarian minister at Boston, a man of deep earnestness, of great eloquence, of splendid courage.

'This collection of books has taken such a hold on the world as no other. The literature of Greece, which goes up like incense from that land of temples and heroic deeds, has not half the influence of this book, from a nation alike despised in ancient and modern times. It is read of a Sunday in all the ten thousand pulpits of our land; in all the temples of Christendom is its voice lifted up week by week. The sun never sets on its gleaming page. It goes equally to the cottage of the plain man and the palace of the king. It is woven into the literature of the scholar, and colours the talk of the street. The barque of the merchant cannot sail the sea without it; no ship of war goes to the conflict but the Bible is there. It enters men's closets; mingles in all the grief and cheerfulness of life. The affianced maiden prays God in Scripture for strength in her new duties. Men are married by Scripture; the Bible attends them in their sickness, when the fever of the world is on them; the aching head finds a softer pillow when the Bible lies underneath; the mariner, escaping from shipwreck, clutches this first of his treasures, and keeps it sacred to God.'

4. *Heinrich von Ewald* was a German scholar of immense learning, who by indefatigable, lifelong study—amid the universal chorus of anathemas from that ' blind and naked Ignorance ' which

> Delivers brawling judgments unashamed
> On all things all day long—

flung more light on the true meaning and history of Scripture than all his assailants put together. One day, when the late Dean Stanley was visiting him, a New Testament which was lying on a little table happened to fall to the ground. He stooped to pick it up, and he laid it again on the table. ' It is impossible,' says Dean Stanley, ' to forget the noble enthusiasm with which this " dangerous heretic," as he was regarded, grasped the small volume, and exclaimed with indescribable emotion, ' *In this little book is contained all the best wisdom of the world.*'

5. Again, the testimony of *Ernest Renan* will not be suspected of religious bias. He was a French sceptic of wide attainments and fascinating style, whose general beliefs were of the loosest and vaguest description. Yet he says: ' Les histoires juives et chrétiennes ont fait la joie de dix-huit siècles; et elles ont une étonnante efficacité

pour améliorer les mœurs. La Bible . . . est, malgré tout, le grand livre consolateur de l'Humanité.'[1]

6. *Professor Huxley* was a man of science, and one of the most eminent. It was he who invented the word 'Agnosticism,' and he accepted the name 'Agnostic.' Yet he pleaded in the School Board for the Bible, as the best source of the highest education for children, and in the 'Contemporary Review' for December 1870 he wrote: 'I have always been strongly in favour of secular education, in the sense of education without theology, but I must confess I have been no less seriously perplexed to know by what practical measures the religious feeling, which is the essential basis of conduct, was to be kept up in the present utterly chaotic state of opinion on these matters without the use of the Bible. The pagan moralists lack life and colour, and even the noble Stoic, Marcus Antoninus, is too high and refined for an ordinary child. Take the Bible as a whole; make the severest deductions which fair criticism can dictate for shortcomings and positive errors; eliminate, as a sensible lay teacher would do if left to himself, all that it is not desirable for children to occupy themselves with; and there still remains in this old literature a vast residuum of moral beauty and grandeur. And then consider the great historical fact that for three centuries this book has been woven into the life of all that is best and noblest in English history; that it has become the national epic of Britain, and is familiar to noble and simple from John o' Groat's House to Land's End, as Dante and Tasso were once to the Italians; that it is written in the noblest and purest English, and abounds in exquisite beauties of a merely literary form; and, finally, that it forbids the veriest hind who never left his village to be

---

[1] *Hist. du Peuple Israël*, p. vii.

ignorant of the existence of other countries and other civilisations, and of a great past, stretching back to the furthest limits of the oldest nations in the world. By the study of what other book could children be so much humanised, and made to feel that each figure in that vast historical procession fills, like themselves, but a momentary space in the interval between two eternities, and earns the blessings or the curses of all time, according to its efforts to do good and hate evil, even as they also are earning their payment for their work?'[1]

Nor is this Professor Huxley's only testimony to the unique glory of the Scriptures. 'It appears to me that if there is anybody more objectionable than the orthodox bibliolater it is the heterodox Philistine who can discover in a literature which in some respects has no superior, nothing but a subject for scoffing and an occasion for the display of his conceited ignorance of the debt he owes to former generations.' 'The Bible,' he says, 'has been the Magna Charta of the poor and of the oppressed; down to modern times no State has had a constitution in which the interests of the people are so largely taken into account; in which the duties, so much more than the privileges of rulers, are insisted on, as that drawn up for Israel; . . . nowhere is the fundamental truth that the welfare of the State in the long run depends on the welfare of the citizen, so strongly laid down. . . . I do not say that even the highest Biblical ideal is exclusive of others or needs no supplement. But I do believe that the human race is not yet, possibly never may be, in a position to dispense with it.'[2]

7. *Mr. Matthew Arnold* was a man with an exquisite gift

<hr>

[1] *Essays on Science and Education*, p. 397.
[2] *Essays on Controverted Questions*, pp. 55–58.

of style and of critical insight. He retained but little faith in the miraculous; his creed was anything but orthodox. Yet the Bible was his chief and his constant study, and he even contributed a most important element to the true principles of its elucidation when he insisted that being a literature it must be interpreted on the fixed principles of literary criticism. His writings abound in passages which witness to his intense reverence and admiration for the Sacred Books.

'As well imagine a man,' he says, 'with a sense for sculpture not cultivating it by the help of the remains of Greek art, and a man with a sense for poetry not cultivating it by the help of Homer and Shakespeare, as a man with a sense for conduct not cultivating it by the help of the Bible.'

II

I will now point to a second group of similar testimonies from men no less separated from each other by their religious beliefs.

1. *F. W. Faber* was a Roman Catholic priest. Speaking of the uncommon beauty and marvellous English of the Authorised Version, he says:

'It lives on the ear like a music that can never be forgotten, like the sound of church bells which the convert scarcely knows how he can forego. Its felicities often seem to be things rather than words. It is part of the national mind, and the anchor of the national seriousness. Nay, it is worshipped with a positive idolatry, in extenuation of whose fanaticism its intrinsic beauty pleads availingly with the scholar. The memory of the dead passes into it. The potent traditions of childhood are stereotyped in its verses. It is the representative of a man's best moments; all that there has been about him of soft and gentle and pure and penitent and good, speaks to him for ever out of his English Bible.   It is his sacred thing which doubt never dimmed and controversy never soiled; and in the length and breadth of the land there is not a Protestant with one spark of religiousness about him whose spiritual biography is not in his Saxon Bible.'

2. Could there be a man whose whole nature furnished a more marked contrast to F. W. Faber than *Jean Jacques Rousseau?*   Yet the French *savant* wrote, 'I must confess to you that the majesty of the Scriptures astonishes me; the holiness of the Evangelists speaks to my heart and has such striking characters of truth, and is, moreover, so perfectly inimitable, that if it had been the invention of men, the inventors would be greater than the greatest heroes.'

3. *Lessing* was a German, a man of letters, of high genius, and a very liberal thinker.   His estimate of the Bible was as follows: 'The Scriptures for 1,700 years have occupied the mind more than all books, have enlightened it more than all other books.'

4. *Goethe* is justly regarded as a type of modern culture, a man of genius, of talents, of scientific insight; a poet and a thinker.   He stood in no very definite relation to any branch of the Christian Church, but he could recognise everything that was wise and beautiful.   He read the Bible so much that his friends reproached him for wasting his time over it.   And this among other things is what he said of it:

'I am convinced that the Bible becomes even more beautiful the more one understands it; that is, the more one gets insight to see that every word which we take generally and make special application of to our own wants, has had, in connection with certain circumstances, with certain relations of time and place, a particular, directly individual reference of its own.'[1]

And, again,

' Let culture and science go on advancing, and the mind progress as it may, it will never go beyond the elevation and moral culture of Christianity as it glistens and shines forth in the Gospels.'[2]

And, again,

'The Bible is a book of eternally effective power.'

And, once more,

'It is to its intrinsic value that the Bible owes the extraordinary veneration in which it is held by so many nations and generations. It is not only a popular book, it is the book of the people. . . . The greater the intellectual progress of ages, the more fully possible will it also become to employ the Bible both as the foundation and as the instrument of education—of that education by which not pedants, but truly wise men are formed.'

'Take the Bible, book after book, and you will find that this Book of Books has been given us in order that, in contact with it, as with a new world, we may study, enlighten, and develop ourselves.'

And as to the place of the Bible in education he said,

'When, in my youth, my imagination, ever active, bore me away, now hither, now thither, and when all this blending of history and fable, of mythology and religion, threatened to unsettle my mind, gladly then did I flee towards those Eastern countries. I buried myself in the

[1] See Goethe, *Conversations*, March 11, 1832 (Eckermann, *Gespräche mit Goethe* (1876), iii. 253-258).

[2] Coleridge said that 'intense study of the Bible will keep any man from being vulgar in point of style.'

first books of Moses, and there, amidst those wandering
tribes, I found myself at once in the grandest of solitudes
and in the grandest of societies.'

5. *R. W. Emerson* during the greater part of his life was
regarded by the religious world in general as an audacious
heretic, a man too liberal and too independent for even
the most liberal of Unitarian congregations. And Emerson was an earnest student, a wide reader of all the best
writings of the world. It was thus that he spoke of the
Bible :

'The most original book in the world is the Bible. This
old collection of the ejaculations of love and dread, of the
supreme desires and contritions of men, proceeding out of
the region of the grand and eternal, seems . . . the alphabet of the nations, and all posterior writings, either
the chronicles of facts under very inferior ideas, or, when
it rises to sentiment, the combinations, analogies, or degradation of this. The elevation of this book may be
measured by observing how certainly all elevation of
thought clothes itself in the words and forms of thought
of that book. . . . Whatever is majestically thought in
a great moral element, instantly approaches this old
Sanskrit. . . . Shakespeare, the first literary genius of
the world, the highest in whom the moral is not the pre-
dominating element, leans on the Bible; his poetry pre-
supposes it. If we examine this brilliant influence—
Shakespeare—as it lies in our mind we shall find it reverent, not only of the letter of this book, but of the whole
frame of society which stood in Europe upon it; deeply
indebted to the traditional morality—in short, compared
with the tone of the Prophets, *secondary*. . . . People
imagine that the place which the Bible owes in the world
it owes to miracles. It owes it simply to the fact that it

came out of a profounder depth of thought than any other book.'

And, long afterwards, he wrote of the Bible in his little poem called 'The Problem':

> Out from the heart of nature rolled
> The burdens of the Bible old;
> The litanies of nations came
> Like the volcano's tongue of flame
> Up from the burning core below—
> The canticles of love and woe.
> The word unto the Prophets spoken
> Was writ on tablets yet unbroken;
> Still floats upon the morning wind,
> Still whispers to the willing mind;
> One accent of the Holy Ghost
> The heedless world has never lost.

6. The French poet *Alfred de Musset* was 'a child of the sunshine and the storm;' and when he died, his old servant pointed to a New Testament and said to a friend who came to inquire about him, 'I know not what Alfred found in that book, but he always latterly had it under his pillow that he might read it when he would.'

7. The Dutch critic *Professor Kuenen* criticised the Old Testament with the most unbiassed freedom, and especially the Prophets; yet he wrote of them:

'As we watch the weaving of the web of Hebrew life we endeavour to trace through it the more conspicuous threads. Long time the eye follows the crimson; it disappears at length; but the golden thread of sacred prophecy continues to the end. The Prophets teach us to live and to struggle; to believe with immovable firmness; to hope even when all is dark around us; to trust the voice of God in our inmost consciousness; to speak with boldness and with power.'

18

8. *Michael Faraday* was one of the greatest men of science whom this age has produced. One day, when he was ill, his friend Sir Henry Acland found him resting his head on a table, on which lay an open book. 'I fear you are worse to-day,' he said. 'No,' answered Faraday, 'it is not that. But why'—he asked, with his hand on the Bible—'why will people go astray, when they have this blessed book to guide them?'

III

I will now proceed to group together a few more of the remarkable testimonies to the unique supremacy of Scripture over all other literature—testimonies gathered from men of every variety of genius and eminence, and from men who, though they differed from each other as widely as possible in their religious standpoint, were at one in their exaltation of Holy Writ.

Let us begin with great authors.

1. *Richard Hooker:*

'There is scarcely any noble part of knowledge worthy of the mind of man, but from Scripture it may have some direction and light.'

2. *Milton:*

'There are no songs to be compared with the songs of Zion, no orations equal to those of the Prophets, and no politics equal to those the Scriptures can teach us.'

And of the Scriptures in general he says:

'I shall wish I may deserve to be reckoned among those who admire and dwell upon them.'

3. The *Translators of 1611*, in their Preface to the Reader, used forcible and eloquent language.

'Men talk much of εἰρεσιώνη how many sweet and goodly things it had hanging on it; of the Philosopher's Stone that it turneth copper into gold; of *Cornu-copia* that it had all things necessary for food in it; of *Panaces* the herb, that it was good for all diseases; of *Catholicon* the drug, that it is instead of all purges; of Vulcanic armour, that it was an armour of proof against all thrusts and all blows. Well, that which they falsely or vainly attributed to these things for bodily good, we may justly and with full measure ascribe unto the Scripture for spiritual. It is not only an armour, but a whole armoury of weapons, both offensive and defensive; whereby we may save ourselves and put the enemy to flight. It is not a herb but a tree, or rather a whole paradise of trees of life which bring forth fruit every month, and the fruit thereof is for meat and the leaves for medicine. It is not a pot of manna or a cruse of oil . . . but as it were a shower of heavenly bread . . . and a whole cellar full of oil vessels. In a word, it is a panary of wholesome food against fenowed traditions, a physician's shop (St. Basil calleth it) of preservatives against poisoned heresies; a pandect of profitable laws against rebellious spirits; a treasury of most costly jewels against beggarly rudiments; finally a fountain of most pure water, springing up into everlasting life.'

'If we be ignorant the Scriptures will instruct us; if out of the way, they will bring us home; if out of order, they will reform us; if in heaviness, comfort us; if dull, quicken us; if cold, inflame us. *Tolle, lege; tolle, lege.*'

4. *Spenser*, we are told, studied the prophetic writings before he wrote the 'Faerie Queen.'

5. *Bacon* has more than seventy allusions to the Bible in twenty-four of his essays.

6. *George Herbert* wrote:

> The Bible? That's the Book. The Book indeed,
>> The Book of Books,
>> On which who looks,
> As he should do, aright, shall never need
>> Wish for a better light
>> To guide him in the night.
>
> . . . . . .
>
> 'Tis heaven in perspective, and the bliss
>> Of glory here,
>> If anywhere,
> By saints on earth anticipated is,
>> Whilst faith to every word
>> Its being doth afford.[1]

7. *George Wither:*

> For many books I care not, and my store
> Might now suffice me, though I had no more
> Than God's two Testaments, and then withal
> That mighty volume which the world we call . . .
> . . . books which better far instruct me can
> Than all the other paper-works of man,
> And some of these I may be reading too
> Where'er I come, or whatsoe'er I do.

8. *Izaak Walton:*

> Every hour
> I read you, kills a sin,
> Or lets a virtue in
> To fight against it.

9. *Sir Isaac Newton:*

'We account the Scriptures of God to be the most sublime philosophy.'

10. *Addison, Johnson, Pope, Young* abound in Scriptural allusions, and that in their most beautiful and impressive passages.

----

[1] *The Synagogue,* 14.

11. *Sir William Jones:*

'I have carefully and regularly perused these Holy Scriptures, and am of opinion that the volume, independently of its Divine origin, contains more sublimity, purer morality, more important history, and finer strains of eloquence, than can be collected from all other books in whatever language they may have been written.'

12. *William Cowper*, comparing the poor Buckinghamshire lace-worker with Voltaire, says:

> Yon cottager who weaves at her own door,
> Pillow and bobbins all her little store,
> Just earns a scanty pittance, and at night
> Lies down secure, her heart and pocket light;
> Just knows, and knows no more, her Bible true,
> A truth the brilliant Frenchman never knew;
> And in that treasure reads with sparkling eyes
> Her title to a mansion in the skies.
> O happy peasant! O unhappy bard!
> His the mere tinsel, hers the rich reward!
> He, praised perhaps for ages yet to come;
> She, never heard of half a mile from home:
> He lost in errors his vain heart prefers,
> She safe in the simplicity of hers.[1]

13. The poet *Collins* in the latter part of his life withdrew from his general studies, and travelled with no other book than an English New Testament, such as children carry to school. Dr. Johnson was anxious to know what companion a man of letters had chosen; the poet said, 'I have only one book, but that book is the best.'

14. *John Wesley:*

'I am a creature of a day, passing through life as an arrow through the air. I am a spirit, coming from God, and returning to God: just hovering over the great gulf;

---

[1] *Truth.*

a few moments hence I am no more seen ; I drop into an unchangeable eternity !   I want to know one thing—the way to heaven : how to land safe on that happy shore. God Himself has condescended to teach the way.   He hath written it down in a book.   O give me that book !   At any price, give me the book of God !   I have it : here is knowledge enough for me.   Let me be a man of one book.   Here, then, I am, far from the busy ways of men. I sit down alone ; only God is here.   In His presence I open, I read His book ; for this end—to find the way to heaven.'

15. *Coleridge :*

'For more than a thousand years the Bible collectively taken has gone hand in hand with civilisation, science, law—in short, with the moral and intellectual cultivation of the species, always supporting and often leading the way.'[1]

16. *Sir Walter Scott :*

> Within this awful volume lies
> The mystery of mysteries :
> Happiest he of human race
> To whom God has given grace
> To read, to fear, to hope, to pray,
> To lift the latch, and learn the way ;
> And better had he ne'er been born
> Who reads to doubt, or reads to scorn.[2]

'Bring me the book,' he said, when he lay dying.   'What book ?' asked Lockhart, his son-in-law.   '*The* Book,' said Sir Walter ; 'the Bible ; there is but one.'

17. *Lord Macaulay,* who knew the Bible well from a child and often refers to it, said :

'The English Bible—a book which, if everything else in our language should perish, would alone suffice to show the whole extent of its beauty and power.'[3]

---

[1] *Confessions of an Enquiring Spirit,* p. 69.

[2] *The Monastery.*   [3] Essay on Dryden.

18. *Charles Dickens* wrote to his son :

'It is my comfort and my sincere conviction that you are going to try the life for which you are best fitted. I think its freedom and wildness more suited to you than any experiment in a study or office would have been. Try to do to others as you would have them do to you, and do not be discouraged if they fail sometimes. It is much better for you that they should fail in obeying the greatest rule laid down by our Saviour, than that you should. I put a New Testament among your books for the very same reasons and with the very same hopes that made me write an easy account of it for you when you were a little child —because it is the best book that ever was or will be known in the world, and because it teaches you the best lessons by which any human creature who tries to be truthful and faithful to duty can possibly be guided.'[1]

19. *Thomas Carlyle*.

Carlyle was a man who prided himself on his absolute veracity. His attitude towards the Church, his attitude to every form of Christianity was one of intellectual aloofness and complete independence. He says of the Bible that it is

'The one Book wherein, for thousands of years, the spirit of man has found light and nourishment, and a response to whatever was deepest in his heart.'

20. *Mr. Ruskin :*

'All that I have taught of Art,' he says, 'everything that I have written, whatever greatness there has been in any thought of mine, whatever I have done in my life, has simply been due to the fact that, when I was a child, my mother daily read with me a part of the Bible, and daily made me learn a part of it by heart.'

'How much I owe,' he says, in the first volume of his 'Præterita,' 'to my mother for having so exercised me in

[1] Forster's *Life of Dickens*, iii. 445.

the Scriptures as to make me grasp them in what my correspondent would call their "concrete whole;" and above all taught me to reverence them as transcending all thought and ordaining all conduct. This she effected, not by her own sayings or personal authority, but simply by compelling me to read the Book thoroughly for myself. As soon as I was able to read with fluency, she began a course of Bible work with me, which never ceased till I went to Oxford. She read alternate verses to me, watching at first every intonation of my voice, and correcting the false ones, till she made me understand the verse, if within my reach, rightly and energetically. It might be beyond me altogether; that she did not care about; but she made sure that as soon as I got hold of it at all, I should get hold of it by the right end. In this way she began with the first verse of Genesis, and went straight through to the last verse of the Apocalypse; hard names, numbers, Levitical law and all; and began again at Genesis next day. If a name was hard, the better the exercise in pronunciation; if a chapter was tiresome, the better the lesson in patience; if loathsome, the better the lesson in faith that there was some use in its being so outspoken. After our chapters (from two to three a day, according to their length, the first thing after breakfast, and no interruption from servants allowed, none from visitors, who either joined in the reading or had to stay upstairs, and none from any visitings or excursions, except real travelling), I had to learn a few verses by heart, or repeat, to make sure I had not lost, something of what was already known; and, with the chapters above enumerated, I had to learn the whole body of the fine old Scottish paraphrases, which are good, melodious, and forceful verse; and to which, together with the Bible itself, I owe the first cultivation of my ear in sound. It is strange that of all the pieces of the Bible that my mother thus taught me, that which cost me most to learn, and which was, to my child's mind, chiefly repulsive—Psalm 119—has now become of all the most precious to me in its overflowing and glorious passion of love for the law of God.'

21. The two greatest poets of our generation, *Browning* and *Tennyson*, abound in loving and reverent allusions to the Bible, which will recur to the memory of every student of their works.

22. *Mr. J. A. Froude*, in his sketch of John Bunyan, writes :

'The Bible thoroughly known is a literature of itself— the rarest and the richest in all departments of thought or imagination which exists.'

23. *Charles Reade* writes that he was astonished at the amazing vividness of impression produced by the sacred writers with a few slight touches. He considered that in a few lines they left a deeper mark than many a writer of genius in a long work of fiction. This consideration suf- ficed, even alone, to impress on him a sense of their tran- scendent value.

24. Speaking of the matchless verve and insight which we find in the delineation of characters in the Bible, an- other of our most eminent modern novelists, *Mr. Robert Louis Stevenson*, says :

'Written in the East, these characters live for ever in the West; written in one province, they pervade the world ; penned in rude times, they are prized more and more as civilisation advances ; product of antiquity, they come home to the business and bosoms of men, women, and children in modern days. Then is it any exaggeration to say that the "characters of Scripture are a marvel of the mind"?'

25. Another eminent novelist, *Mr. Hall Caine*, writes in 'McClure's Magazine':

'I think that I know my Bible as few literary men know it. There is no book in the world like it, and the finest novels ever written fall far short in interest of any one of the stories it tells. Whatever strong situations I have in my books are not of my creation, but are taken from the Bible. "The Deemster" is the story of the Prodigal Son. "The Bondman" is the story of Esau and Jacob. "The Scapegoat" is the story of Eli and his sons, but with Samuel as a little girl; and "The Manxman" is the story of David and Uriah.'

26. *Mr. J. H. Green* wrote his admirable history of England without the smallest touch of clerical bias, and, speaking simply as an observer and an impartial historian, he records the memorably noble effects produced upon England by the possession of the Scriptures in a language which the people could understand.

'England became the people of a Book, and that Book was the Bible. It was, as yet, the one English book which was familiar to every Englishman. It was read in churches, and it was read at home, and everywhere its words, as they fell on ears which custom had not deadened to their force and beauty, kindled a startling enthusiasm. . . . Elizabeth might silence or tune the pulpits, but it was impossible for her to silence or tune the great preachers of justice, and mercy, and truth, who spoke from the Book which the Lord again opened to the people. . . . The effect of the Bible in this way was simply amazing. The whole temper of the nation was changed. A new conception of life and of man superseded the old. A new moral and religious impulse spread through every class. . . . Theology rules there, said Grotius of England, only ten years after Elizabeth's death. The whole nation, in fact, becomes a Church.'

IV

Let us now adduce the opinions of a few kings and statesmen.

1. *St. Louis the Ninth of France* 'Sanctorum Bibliorum lectione mire delectabatur.'

2. *Henry the Sixth* 'in orationibus aut in Scripturarum lectionibus assidue erat occupatus.'

3. *John the Second*, King of Castile, was a constant Bible reader.

4. *Alonso the Fifth of Aragon* gloried in having read the Bible fourteen times, with glosses and notes.[1]

5. *King Edward the Sixth*. At the coronation of the young King Edward VI., three swords were brought to be carried before him, as signs of his being head of three kingdoms. 'There is one sword yet lacking,' said the king, 'the Bible. That book is the sword of the Spirit, and to be preferred before any other. Without that sword we can do nothing, we have no power.' And, so it is said, at his command, the Bible was also carried before him in the procession.[2]

---

[1] I quote these four instances from Father Clarke (in *The Tablet*, January 5, 1889).

[1] In the Coronation Service the Dean of Westminster is directed, after the actual coronation, 'to take from off the altar the Holy Bible which was carried in the procession, and deliver it to the Archbishop, who shall present it to the Queen, first saying these words to her: "Our gracious Queen, we present you with this book, the most valuable thing that this world affords. Here is wisdom: this is the royal law: these are the holy oracles of God."' Bishop Westcott thinks that the custom was first introduced at the coronation of William and Mary.

6. Very remarkable was the emphatic testimony of *Napoleon I.* to the Bible as recorded in Bertrand's *Memoirs.* 'Behold it upon this table' (here he solemnly placed his hand upon it). 'I never omit to read it, and every day with the same pleasure. Nowhere is to be found such a series of beautiful ideas, admirable moral maxims, which produce in one's soul the same emotion which one experiences in contemplating the infinite expanse of the skies resplendent upon a summer's night with all the brilliance of the stars. Not only is one's mind absorbed, it is controlled, and the soul can never go astray with this book for its guide.'[1]

7. *Lord Bacon*—'The Student's Prayer':

'To God the Father, God the Word, God the Spirit we pour forth most humble and hearty supplications that He, remembering the calamities of mankind, and the pilgrimage of this our life, in which we wear out days few and evil, would please to open to us new refreshments out of the fountain of IIis goodness for the alleviating of our miseries. This also we humbly and earnestly beg, that human things may not prejudice such as are Divine; neither that from the unlocking of the gates of sense and the kindling of a greater natural light anything of incredulity or intellectual night may arise in our minds towards Divine mysteries; but rather that by our minds thoroughly cleansed and purged from fancy and vanities, and yet subject and perfectly given up to the Divine oracles, there may be given unto faith such things as are faith's.'

8. *John Selden :* 'I have surveyed most of the learning found among the sons of men; but I can stay my soul on none of them but the Bible.'

9. *Sir Matthew Hale* (Lord Chief Justice) : 'Every morn-

---

[1] See *Table Talk of Napoleon I.* p. 120.

ing read seriously and reverently a portion of the Holy
Scripture, and acquaint yourself with the doctrine thereof.
It is a book full of light and wisdom, and will make you
wise to eternal life.'

10. *Judge Blackstone*, in his famous 'Commentaries on
the Laws of England,' says that 'the Bible has always
been regarded as part of the Common Law of England.'

11. *Edmund Burke:* 'The Bible is not a book, but a
literature, and indeed an infinite collection of the most
varied and the most venerable literature.'

12. *William Wilberforce:* 'Through all my perplexities
and distresses, I seldom read any other book, and I as
rarely have felt the want of any other. It has been my
hourly study.'

13. *Mr. Gladstone:* 'It is supremacy, not precedence,
that we ask for the Bible; it is contrast as well as resemblance, that we must feel compelled to insist on. The
Bible is stamped with speciality of origin, and an immeasurable distance separates it from all competitors.

'Who doubts that, times without number, particular
portions of Scripture find their way to the human soul as
if they were embassies from on high, each with its own
commission of comfort, of guidance, or of warning? What
crisis, what trouble, what perplexity of life has failed or
can fail to draw from this inexhaustible treasure-house its
proper supply? What profession, what position, is not
daily and hourly enriched by these words which repetition
never weakens, which carry with them now, as in the days
of their first utterance, the freshness of youth and immortality? When the solitary student opens all his heart to
drink them in, they will reward his toil. And in forms
yet more hidden and withdrawn, in the retirement of the
chamber, in the stillness of the night season, upon the bed

of sickness, and in the face of death, the Bible will be
there, its several words how often winged with their several
and special messages to heal and to soothe, to uplift and
uphold, to invigorate and stir. Nay, more, perhaps, than
this: amid the crowds of the court, or the forum, or the
street, or the market-place, where every thought of every
soul seems to be set upon the excitements of ambition, or
of business, or of pleasure, there too, even there, the still
small voice of the Holy Bible will be heard, and the soul,
aided by some blessed word, may find wings like a dove,
may flee away and be at rest.'

V

Of American statesmen and writers we may adduce,

1. *President John Quincy Adams:*

'The first and almost the only book deserving of universal attention is the Bible. The Bible is the book of all
others to be read at all ages and in all conditions of human
life; not to be read once or twice through and then laid
aside, but to be read in small portions of one or two chapters every day, and never to be intermitted except by
some overruling necessity. I speak as a man of the world
to men of the world, and I say to you, "Search the Scriptures."

'I have for many years made it a practice to read through
the Bible once a year. . . . It is an invaluable and inexhaustible mine of knowledge and virtue.'

2. *Andrew Jackson*, President of the United States.
When he lay on his deathbed he pointed to the Family
Bible which lay on the table beside him, and said to his
physician:

'That book, sir, is the rock on which our Republic rests.'

3. *Senator W. B. Leigh*, a famous Virginian lawyer:

'I advise every man to read his Bible. I speak of it here as a book which it behoves a lawyer to make himself thoroughly acquainted with. It is the code of ethics of every Christian country on the globe, and tends, above all other books, to elucidate the spirit of law throughout the Christian world. It is, in fact, a part of the practical law of every Christian nation, whether recognised as such or not.'

4. *Daniel Webster*, the great American orator:

'From the time that, at my mother's feet or on my father's knee, I first learned to lisp verses from the sacred writings, they have been my daily study and vigilant contemplation. If there be anything in my style or thoughts to be commended, the credit is due to my kind parents in instilling into my mind an early love of the Scriptures.'

And, again,

'If we abide by the principles taught in the Bible, our country will go on prospering and to prosper; but if we and our posterity neglect its instructions and authority, no man can tell how sudden a catastrophe may overwhelm us and bury our glory in profound obscurity.'

And in his speech on the completion of the Bunker Hill Monument (1843), he said, 'The Bible is a book of faith, and a book of doctrine, and a book of morals, and a book of religion, of especial revelation from God.'

When he lay on his deathbed his physician quoted to him the verse of Psalm xxiii.—'Yea, though I walk through the valley of the shadow of death, I will fear no evil: for Thou art with me; Thy rod and Thy staff they comfort me.' And the great strong man faltered out, 'Yes; that is what I want. Thy rod, Thy rod; Thy staff, Thy staff.' They were the last words he spoke.

5. *Secretary Seward :* 'The whole life of human progress is suspended on the ever-growing influence of the Bible.'

6. *General Grant*, President of the United States, sent a message to this effect to the Sunday-school children of America in 1876: 'Hold fast to the Bible as the sheet anchor to your liberties. Write its precepts in your heart and practise them in your lives. To the influence of this book we are indebted for all the progress made in true civilisation, and to this we must look as our guide in the future.'

7. *William Lloyd Garrison*, who did more than any man to sweep away the curse of American slavery, and who often had the Bible flung in his face by its 'religious' supporters, grew indeed to a clearer apprehension of what the Bible is and what it is not, and yet he said, 'Take away the Bible from us, and our warfare against intemperance, and impurity, and oppression, and infidelity, and crime is at an end. We have no authority to speak, no courage to act.' Who, then, can adequately estimate its immeasurable influence on the world's greatest literature?

8. 'Of all books,' said *Mr. Dana* to the students of Union College, 'of all books, the most indispensable and the most useful, the one whose knowledge is most effective, is the Bible. There is no book from which more valuable lessons can be learned. I am considering it now not as a religious book, but as a manual of utility, of professional preparation and professional use for a journalist. There is, perhaps, no book whose style is more suggestive and more instructive, from which you learn more directly that sublime simplicity which never exaggerates, which recounts the greatest event with solemnity, of course, but without sentimentality or affectation, none which you open with such confidence and lay down with such reverence. There is no book like the Bible.'

9. *Mr. Charles Dudley Warner* wrote recently in 'Harper's Magazine':

'Wholly apart from its religious or from its ethical value, the Bible is the one book that no intelligent person who wishes to come into contact with the world of thought and to share the ideas of the great minds of the Christian era can afford to be ignorant of. All modern literature and all art are permeated with it. There is scarcely a great work in the language that can be fully understood and enjoyed without this knowledge, so full is it of allusions and illustrations from the Bible. This is true of fiction, of poetry, of economic and philosophic works, and also of the scientific and even agnostic treatises. It is not at all a question of religion, or theology, or of dogma; it is a question of general intelligence. A boy or girl at college in the presence of the works set for either to master, without a fair knowledge of the Bible is an ignoramus, and is disadvantaged accordingly. It is in itself almost a liberal education, as many great masters in literature have testified. It has so entered into law, literature, thought, the whole modern life of the Christian world, that ignorance of it is a most serious disadvantage to the student.'

10. We should perhaps hardly have expected a glowing eulogy of the Bible from *Mr. Walt Whitman*. Yet in his 'November Boughs' he wrote:

'The Bible as Poetry. I've said nothing yet of the cumulus of associations of the Bible as a poetic entity, and of every portion of it. Not the old edifice only—the congeries also of events, and struggles, and surroundings, of which it has been the scene and motive—even the horrors, dreads, deaths. How many ages and generations have brooded and wept and agonised over this book!

19

What untellable joys and ecstasies, what support to martyrs at the stake, from it!   To what myriads has it been the shore and rock of safety—the refuge from driving tempest and wreck!   Translated in all languages, how it has united this diverse world!   Of civilised lands to-day, whose of our retrospects has it not interwoven and linked and permeated?   Not only does it bring us what is clasped within its covers: nay, that is the least of what it brings. Of its thousands there is not a verse, not a word, but is thick-studded with human emotion.   Successions of fathers and sons, mothers and daughters, of our own antecedents, inseparable from that background of us, on which, phantasmal as it is, all that we are to-day inevitably depends—our ancestry, our past.'

11. Let me add the testimony of one of the best known of the great philanthropists of America.

It is related of *George Peabody* that when he was quite an old man, sitting in his office one day in London, a boy brought him a New Testament for some purpose, I know not what; but the old man, looking up, said: 'My boy, you carry that book easily in your youth, but when you are as old as I am it must carry you.'

After reading so many and such varied testimonies, may we not well say with Tertullian:

'ADORO SCRIPTURÆ PLENITUDINEM'?[1]

[1] Tert. *c. Hermog.* 24.

CHAPTER XIX

THE BIBLE AND INDIVIDUAL SOULS.

O that I knew how all thy lights combine,
And the configurations of their glorie!
Seeing not only how each verse doth shine,
But all the constellations of the storie.

G. HERBERT.

I WILL now furnish a few instances in which isolated words
and passages of the Bible have had an overwhelming
influence for good upon individual souls, who, after having
been themselves won, mastered, converted by those texts,
have, in some cases, swayed the tendencies of generations
of mankind for long centuries.

A poet tells us that he was once walking over a wide
moor; at one point of it he picked up an eagle's feather;
well, he forgot the rest of his journey, but that spot was
imprinted on his mind. I once stood upon a pier and was
struck, as I had never been before, by the way in which
each separate wave seemed to flash up into the sunshine a
handful of diamonds. I shall never forget those particular
waves.

We may sometimes walk on long shores of yellow sand,
and here and there one single sand-grain out of the innumerable multitudes may seem to flame out into a ruby or
an emerald, because a sunbeam has smitten it and trans-

figured it! So in Holy Writ: words of it, expressions of it,
separate points of it, by themselves, may sometimes create an
indelible impression. The Jewish High Priest wore on his
ephod a breastplate, 'ardent with gems oracular,' to which
was, in some mysterious way, attached an oracle, the whole
being called Urim and Thummim, or 'Lights and Truths.'
The old Rabbis said that the way in which the High Priest
ascertained the will of God from the Urim, was, that he
gazed on the graven names of the tribes of Israel, until a
fire of God stole in mysterious gleams over the letters, and
spelt out words of guidance. The Holy Scriptures are, if
we make them so, such a Urim and Thummim; such mani-
festations of truths, such gleams and flashes of Holy Light.
Sometimes the Spirit of God, without our desire, may, as
it were, flame out before us, in letters of intense revelation,
on the emerald or chrysolite of some familiar text; sometimes in the night of meditation, it may vivify with celestial
glimmerings some long-remembered but hitherto inopera-
tive words.

Let me illustrate the fact by actual transcripts from
human experience.

i. Fifteen hundred and seven years ago there was a dark,
brilliant, beautiful, hot-blooded youth, born in Tagaste:

> Into the presence of the lad did pass
> An influence from a climate as of flame;
> And in those lustrous eyes of his there was
> A tint of flowers and oceans far away
> Amid the woods and waves of Africa.

This youth had a heathen father, but a saintly mother.
He had been under religious teaching from earliest years;
but, overpowered by the seductions of sensuality, he had
lived an impure life, and forged for himself fatal fetters

of habit which he could not break, and which he thought that no force on earth could ever break. At Milan he was influenced by the great Bishop St. Ambrose, 'having been led unknowingly by God to him, that he might knowingly be led to God by him.' One day the story of the lives of some saints of God had flung this youth into a tumult of agitation beyond all wont. His forehead, cheeks, eyes, colour, and tone of voice were more eloquent than his words. He rushed into his little garden to fight out the battle with his own tumultuous soul. 'A violent storm,' he says, 'raged within me, bringing with it a flood of tears. Rising, I flung myself under a fig-tree in an agony of remorse, exclaiming, "How long, O Lord? how long? Remember not my former sins! To-morrow? and to-morrow?—why should there not be in this very hour an end to my baseness?"' In the midst of his agitated prayer, he heard the voice of a child—whether boy or girl he knew not—singing, again and again, the words ' *Tolle, lege ; tolle, lege.*' Believing this to be a voice from God, bidding him to open a book, and read the first verse on which he lighted, he repressed his tears, and rushing back to the place where he had left his friend Alypius sitting, he opened the MS. of St. Paul which was lying there, and read in silence the verse on which his eyes first fell. It was, 'Not in rioting and drunkenness, not in chambering and wantonness. But put ye on the Lord Jesus Christ, and make not provision for the flesh to fulfil the lusts thereof.' 'I wished,' he said, 'to read no more. There was no need. For, instantly, as though the light of salvation had been poured into my heart, with the close of this sentence, all the darkness of my doubts had fled away.'

The name of that youth was St. Augustine; that Divine lightning flash fused the sensualist into the saint; that

one text rescued him, and since then he has exercised un-
told influence over thousands of human souls.

ii. A second instance. Just 387 years ago, in 1510, a
German youth, a pious monk, full of intense ardour and
enthusiasm, went on a pilgrimage to Rome. His visit
frightfully disenchanted him. He found a hollow religion
—a form which evinced no corresponding reality. He
found Popes, Cardinals, and Priests tainted with atheism
and indifference, amid the terrible prevalence of unblush-
ing immorality. There is at Rome a staircase, called the
Santa Scala, which professes to be that which Christ ascended to the judgment seat of Pilate. No one is allowed
to go up except upon his knees; and to every one who as-
cends it on his knees are promised, I know not how many
Papal Indulgences. This earnest and devout German
youth—a youth terribly in earnest, a youth who could not
live on gilded shams—began the ascent on his knees; but
when he was half-way up, there burst upon his soul, like
the rush of an avalanche, the text, 'The just shall live
by faith.' By faith, not by sham penances; by faith, not
by will worship and voluntary humility; by faith, not by
external mechanical acts. Of what use to him, in compari-
son with even one of the sacrifices which God approves,
would be 100,000 years of such indulgences as such priests
as he saw at Rome, or as all the priests in the whole world,
could idly promise? They were not worth the breath that
uttered them or the paper on which they were written.

He who hears the voice of God in his soul can listen no
longer to the lies of man. Luther, for it was Martin
Luther, the son of the German miner of Eisenach, rose
from his knees, walked down the steps; and by that one
text, the glory of the bright and blissful Reformation—in
which 'the sweet odour of the returning Gospel of Christ

has embathed men's souls in the fragrancy of heaven,'
and emancipated millions from Egyptian darkness—was
kindled in his soul.

iii. Yet a third instance. Nearly four centuries ago,
there was, in the University of Paris, a gay young nobleman of Navarre, who charmed all by his eloquence and
knowledge, whose beautiful face beamed with genius, and
whose bright temperament made him delight in scenes of
festivity and mirth. With him was a stern Spaniard, who
had been a soldier and a student of romance; but who,
having been crippled and wounded in the siege of Pam-
peluna, suffered months of torture and devoted himself
to spiritual warfare. Wherever the gay noble went the
Spanish soldier limped after him; and, whenever he was
flushed with enjoyment and gratified vanity, said to him,
'Yes! but what shall it profit a man if he gain the whole
world and lose his own soul?' At last the oft-repeated
words of Christ burnt themselves on the young man's
soul. 'Ah, what would it profit? What is our life? Is
it not as vapour, so soon passeth it away, and we are
gone?'

And so the gay young noble, disillusioned of the lower
temptations, and brought to his knees, resolved not to live
to the world, or for pleasure, but to give his heart to God.
That youth was Francis Xavier; that Spanish soldier was
Ignatius Loyola; and in the power of that one text—seizing a heart which would not make, as we most of us make,
'the great refusal'—lay the first mighty work of modern
missions to the heathen in Ceylon, in India, in China, in
Japan.

iv. I might give many instances more; but my last shall
be told in the homely words of a living traveller. 'I have
been in Africa seventeen years,' he said to a newspaper

correspondent. 'In 1871 I went to Africa as prejudiced as the biggest atheist in London. But there came for me a long time for reflection. I was out there, away from a worldly world. I saw a solitary old man there, and asked, "Why on earth does he stop here? Is he cracked, or what? What is it that inspires him?" For months after we met, I simply found myself listening to him, wondering at him, as he carried out all that was said in the Bible: "Leave all that ye have, and follow me." But, little by little, his sympathy became contagious. Seeing his piety, his gentleness, his zeal, his earnestness, and how quietly he did his duty, I was converted by him, though he had not tried to do it.'

Not long after, in 1873, that old man was found dead on his knees, by the side of his lowly cot, in his mud hut, in the heart of Africa, with none but black faces round him. And the faithful blacks, for whose sake he had left all and succumbed to his endless hardships, smeared his corpse with pitch, and covered it with palm-leaves, and carried it on their shoulders, 300 miles to Zanzibar. A ship bore it to England, and it was buried, amid the tears of the noble and the great, in the nave of Westminster Abbey. The traveller was Mr. H. M. Stanley; the aged missionary, whose life is the pledge of future regeneration for miserable and distracted Africa, was David Livingstone. And though he died and saw no fruit of his labours, it is to him and to the text which had grown so luminous to him that we owe the translation of the Bible since his death into fourteen languages of Africa, and the extension of the British protectorate over 170,000 square miles.

These are avowedly but chance and casual examples; but the instances are numberless in which single texts have thus become luminous and vivifying for individual souls. And hence we may see that the Bible is no mere earthly volume, but resembles some great ocean, upon which the Spirit, 'dovelike, sits brooding o'er the vast abyss;' no mere earthly volume, but rather like some great collection of Sibylline oracles, pregnant with the fate of nations; like some field of the bread of life, over the billows of whose golden grain pass the breathings of the Holy Spirit of God; like some magic palimpsest 'whose leaves are, as it were, blown to and fro by the winds of destiny.'

It will not even be pretended that any book in the world, or all the books in the world put together, have wrought such vast and beneficent conversions—such deliverances from darkness unto light, and from the power of Satan unto God—as have been and are day by day being wrought by the voice of God speaking to us from the Holy Scriptures. Is not this single fact sufficient to prove their unique preciousness, their transcendent supremacy?

CHAPTER XX

THE BIBLE THE CHIEF SOURCE OF HUMAN CONSOLATION.

'Comfort ye, comfort ye my people, saith your God.'—Is. xl. 1.

'Blessed are they that mourn: for they shall be comforted.'—Matt. v. 4.

THE story is told that some great Sultan once bade his Grand Vizier write or compile a history of the human race. With long toil the task was accomplished, and the Grand Vizier went to the Sultan with fivescore asses laden with five hundred volumes of historic lore. 'Abridge! abridge!' said the alarmed potentate. 'Sire,' answered the Vizier, 'all these volumes may be compressed into a single line—"They were born; they suffered; they died."'

Without pressing to wrong and exaggerated conclusions the verse of Job, 'Man is born to trouble, as the sparks fly upwards;'[1] without accepting this as in any sense a complete epitome of life; maintaining that in human life the elements of natural and innocent happiness do, or, but for our own fault, *may* preponderate; still pain and misfortune and mental anguish belong so completely to the universal experience of mankind, that any source whence we may derive comfort either in the form of an immediate alleviation for misery, or of a sure and certain hope of

[1] Job v. 7.

something which lies beyond this dark horizon, cannot but be inestimably precious to the suffering race of man.

'The Persian king,' it has been said, 'could not find the names of even three happy men to write on his wife's tomb, or the philosopher would have recalled her from death. Every son of Adam has his task to toil at, and his stripes to bear for doing it badly.' Well may the poet exclaim :

> O purblind race of miserable men !
> How many among us at this very hour
> Do forge a lifelong trouble for ourselves,
> By taking true for false, or false for true ;
> Here, thro' the feeble twilight of this world
> Groping—how many—until we pass and reach
> That other, where we see as we are seen ![1]

I have already quoted the unsuspected testimony of Ernest Renan, who says that, after all, the Bible is the great Book of Consolation for Humanity. Dwelling as I am on the matchless value of the Holy Book, it may help us to realise this element of its preciousness if I give some instances to show how it may bring us peace, when no other book can lead us so directly to the source of peace, during this 'peevish April day' of life, when so often even after the rain the clouds return.

'Our finite miseries,' said Victor Hugo, 'shrink into nothing before the infinitude of hope !' Yes, that is true, and is an eminently Christian sentiment : but hope for the future is not, when taken alone, sufficient to give us blessedness and peace in the present. Yet that unbroken blessedness and peace—like the stillness of the inmost heart of the ocean, however fiercely the billows may roll over its storm-swept surface—is what the true Christian

---

[1] Tennyson, *Enid and Geraint.*

can learn from the Book of God. The consolation really offered by the writer of the Epistle to the Hebrews to his despoiled and suffering brethren is not (as in the erroneous and weakened reading of our Authorised Version) that they had a better and abiding substance in heaven, but that they had *themselves*—their own ennobled and purified personality—for a possession better than any which earth could either give or take away, and abiding.[1]

This is strikingly expressed in a scene described in a great work of fiction. A faithful but humble enthusiast, ragged, beaten, crushed, breathless, in peril of violent death at the hands of a bloodthirsty and howling crowd, looks up amid the glare of lanterns, and sees that he has been rescued by the exertions of a beautiful youth in authority, who has kept back the raging mob. Next day, while still a prisoner, he is visited by this generous youth, and says to him : 'Do you think that when I saw you last night, in your courtier's dress of lace and silver, calm, beneficent, and powerful for good, you did not seem to my weak human nature and my poor human instincts, beautiful as an angel of light? Truly you did. Yet I tell you—speaking by a nature and in a voice more unerring than mine—to the Divine Vision, of us two at that moment you were the one to be pitied; you were the outcast, the tortured of demons, the bound hand and foot, whose portion is in this life, who, if this fleeting hour be left unheeded, will be tormented in the life to come.'[2]

Yes ! Faith alters the perspective, reverses the appearances of life; it strips the seemingly happy of their guise of bliss, and robes the seemingly naked in royal apparel. It says in no uncertain voice, 'Sperate miseri;

[1] Heb. x. 34, reading ἑαυτούς, and omitting ἐν οὐρανῷ.
[2] *John Inglesant.*

cavete felices!' It transforms sorrow into triumph; the crown of thorns into a crown of stars; the Cross into a glory, and a rod of power. It turns martyrdom into rapture, and malediction into a beatitude. And the secret of these Divine transformations is best learnt—is learnt all but exclusively—from Holy Writ. Faith in facts, faith in a Person, involves the secret of all consolation. They who have learnt that secret from the Bible have learnt the true inner meaning of all life. Though weak they are strong; though destitute they are rich; having nothing, they possess all things; they are persecuted, yet not forsaken; cast down, but not destroyed. They are, as Dante said: 'Contenti nel fuoco'—happy in the very fire.[1]

1. The Scriptures supply us with many instances. Let us take the single case of *St. Paul*. He cherished no illusions; he trusted to no chances. He did not, in the language of Isaiah, prepare a table for Fortune and pour out a drink-offering to Destiny.[2] Following the footsteps of his Lord, ready to drink to the dregs the cup of trembling which his Father had prepared for him, he walked with open eyes to the edge of the terrible abyss which yawned before him. He was perfectly aware that in every city bonds and imprisonment awaited him. He regarded his life as a libation which was to be poured out upon the altar of his God.[3] He placed no reliance on the arctic temperature of most human friendships; he had fathomed the depths of human selfishness; he did not complain that his life of love lost itself, like some bright river, in the sands

---

[1] Dante, *Purg.* i. 118.

[2] Is. lxv. 11. Heb.: Gad, Meni. A.V.: 'a table for that troop . . . and a drink-offering unto that number.'

[3] 2 Tim. iv. 6: 'I am already being poured out as a libation.' A.V.: 'I am now ready to be offered.'

and marshes of hatred, or that the boundless self-sacrifice of his efforts had been cast into a Dead Sea of callousness. Did his sad lot make him murmur against God? Nay, he would not have changed his rags for Nero's purple, or his fetters for Nero's gems. In some acute crisis of mental agony, he yet wrote to the Corinthians that God 'comforteth us in all our tribulation, that we may be able to comfort them who are in any trouble, by the comfort wherewith we ourselves are comforted of God. For as the sufferings of Christ abound unto us, so our comfort also aboundeth through Christ. And our hope for you is stedfast; knowing that, as ye are partakers of the sufferings, so also are ye of the comfort.'[1] And from his lonely Roman dungeon, he wrote to the Philippians a letter radiant with inward joy, in which he has almost to apologise for the exuberant iteration of his gladness when he says, 'Rejoice in the Lord alway: again I will say, Rejoice.'[2] And in his last recorded words, his last will and testament so to speak—when he wrote to the dear Lycaonian youth who had shared the hardships of his travels— though he was about to perish, almost without a friend, not a murmur, not a sigh escapes him, but words of noblest and calmest resignation, of peace, and hope, and joy in believing.

2. Or take the case of the Martyrs. They had the same feelings as other men. They were of the same flesh and blood as we. 'Whence came this tremendous spirit?' asks Cardinal Newman; 'they shrank from suffering like other men, but such shrinking was incommensurable with apostasy. No intensity of torture had any means of affecting

---

[1] 2 Cor. i. 4–7. The A.V. is much weakened by rendering the same word now 'comfort' and now 'consolation.'

[2] Phil. iv. 4.

what was a mental conviction; and the sovereign thought in which they had lived was their adequate support and consolation in their death.' What enabled them to enter the dark river and its still waters with a smile upon their faces? Was it not because they had learnt from God's promises that underneath them were the everlasting arms? 'I know what is my gain,' said the martyr Ignatius; 'of nothing visible or invisible am I ambitious, save to gain Christ. Whether it is fire, or the cross, the assault of wild beasts, the wrenching of my bones, the crunching of my limbs, the crushing of my whole body, let the tortures of the devil all assail me if I do but gain Jesus.'

3. The same fearless joy is found even in boys and tender women. They did not quail before the seven-times heated furnace because they knew that the Spirit of God would be with them as 'a moist whistling wind' amid the flames;[1] that God would send to them His Angel of the Dew to beat back the fiery surge, and that while they walked unbound in the midst of the fire the form of Him who walked with them would be the form of the Son of God. And how soon would it end!

Waft of soul's wing!—
What lies above?
Sunshine and Spring,
Skyblue and love!

4. So we read of *St. Perpetua:* '"Have pity on thy babe!" they cried to her. "Have pity on the white hairs of thy father, and the infancy of thy child." I replied, "I will not." "Art thou then a Christian?" and I answered, "Yes, I am a Christian;" and as my father would have drawn me away, Hilarianus ordered him to be driven off.

---

[1] *Song of the Three Children,* 27.

Then sentence was pronounced and we were condemned to the beasts, and with hearts full of joy we returned to our prison.'[1]

5. Or come down the centuries and read of the death of *Savonarola*. He suffered—as wellnigh every preacher of righteousness has had to suffer since the days of Noah and Isaiah, and as the Lord of Glory Himself suffered—in a wickedly depraved world and a Church which (by its own confession) had fallen into deep corruption. His enemies hurled him from his pulpit, excommunicated him, lied about him, imprisoned him, infamously tortured him; finally they hung him in chains and burnt him in the public square at Florence. Now as Savonarola lay in his dungeon, with his cruelly racked frame, his name branded as that of an impostor and a traitor, his work apparently annihilated, deserted by his friends, abandoned to his foes—where alone did he find consolation? Hear his own words. 'Whatever I see, whatever I hear,' he wrote shortly before his judicial murder, 'carries the banner of sorrow. The remembrance of my friends saddens me; the recollection of my sins afflicts me; the consideration of my cloister and my cell torments me; the memory of my studies pains me; the thought of my sins weighs me down—all things are to me turned to mourning and sorrow. Who will succour me? Whither shall I go? How shall I escape? . . . Hearken! does not the Prophet say, "Thou, O Lord, art my hope; Thou hast set my house of defence very high!"' And so—with a hand left undislocated that he might sign documents full of lies which were passed off as his confessions—he turned to Scripture and occupied his last days in writing a comment upon the 31st and 51st Psalms.

6. Who, again, has not been touched as he read the

---

[1] *Acts of St. Perpetua.*

scene of the death by fire of the Bohemian Reformer *John Huss?* In all the infuriated insults heaped upon him, in all the agonies to which he was subjected, the words of Scripture were his firm support. When they placed on his head the cap painted with demons, he exclaimed, 'Most joyfully will I wear this crown of shame for Thy sake, O Jesus, who for me didst wear a crown of thorns;' and during all the preparation of the stake, and amid the consuming flames, he still cried repeatedly, 'Jesus, Thou Son of David, have mercy upon me! Lord Jesus, into Thy hands I commend my spirit.'

7. In 1677 Wigtown saw a deeply pathetic spectacle. An elderly woman named *Margaret Lachlan* was tied to a stake in the path of the advancing tide, as it swept upwards swift and strong in the waters of the Bladenoch. And nearer inland, that she might witness the agonising death struggles of the elder sufferer, a young girl of twenty, named *Margaret Wilson*, was tied to another stake. Their sole crime in the eyes of the brutal and tyrannous bigots who doomed them to death was that their consciences forbade them to take a test which they regarded as wrong; and that they had attended conventicles and field-preachings to worship the God of their fathers in the way which they found most profitable to their souls.

The rolling tide came up along the sand,
And round and round the sand
And o'er and o'er the sand
As far as eye could see,

and poor Margaret Lachlan was drowned. Then they unbound the girl, Margaret Wilson, that they might tempt her to apostatise and succumb. But she refused to give way. She was tied to the stake again. The cruel crawling

20

foam reached her feet; slowly, slowly it rose to her ankles, to her knees, to her breast, to her lips. She was face to face with the horror of violent death, yet she would not give way. What sustained her? Clear and high her voice was heard singing the words of the 25th Psalm—'Remember not the sins of my youth, nor my transgressions. Let me not be ashamed, for I put my trust in Thee.'

8. Again, in 1679, two Scotchmen were executed on the false charge of complicity in the murder of Archbishop Sharp, whom neither of them had ever seen. They were poor, uneducated men, and they walked side by side to the terrible scaffold without a tremor or a complaint. What sustained them? It was the nineteenth verse of the 34th Psalm—'Many are the troubles of the righteous: but the Lord delivereth him out of them all.' 'God hath not promised,' said one of them, 'to keep us from trouble, but to be with us in it; and what needs more? I bless the Lord for keeping me to this very hour; for little would I have thought a twelvemonth since, that the Lord would have taken *me*, a poor ploughman lad, and have honoured me so highly as to have made me first appear for Him, and now hath keeped me to this very hour to lay down my life for Him.'

9. But there are forms of slow-consuming agony and long-continued horror which are more terrible to bear in every way than the brief spasm of martyrdom; and even under such awful burdens of anguish the promises contained in the Scriptures have been found all-sufficient to support and to console.

During the Indian Mutiny in 1857, not a few of the sufferers realised what a new force came into the words of Scripture at the hour of need. 'A young English baronet, Sir Mountstuart Jackson, with Lieutenant Burnes, Mrs.

Orr, Miss Jackson, and some little children were trying to escape from Seetapore, and went through sufferings almost unspeakable, as they struggled forward, mostly by night, ragged, tattered, ill, and with matted hair. The only comfort which came to them in their tribulation came from the Word of God. They had no Bible among them, but, one day, some native medicines were brought to Mrs. Orr wrapped in a piece of printed paper which proved to be part of a leaf of the Book of Isaiah. And the message which came to them through Mohammedan hands was this: . . . "they shall obtain gladness and joy; and sorrow and mourning shall flee away. I, even I, am He that comforteth you: who art thou, that thou shouldest be afraid of a man that shall die, and of the son of man which shall be made as grass; and forgettest the Lord thy maker, . . . and hast feared continually every day because of the fury of the oppressor, as if he were ready to destroy? and where is the fury of the oppressor? The captive exile hasteneth that he may be loosed, and that he should not die in the pit, nor that . . ." [1]—and there the bit of paper was torn off. But the words of love thus strangely and mysteriously brought to them, comforted and strengthened them in the midst of their sorrow. The torn fragment of a text which came to them through heathen hands seemed like a promise of deliverance.' [2]

10. Can there be abysses of misery deeper even than this? Yes! one of the most tragic death-scenes of which I have ever read was that of *Captain Allen Francis Gardiner* and his poor companions on Picton Island in 1851. They died of slow starvation. While thousands of useless men live in hard-hearted self-indulgence, this brave and blameless sailor was actuated by the one burning desire to

[1] Is. li. 11–14.　　　　[2] Sir J. Kaye, *Sepoy War*, iii. 488.

spread the truth of God among the degraded heathen of
Patagonia and Tierra del Fuego, who are some of the very
lowest of the human race.   Landing with one or two companions on the wintry, storm-swept, hungry coast of Picton
Island, deserted and abandoned by the rescue which should
have come, these poor men slowly starved to death in long-
continued agony.   Did their faith fail under those frightful
circumstances?   It failed not!   They continued in mutual
and jubilant trust in God.   'Asleep or awake,' wrote one of
them—poor Richard Williams—in his diary, 'I am happy
beyond the poor compass of words to tell.'   In August 1851,
after weeks of ravening hunger and freezing cold, Allen
Gardiner wrote, 'God has kept me in perfect peace.'   And
so, unmurmuringly trustful to the last, they died of hunger,
and when their bodies were found a month afterwards,
the captain and sailors who had gone too late to rescue
them, cried like children; but it was found that Allen
Gardiner had painted upon a rock beside the cavern in
which these hapless ones had taken refuge, a hand pointing downwards, and underneath it the words, 'My soul,
wait thou only upon God.'   Surely before that royal throne
of unmoved affliction kings might lay down their crowns,
and bow their heads in humblest reverence!

11. And even when death comes upon men suddenly, 'terrible and with a tiger's leaps,' it is in the words of Scripture that they find their strength and hope.   Even at such
awful moments they have been enabled to exclaim,
'Though He slay me, yet will I trust in Him.'

In 1863 there was a terrible earthquake in Manilla.
The great cathedral of the city was shaken down over the
heads of the worshippers assembled in it.   Owing to some
peculiarity of the vaulted roof, which for a time upheld the
masses of superincumbent ruin, some of the congregation

were not immediately killed, though they were maimed and terrified. But the rescue of the survivors was at once seen to be hopeless. To touch the ruins was to bury them alive. A throng of people was assembled outside the walls, and they distinctly heard the voices of the doomed multitude within. A low, deep, bass voice, doubtless that of the priest, was heard within, uttering the words, 'Blessed are the dead that die in the Lord;' at which the hearers burst into a passion of sobs, for deep groans were wrung from the speaker by some intense pain. But, immediately afterwards, the same voice spoke to those who were thus in the very valley of the shadow of death. It spoke in a calm and even tone, and the listeners outside distinctly heard the words, 'The Lord Himself shall descend from Heaven with a shout . . and the dead in Christ shall rise first.'

12. In the Civil War between the Northern and Southern States of America, after one of those disastrous battles, they found the body of a poor Southern soldier. He was a youth, and he had been shot on the field ; but as he lay there with the life-blood ebbing from his wounds, he had drawn out his Bible and it was found in his dead hands, and the rigid fingers were still pressed upon the words, ' Yea, though I walk through the valley of the shadow of death I will fear no evil. For Thou art with me. Thy rod and Thy staff they comfort me.'

'What a history a collection of Bibles would give us,' says the Archbishop of Armagh, 'if we could only have it ! One would represent to us the sigh from a penitent, and one the song from a saint, and one would have its story of strength for some one who was tempted, and through one Christ's heart of fire melted the icicles round some heart of ice.'

CHAPTER XXI

SPECIAL CONSOLATIONS OF SCRIPTURE.

'That through patience and comfort of the Scriptures we might have hope.'—Rom. xv. 4.

'I see that the Bible fits into every fold and crevice of the human heart. I am a man, and I believe that this is God's book because it is man's book.'—HALLAM.

MARTYRDOM and the accumulations of overwhelming tragedy only befall the few; but many forms of sorrow —'bitter arrows from the gentle hands of God'—strike the lives of every one of us. Shakespeare, in his all-observing genius, has twice enumerated some of them. Thus in 'Hamlet' he says,

There's the respect
That makes calamity of so long life;
For who would bear the whips and scorns of time,
The oppressor's wrong, the proud man's contumely,
The pangs of despised love, the law's delay,
The insolence of office, and the spurns
That patient merit of the unworthy takes,
When he himself might his quietus make
With a bare bodkin? who would these fardels bear,
To grunt and sweat under a weary life,
But that the dread of something after death,
The undiscovered country from whose bourn
No traveller returns, puzzles the will,

And makes us rather bear those ills we have
Than fly to others that we know not of?

And in his famous sonnet he sings,

Tired of all these, for restful death I cry;—
As to behold desert a beggar born,
And needy nothing trimm'd in jollity,
And purest faith unhappily forsworn,
And gilded honour shamefully misplaced,
And maiden virtue rudely strumpeted,
And right perfection wrongfully disgraced,
And strength by limping sway disabled,
And art made tongue-tied by authority,
And folly (doctor-like) controlling skill,
And simple truth miscalled simplicity,
And captive good attending captain ill:
Tired with all these, from these would I be gone.

Let us then glance at some of the commonest forms of human sorrow, and note how in their extreme incidence men have learnt best how to bear them by calling to mind the promises of Holy Writ. Some of these manifold sorrows are occasional; some continuous. Some are exceptional, others universal: but for all alike—both for those which are overwhelming in their permanence and almost inconceivable in their intensity, and for those which, though less acute, benumb and paralyse our souls as with the touch of a torpedo—there is balm in the Gilead of Scripture and there is a physician there. To the anodynes which God there prescribes for us, there is no such thing as an incurable disease.

1. Take the universal, inevitable sorrow of bereavement. In that dark hour, what consolation can be distinctly compared to those which we derive from the words of Scripture read in the light of Christ's Resurrection? We

remember that our beloved ones have but entered a valley which, if it be dark, has yet been illuminated by Christ's footsteps; and over their graves we proclaim, in the thought of His victory, 'Thy dead men shall live; together with my dead body shall they arise! Awake, and sing ye that dwell in the dust, for thy dew is as the dew of herbs, and the earth shall disclose her dead.' We remember that it is God who giveth His beloved sleep. 'I saw,' says George Fox, 'that there was an ocean of darkness and death; but an infinite ocean of Light and Love flowed over the ocean of Darkness: and in that I saw the infinite love of God.'

Aaron, when his two sons were stricken with death—Ezekiel, when the delight of his eyes was taken from him at a stroke—bowed their heads and held their peace. When the boy of the Lady of Shunem lay dead in the upper chamber of her home, she was met by Gehazi with the questions, 'Is it well with thee? Is it well with thy husband? Is it well with the child?' Ah! her heart was breaking, and her husband's heart was very sore, and the dear little lad, her only son, lay dead in the Prophet's chamber: yet she would not let her voice break with sobs as she answered, '*It is well!*' Not a few parents, crushed in their deep sorrow by such a narrative as this, have carved upon the tombs of their dead sons the words, 'Is it well with the child? It is well!'

2. Again, there are few who escape all through life the wearing pain of severe sickness, and the depression which accompanies it. Do not Christian sufferers again and again find comfort in the verse, 'Thou shalt make all his bed in his sickness'? Can there be a malady more hopelessly loathsome than leprosy? There is one of the Sandwich Islands, called Molokai, which is consigned exclusively

to lepers, and more than 800 lepers are living there. The sun rises on no more distressful and revolting scene of human abjectness and misery. And yet the young Belgian priest, Father Damien, voluntarily offered himself in 1873 to serve in that island, among its horde of hapless and hopeless lepers, with the practical certainty that he would himself succumb to that obliterating horror. There for thirteen years he continued to be the doctor, nurse, magistrate, teacher, carpenter, gardener, cook, sometimes even the grave-digger of those awfully afflicted wrecks of humanity. At last he contracted the foul disease, and died of it. Hear his own touching words: 'I am now the only priest in Molokai. Impossible for me to go any more to Honolulu, on account of the leprosy breaking out upon me. Having no doubt of the true character of my disease, I feel calm, resigned, and happier among my own people. Almighty God knows what is best for my own sanctification, and with that conviction I say daily, "Thy will be done." Please pray for your afflicted friend, and recommend me and my unhappy people to all servants of the Lord.'

3. Or take the common case of pecuniary anxiety and care for the means of sustenance. How many a father of a family, full of misgiving for his children, feels this care constantly flapping its wings about him in the pauses of the day and the silent watches of the night? How many a young man feels with a sense of anguish that he has 'no prospects;' that he cannot make his way; that he will never be able with honour or prudence to marry or make himself a home. 'I shall be chained,' he says, 'to dust and deskwork, a miserable drudge, for all the dreary to-morrows which shall be no better than the dreary yesterdays.' What remedy is there but faith in the promises of

God? If he be honest, upright, temperate, strenuous, he will yet live to say, 'I have been young, and now am old, yet never saw I the righteous forsaken, nor his seed begging their bread.' He learns to trust Him without whom not even the little brown sparrow falleth to the ground, and to cast all his care upon God, because God careth for him.

4. Again, how many suffer for long years from the gnawings of the viper's tooth of envy; how many, all their lives long, are the victims of hatred, malice, calumny, slander, and all uncharitableness. Yes, for there are multitudes of men through whom 'misunderstanding of everything passes like the mudcast of the earthworm.' Those are specially liable to suffer thus who always speak the truth and boldly rebuke vice, and those also who rise ever so little above their fellow-men.

> Every age on him who strays
> From its broad and beaten ways
> Pours its sevenfold vial.[1]

In such hours is it no comfort to the Christian to recall his Lord's words, 'Blessed are ye when men shall revile you, and persecute you, and shall say all manner of evil against you falsely, for My sake. Rejoice, and be exceeding glad: for great is your reward in heaven: for so persecuted they the prophets which were before you;' and 'If they have called the master of the house Beelzebub, how much more them of his household?' How can the servant escape when the sinless Master was described by priests as a deceiver and a blasphemer, and by Pharisees as a gluttonous man and a winebibber, a Samaritan, a traitor, a demoniac? How many of God's best saints

[1] J. G. Whittier, *Barclay of Ury.*

have shared the lot of their Lord? St. Athanasius was accused of magic and murder; St. Jerome of impurity; St. Gregory of Nyssa of base embezzlement; St. Chrysostom of gluttony, fraud, and hypocrisy; St. Basil of heresy and treason; Luther of every kind of crime; Richard Hooker of adultery; St. Vincent de Paul of theft. Milton was called a venomous serpent and a foul-mouthed Zoilus; William the Silent was accused of having murdered his own wife. As for the saintly Whitfield, he

> Stood pilloried on Infamy's high stage
> And bore the pelting scorn of half an age.
> The man who mentioned him at once dismissed
> All mercy from his lips, and sneered and hissed:
> His crimes were such as Sodom never knew,
> And Perjury stood up to swear all true.

They could bear this, as all good men can bear it, because they believe in the day when Christ's *Ite* or *Venite* shall decide all judgments and all controversies for ever. They calmly commit their way unto the Lord, and are content to feel that, according to His warning, to be near Him in this life is to be near the fire and near the sword.[1]

5. And it is no very uncommon case for men to lose their all. In 1830 the ship which was taking to India the excellent missionary Dr. Duff was wrecked in the breakers on the desolate shore of a little island. The crew escaped in small boats with nothing but their lives. A sailor saw something lying on the shore, and picking it up found that it was a small Bible of Dr. Duff's, the sole book left of 800 volumes which he was taking out with him. Dr. Duff, undismayed at the loss of all he possessed, knelt down on the white surf-beaten sand with the forlorn sur-

---

[1] Quoted by Origen, *Hom. in Jerem.* iii. 778.

vivors of the wreck, and their hearts burned with fresh hope within them, as he read to them the four deliverances of the 107th Psalm, ending with the words, 'Whoso is wise will ponder these things, and they shall understand the loving kindness of the Lord.'

6. Sometimes, too, personal ruin is the accompaniment of overwhelming national disaster. It was so when after the fearful defeat of Jena in 1806 Prussia went down before the cruel and reckless ambition of Napoleon. On no heart did the throe of a nation's anguish fall with more agonising incidence than upon the young and beautiful *Queen Louise.* It meant the utter ruin of all her hopes. When she heard the news, she burst into uncontrollable weeping. How did she calm her anguish? It was the pious custom in Germany when a pupil left the school, to accompany him, singing the 37th Psalm—'Fret not thyself because of evil-doers'—of which the fifth verse is, 'Commit thy way unto the Lord; trust also in Him, and He shall bring it to pass.' The young Queen sat down to her piano, and softly sang the Psalm. When she rose, we are told her eye was clear, her spirits tranquil. That same verse was the constant comfort of David Livingstone also, during all his perils and fevers and hungry wanderings in scorching Africa and its desert wastes.

7. There is one very terrible form of agony which affects some of the noblest souls: it is the sense of Sin, which sometimes drives men into deep religious despondency.

Let us take the case of *John Bunyan.*

'One morning when I was again at prayer, and trembling under the fear that no word of God could help me, that piece of a sentence darted into my mind, "My grace is sufficient." At this methought I felt some stay as though there might be hopes. But oh how good a thing it is for God to send His Word! For about a fortnight before I was looking at this very place, and then I thought it could not come near my soul with comfort; therefore I threw down the book in a pet. Then I thought it was not large enough for me; no, not large enough; but now it was as if it had arms of grace so wide that it could not only enclose me, but many more besides, and one day as I was in a meeting of God's people, full of sadness and terror—for my fears again were strong upon me—these words did suddenly with great power break in upon me, "My grace is sufficient for *thee!*" (three times together); and oh methought that every word was a mighty word unto me, as "My" and "grace" and "sufficient" and "for thee." At which time my understanding was so enlightened that I was as though I had seen the Lord Jesus look down from heaven through the tiles upon me, and direct these words unto me. This sent me mourning home. It broke my heart and filled me full of joy, and laid me low in the dust.'[1]

'Search the Scriptures,' says an old bishop, 'and say if things ran not thus as their ordinary course. God commandeth and man disobeyeth. Man disobeyeth and God threateneth. God threateneth and man repenteth. Man repenteth and God forgiveth. "Abimelech! thou art but a dead man, because of Sarah whom thou hast taken;" but Abimelech restoreth the Prophet his wife, and God spareth him, and he dieth not. "Hezekiah! put thine house in order, for thou shalt die and not live;" but Hezekiah turneth his face to the wall, and prayeth and weepeth.

[1] Bunyan, *Grace Abounding*, pp. 206, 207.

and God addeth to his days fifteen years. "Nineveh! prepare for desolation; for now but forty days and Nineveh shall be destroyed!" but Nineveh fasted and prayed and repented, and Nineveh stood for more than forty years twice told. To show compassion and to forgive is the thing in which God most of all delighteth, but to punish and to take vengeance is (as some explain that passage in Isaiah) "His strange work," a thing He taketh no pleasure in. As the bee laboureth busily all the day long, and seeketh to every flower and every weed for honey, but stingeth not once unless she be ill provoked; so God bestirreth Himself, and He yearns to show compassion. Vengeance cometh on slowly and unwillingly, and draweth a sigh from Him. "Ah! I must—I see there is no remedy—I must ease Me of Mine adversaries. Yet how shall I give thee up, O Ephraim? Is Ephraim My dear son? Is he a pleasant child? for since I spake against him, I do earnestly remember him still: therefore My heart is troubled for him; I will surely have mercy upon him, saith the Lord." Consider this, and take comfort, all ye that mourn in Zion, and groan under the weight of God's heavy displeasure. Why do ye spend your strength and spirit in gazing altogether with broad eyes on God's justice? Take them off a little and refresh them by fastening them another while on His mercy. Consider not only what He threateneth, but why He threateneth. It is unless you repent. He threateneth to cast down indeed, but into humiliation, not into despair. He shooteth out His arrow, but as Jonathan's arrow for warning, not for destruction. "Yea, but who am I," will some disconsolate soul say, "that I should make God's threatening void? or what my repentance that it should cancel the oracles of truth?" Poor and distressed soul that thus disputest against thine own peace, but seest not the while the unfathomed depths of God's mercy, and the wonderful dispensations of His truth!'

Can it be true the grace He is declaring?
  O let us trust Him, for His words are fair!
Man, what is this? and why art thou despairing?
  God shall forgive thee all but thy despair!

CHAPTER XXII

THE BIBLE AND THE NATIONS.

'So shall my word be that goeth forth out of my mouth: it shall not return unto me void, but it shall accomplish that which I please, and it shall prosper in the thing whereto I sent it.'—Is. lv. 11.

'Upon the onely Scripture doth our Church Foundation lay,
Let Patriarchs, Prophets, Gospels, and the Apostles for us say:
For soul and body we affirm are all-sufficient they.'
WARNER, Albion's England, ix. 32.

I SHOWED in the last chapters that the separate phrases of Scripture have been, as it were, blazoned in letters of gold upon the souls of individuals. They have been no less mighty in their power to sway the destiny of entire nations. In the Bible, more clearly than from any other source, men have heard 'the voice of God sounding across the centuries the eternal distinctions of right and wrong'—for it was in the Bible that the voice of God taught us three thousand years ago that 'Righteousness exalteth a nation, but Sin is the reproach of any people.'

'No Book has been so often printed as the Bible. No fewer than 1,326 editions were published in the sixteenth century. Down to 1896 the British Bible Society printed no fewer than 147,366,660 copies of the Scriptures, and the American 61,705,000. The British Society issues 4,000,-000 copies yearly, and the American 1,750,000.'

320

The Bible has been the guide, the inspiration, the ennoblement, the statesman's manual of the greatest nations in the world.

1. The Old Testament is the Bible of *the Jews;* and see what it did for them! It enshrined the code of their great lawgiver; it preserved the burning words of their mighty prophets; it presented them with a history prolific in heroic examples; it gave them a harp, which, soft as Memnon's at morning, furnished their worship with golden canticles, and throbbed with every spontaneous emotion of their joy and their despair. And what else has preserved their immemorial continuity as the most imperishable of the nations of the world? Why have revolutions thundered in vain over their heads? Judæa saw many a mighty empire rise and fall; she was herself but a petty kingdom, hardly more extensive, and not nearly so populous, as many an English county. The hosts of Assyria trampled her into the mire; Babylonia swept her into hopeless exile; Persia imprisoned her in the iron network of her cruel satrapies; the kings of Syria and Egypt made her the football of their fierce contentions; Republican Rome put her under a procurator who was the son of a slave; Imperial Rome burnt her to ashes and reared a temple to Venus on the platform of the revived shrine of God. The nations of Europe, with their Torquemadas and Borgias and devilish Inquisitions, in Italy and England, and miserable Spain, tortured and insulted her. The Moslim have held her land and city for twelve centuries and a half under their effete and somnolent despotism—but where are her enemies?

'Assyria, Greece, Rome, Carthage, where are they?' 'They are dead; they shall not live; they are deceased, they shall not rise.' Even brilliant Greece, with her poetry and her art and her science, perished of her own lusts. Even Imperial Rome, with her legions and her luxuries, sickened of imported corruption. But because Israel had her Bible, and clung to it—because, amid all her miserable failings, she was 'the lifter up to the nations of the banner of righteousness'—they have perished, and she remaineth. The word of the Lord, given to her in her Scriptures, has been fulfilled to her in the letter, 'Fear not, thou worm Jacob, and thou handful Israel. I will help thee, saith the Eternal. Behold, I have graven thee upon the palms of My hands!'

2. Again, when the civilisation of the older world was perishing with the dry rot of luxury, sensuality, and greed; when it had poisoned all the wholesome air of the world; when

> Rome, whom mightiest kingdoms curtsied to,
> Like a forlorn and desperate castaway,
> Did shameful execution on herself;

then God poured into the effete veins of the empire the purer blood of the Northern nations. What saved Europe in that day under the Providence of God? *The Goths—* the noblest of all the barbarian invaders, a strong manly race, tall of stature, of bright complexion, blue eyes and fair hair—had among them a little captive Cappadocian boy. They called him Wulfila—'the little wolf.' They all loved him, and said that he was so good that he could do no wrong. Gloriously did he repay their affection! When he grew up he invented a Gothic alphabet and characters, and translated for them almost the whole Bible into Gothic. A single precious copy of that translation, written in silver letters on purple vellum, which still exists at Upsala in Sweden, is the sole surviving monument of the people and their language! It was the means of converting them to Christianity; and their conversion saved the Christian fortunes of the world, when Alaric and his Goths, humanised and ennobled by the oracles of God, burst into the burning streets of Rome and bowed her glories to the dust.

3. I might speak of *Germany*—owing her freedom, her manliness, her supremacy, her pure and wholesome home-life to that Bible which Martin Luther found in the monastery of Erfurt, which in the bright and blissful Reformation, translated by Luther for the German people, emancipated Germany from the yoke of priestcraft. All the power of the German language, and all the greatest literature of the German nation, and all its foremost men, and all its most imperial progress, date from its possession of the Book of God.[1]

4. But turn to our own beloved *England*. Before the Reformation Wycliffe had endeavoured to put the English Bible into the hands of the people. 'O Christ,' he exclaimed, 'Thy Law is hidden in the sepulchre; when wilt Thou send Thine angel to remove the stone, and show Thy truth unto Thy flock?' Wycliffe, strange to say, died in his bed, and not on the rack or at the stake. But the English Bible, condemned in 1408 by Archbishop Arundel, was to all intents and purposes suppressed; and Pope Martin V. ordered the exhumed remains of this saint of God to be burnt and flung into the Swift. Yet God's word did not return unto Him void.

In the Netherlands, an Emperor who lived in adultery

---

[1] *Gespräche mit Goethe*, iii. 256. To this fact Goethe is an unexceptionable witness. '"Wir wissen gar nicht," fuhr Goethe fort, "was wir Luthern und der Reformation im allgemeinen alles zu danken haben. Wir sind frei geworden von den Fesseln geistiger Bornirtheit, wir sind infolge unserer fortwachsenden Cultur fähig geworden, zur Quelle zurück zukehren und das Christenthum in seiner Reinheit zu fassen."'

and was steeped in lies, burned and massacred his subjects
if they sung the Psalms in their own tongue; and in England, even under Henry VIII., it was a crime punishable
with death to read the Bible in a language which they
understood. It was for the crime of translating the Bible
into the vernacular that one of the purest and noblest of
Englishmen, William Tyndale, whose version is the chief
element in our Authorised Version, was imprisoned,
strangled, and burnt in 1536. His last words before he
died were, 'O Lord, open the King of England's eyes.'
That prayer was answered. The very next year Henry
VIII. permitted Cranmer to circulate the Bible in English.
Thenceforward England became more and more the people
of one book. The influence exercised by the open Bible
was prodigious. An Italian writer, Signor Zumbini, says
it was due to 'the most complete assimilation ever made
by individual or people of a series of ideas and conceptions not their own.'[1] Manhood springing up in its
untrammelled nobleness, deepened in disemprisoned human souls, the sense of personal duty which will no
longer be content with functional and vicarious religion.
'In the days of the father of Elizabeth,' wrote a Romish
priest, 'the whole kingdom was content to take its beliefs
from a tyrant's word: now boys and women boldly refuse
to make the slightest concession even at the threat of
death.' That was the heroic England which shattered the
Invincible Armada; that was the England of Drake, of
Bacon, of Hooker, of Shakespeare, of Sydney, of Raleigh,
and of Spenser; that was the England which under the
freshly applied goad of civil and ecclesiastical oppression

---

[1] Zumbini, *Saggi Critici* (Morano, 1876): 'The constant reading of
the Bible in public and in private has contributed to a unity of the
language, alike in time and in use, by all sorts and conditions of men.'

awoke the burning righteousness of Puritanism, shattered the tyranny of the Stuarts, suppressed the odious Star Chamber, sent its soldiers to battle with Bibles in their knapsacks, and made the Pope cease to roll God's slaughtered saints down the rocks of Piedmont lest Cromwell 'should make the guns of England heard in the Castle of St. Angelo.'

It was the Bible which created the prose literature of England, of which its Authorised Version was the noblest monument; it was the Bible which gave fire and nobleness to her language; it was the Bible which turned a dead oppression into a living Church; it was the Bible which put to flight the nightmare of ignorance before the rosy dawn of progress; it was the Bible which made each free Christian man feel some grandeur in the beatings of his own heart, as of a being who stood face to face with God, responsible to Him alone, having 'the dignity of God's image upon him, and the sign of His redemption marked visibly upon his forehead.' It was the Bible which saved England from sinking into a tenth-rate power as a vassal of cruel, ignorant, superstitious Spain, whose Dominicans and tyrants would have turned her fields into slaughter-houses as they turned those of the Netherlands, and would have made her cities reek as she made Seville reek with the bale-fires of her Inquisition.

5. And what the Bible did for England, it did for the *United States of America.* It was the Bible that made America what she is. It was the Bible, and the preference of its pure unadulterated lessons to subservience to the tyranny of bishops, which sent the Pilgrim Fathers in the *Mayflower* to the New England they were to make so great.

6. And so rich, so marvellous is the universal adaptability of the Bible to every rank and order of human

minds, that it is equally fitted to rouse the barbarian from savagery, and to uplift the civilised into the foremost nations of the world. In the Bible Society's offices may be seen a copy of St. John's Gospel, beautifully written out in 1820 by King Pomare II., King of the Pacific isle of *Tahiti*, because he could not procure a printed copy. The Bible redeemed his people from savage wickedness to reverence and honour.

7. In *New Zealand*, when an unbeliever was sneering at the Bible to a native chief, the chief pointed to him a great stone, and said, 'My fathers and I were once blood-thirsty cannibals. On that stone we slaughtered and roasted and devoured our human victims. We are Christians now. What raised us to what we are from what we were? The Bible at which you scoff.'

8. The late saintly Bishop of Moosonee told me that once, in a small gathering of *North American Indians* on the coast of Hudson's Bay, he found that there was scarcely one of those present who had not, according to their custom, murdered his own mother when she became too old to work; 'and now,' he said, 'if you visited their wigwams you would find each of them in possession of a Bible, and each of them a humble reader of it.' Yes! because it came from true human hearts, it will ever thrill like electric flame into the hearts of men who are men indeed. That is because the Bible contains God's words for all the world. That is why in century after century it renews its youth as the eagle. That is why 'the sun never sets upon its gleaming page.'

9. Let us now turn to *Japan*. Christianity was first introduced among the Japanese in 1549, by Francis Xavier, and for a time Christianity spread considerably

among the people. But soon, through the meddling of Jesuits, there arose very serious quarrels and disturbances, and at last many Christians were cruelly put to death. Persecutions went on more or less for a long period of time; almost all the remaining Christians in Japan were murdered; and in 1637 Japan was closed 'for ever' to foreigners and to Christianity. There was a public inscription put up to the effect that anybody who taught the 'vile Jesus doctrine,' as it was called, should be executed. Who was it who reintroduced Christianity into Japan? It was a Japanese nobleman. One day he saw in the Bay of Yeddo something floating on the water, which proved to be a Bible. He did not, however, know what it was, but was told that it was a book which had been dropped from some English or American vessel. He became interested in it and anxious to know more about it. He then sent it to Shanghai to have it interpreted for him. His study of the truth was sanctified to him; he was converted, and, in 1857, was the first Japanese who was baptised. Two others were baptised with him, and from that time Christianity has been a living and growing power in the empire. The first great impulse was given by that single Bible.

10. One more instance only out of many, to show that this efficacy of the Bible is not due only to its human expounders. Let us look at a lonely and once desert island, only discovered in 1767. In 1790 the crew of an English vessel named *The Bounty* mutinied, mastered the vessel, and turned their officers adrift. Nine of the mutineers, with six men and twelve women of Tahiti, landed on this uninhabited *Pitcairn's Island*. One of them unhappily learned how to make spirits from an indigenous root, and

that little spot, only seven miles in circumference, became at once, in consequence of the drink, a hell on earth. Drunkenness made its Paradise a scene of devilish orgies and bloody massacres, till, by the year 1800, all the Tahitian men, and all the English but one had perished. That one English survivor was John Adams. He found a Bible in the wreck of *The Bounty;* read it; was struck with remorse for his crimes, and from it he taught the Tahitian women and their children. He became the head of a patriarchal community, which, though half-caste and the offspring of mutineers, murderers, and savages, became, through the teaching of the Bible, renowned throughout the world for the kindness and gentleness of their character, the simplicity and virtue of their lives.

In that desert island was re-enacted the immemorial story of the human race: the story of Eve and the tree of the Knowledge of Evil; the story of Cain, his brother's murderer; the story of Noah's intoxicated shame; the story of a community plunged into destruction by drink and sensuality, saved, ennobled, regenerated by the simple Word of God.

11. I need not give any further instances. But this is certain: so far as, and so long as, *England* remains true to that simple, unadulterated Word of God which has been purchased for us by the misery of exiles and the blood of martyrs; so far and so long as she stands fast in the freedom wherewith God has made her free, and is not again entangled with the yoke of bondage—so far and so long as she refuses to be either driven into indifference by disgust, or seduced into delusion by false religion; so far and so long will she maintain the honours of this great people. All else—call itself by what sounding name it will—will prove to be but booming brass and tinkling

cymbal. Let England cling to her open Bible; [1] let her
learn from it the broad truths of primitive Christianity,
and be faithful to them; let her teach it to her children,
and her children to their children, and their children to
generations yet unborn, and then no wind that blows, no
storm that beats, will shake her invincible foundations,
for she will be founded upon a rock! But let her apostatise from its pure lessons into humanly invented falsities,
and I would not give fifty years' purchase either for her
greatness or for the stability of her Church. 'The world
has no other trumpet of peace save Holy Scripture for
souls at war; no other weapon to slay terrible passions;
no other teaching to quench the heart's raging fires. This
book alone makes mortals immortal, makes immortals
gods.'

The Bible will ever continue to be a lamp to our individual feet and a light to our individual paths. It has
often saved nations in their decadence, and Churches from
their corruption. 'If it be a crime to make known the
Scriptures,' said the Bishop of Cloyne, 'it is one of a very
singular nature; for our Saviour set the example: the
Apostles followed it, and God Himself has commanded
and sanctioned it.'

> Stars are poor books, and oftentimes do miss;
> This book of stars lights to eternal bliss.

[1] The Council of Trent said : 'Indiscriminata lectio Sacræ Scripturæ
interdicta est.' So the Pope in 1816 said : 'Si Sacra Biblia vulgari
lingua passim sine discrimine permittantur, plus inde detrimenti
quam utilitatis oriri.' Pope Pius VI. spoke of the Scriptures as
'fontes uberrimi qui CUIQUE patere debent,' but Pope Pius VII., op-
posing the Bible Society in Poland, expressed his 'horror at this most
subtle attempt to undermine the very foundation of religion.'

CHAPTER XXIII

CONCLUSION.

'And with that he held his peace. And all the people then shouted and said, GREAT IS TRUTH, AND MIGHTY ABOVE ALL THINGS.'—1 Esdras iv. 41.

'Ama Scripturas et amabit te sapientia.'—ST. JEROME.

'It is the king's best copy, the magistrate's best rule, the house-wife's best guide, the servant's best directory, and the young man's best companion.'—HUNTINGTON.

To point out all the ways and the extent to which Scripture has been a priceless boon to the race of man would be a task without end. The ways are manifold, the extent infinite. When Bishop Watson published his 'Apology for the Bible,' George III. remarked 'that he did not know the Bible wanted any apology.' The Bible needs no apology, for humanity has set its seal thereto, and can never be robbed of its treasured blessedness. *Securus judicat orbis terrarum.*

'What truth, what saving truth without the Word of God?' ask King James's translators. 'What word of God whereof we may be sure without the Scripture?'

And, again, 'The Scriptures being acknowledged to be so good and so perfect, how can we excuse ourselves of negligence if we do not study them? of curiosity if we be not content with them?'

330

There may be some who would pronounce such eulogies somewhat vague, rhetorical, and indiscriminating; but they come from full and sincere hearts, and they correspond to many phases of universal experience.

Writing of the Bible, as he always does with earnest enthusiasm, Mr. Ruskin says:

'Match, if you can, its Table of Contents!

'First you have

'1. The story of the Fall and of the Flood, grandest of human traditions founded on a true horror of sin.

'2. The story of the Patriarchs.

'3. The story of Moses, with the results of that tradition on the moral law of all the civilised world.

'4. The story of the Kings; virtually that of all kinghood in David, and all philosophy in Solomon, culminating in the Psalms and Proverbs, and the still more close and practical wisdom of Ecclesiastes and the son of Sirach.

'5. The story of the Prophets; virtually the deepest mystery, tragedy, and permanent fate of national existence.

'6. The story of Christ.

'7. The moral law of St. John and his closing Apocalypse of its fulfilment.' [1]

Yet some features of Scripture as a whole are so striking that we may well touch specially upon them.

St. Paul mentions three of them. He says that 'Whatsoever things were written aforetime were written for our learning, that we through patience, and comfort of the Scriptures, might have our hope.' Instruction, endurance, consolation—those three blessings we may always find.

1. We may find Instruction. Solomon tells us that he wrote his Proverbs 'to know wisdom and instruction, to

---

[1] Ruskin, *Bible of Amiens*, p. 133.

perceive the words of understanding; to receive the instruction of wisdom, justice, and right, and equity; to give subtlety to the simple, to the young man knowledge and discretion. A wise man will hear and will increase in learning; and a man of understanding shall attain unto wise counsels.'

The instructiveness of the Bible is largely due to the universality on which I have already dwelt. In the rigid systems of modern sectaries we are often stifled, we are sickened, we pant for God's free air, we are overshadowed by man's pettiness and gloom. All is narrow suspicion, dreary function, and self-satisfied intolerance. Life in its largeness and beauty is dwarfed into a selfish struggle after individual salvation; the world becomes a sea strewn with shipwrecks where our sole business is to seize a plank. The Bible in its immensity and its ever-broadening horizon is one magnificent protest against this poverty of conception. Instead of dimly groping round the narrow circle of opinionative intolerance it sets our feet upon the mountain and turns our eyes towards the sun. From the formless chaos of Genesis to the new heaven of Revelation it overarches the throne of God with a rainbow of mercy in sight like unto an emerald.

It is not a book for religiosity, or Pharisaism, or outward forms, or repeated shibboleths, or rigid scholasticism. It recognises that true religion is morality and large-heartedness and love. In it, as by the outpouring of a perpetual Pentecost, we listen to the voices of men and nations, and we do hear them speak in our tongue the wonderful works of God.

And this central idea of Scripture accounts for the fact that with all its diversity and universality it is gifted also with a Divine adaptability. The Bible is beyond all other books the Book of the World. Other books are for special times or separate races; this book has been dear in every age to men of all races. Other books are for the poor or for the rich; this book regards poor and rich alike, not under the inch-high differences of wealth and rank, but as heirs alike of the common mysteries of Life and Death, of Redemption and Immortality. Other books are for the mature or the youthful; this book alone neither wearies the aged nor repels the young. Other books are only for the learned, or only for the ignorant; this book, in the sweetest and simplest elements of its revelation, is as dear to the German philosopher as to the negro's child. In it mind speaks to mind and heart to heart, soul to soul. 'It is no light thing,' it has been said, 'to hold with an electric chain, be it but for one hour, even a hundred hearts; but this book has held millions of hearts, and that for centuries. Thousands of writers come up in one generation to be totally forgotten in the next, but the silver cord of the Bible is not loosed, nor its golden bowl broken, as Time chronicles its tens of centuries passed by.'

2. In old days a Bible cost almost as much as a king's ransom. A load of hay was thought a cheap price for a few leaves of it. In these days we may buy a good copy of the Bible for eighteenpence; but to buy it is one thing, to possess, to know it, to understand it, to make it a lamp unto the feet, and a light unto the path is quite another. 'It is not to be had,' says Mr. Ruskin, 'at that low figure, the whole 119th Psalm being little more than one agonising prayer for the gift of it, and a man's life is well spent if he has truly received and learned to read ever so little a part of it.'

3. And whether to any good purpose we understand it or not, depends wholly on the spirit with which we read it.

In his last sickness, Archbishop Usher was observed, one day, sitting in his wheel-chair with his Bible in his lap, and moving his position as the sun stole round to the westward so as to let the light always fall on the sacred page. That is a symbol of the right use of the Bible.

It is truly said, 'Read it in the sunshine of love, and love will shine forth from its gleaming page.'

The sunshine may sometimes fail us, but surely we may always find some glow-worm light whereby to read.

'This evening,' says a pleasant writer, 'I have been turning glow-worms to a use which probably no naturalist ever thought of—reading the Psalms by their cool green radiance. I placed six of the most luminous insects I could find at the top of the page, moving them from verse to verse as I descended. The experiment was perfectly successful. Each letter became clear and legible, making me feel deeply and gratefully the inner life of the Psalmist's adoration: "Oh Lord! how manifold are Thy works! in wisdom hast Thou made them all; the earth is full of Thy riches." By the help of this emerald of the hedgerow I can read not only the hymns of saints to God, but God's message to me. I could not have read evensong among the trees by night, unless I had moved the lamp up and down. One verse shone while the rest of the page was dark. Patience alone was needed. Line by line the whole Psalm grew bright. The sequestered paths of the Gospel garden are studded with glow-worms. I have only to stoop and find them. These recollections are my lanterns in the dark. The past lights up the present. I move my glow-worm lower on the page and read to-day by yesterday.'[1]

Cromwell quoted the two verses of the 117th Psalm—'O

[1] R. S. Wilmot, *Summer Time in the Country.*

praise the Lord, all ye nations: praise Him, all ye people. For His merciful kindness is great towards us: and the truth of the Lord endureth for ever'—after the victory at Dunbar. The fourteenth verse of the 118th Psalm—'The Lord is my strength and song, and is become my salvation'—was chosen for the text of the sermon preached by Carstairs at Torbay in 1688, after the landing of William III. The sixth verse of the same Psalm—'The Lord is on my side; I will not fear: what can man do unto me?'—cheered the Protestants on the day of St. Bartholomew; the twenty-third verse—'This is the Lord's doing'—was quoted by Queen Elizabeth when she heard of her accession. The 119th was being chanted by the monks at the Certosa in 1515, when Francis was taken prisoner at Pavia; and when they came to the nineteenth verse—'I am a stranger in the earth: hide not Thy commandments from me'—he joined his voice with theirs. The 122nd Psalm furnished Bishop Grafton with his text—'I was glad when they said unto me, Let us go into the house of the Lord'—at St. Paul's Cathedral after the Great Fire, and was again the text after the Peace of Ryswick. The first verse of the 137th—'By the rivers of Babylon, there we sat down, yea, we wept, when we remembered Zion'—comforted John, King of France, when he was taken captive at Poictiers. The second verse of the 146th—'While I live will I praise the Lord'—was quoted by the Earl of Strafford as he stood on the scaffold. The sixth verse of the 149th—'Let the high praises of God be in their mouth, and a two-edged sword in their hand'—was the text of Wishart's sermon before the Battle of Bothwell Bridge.

These are remarkable instances, yet they do not represent a thousandth part of the spell exercised by special Psalms, and particular verses of them, throughout the

entire period of English history.   The first verse of Psalm
xxiv.—'The earth is the Lord's, and the fulness thereof;
the world, and they that dwell therein'—was the motto
chosen by Prince Albert for the Great Exhibition of 1851.
The first verse of the 27th—'The Lord is my light and my
salvation; whom shall I fear?   The Lord is the strength
of my life, of whom shall I be afraid?'—is the motto of
the University of Oxford.[1]

If, then, we merely take the Psalter alone, was not St.
Athanasius right in calling the Psalms 'a mirror of the
soul'? and St. Ambrose in saying that 'the Psalter is the
praise of God, the weal of man, the voice of the Church,
the best confession of faith'?   'They are read in all the
world,' says St. Augustine, 'and there is nothing hid from
the heat thereof.'   Such testimonies abound in all ages of
Christian history.   'The choice and flower of all things
profitable in other books,' says Hooper, 'the Psalms do
both more briefly contain, and more movingly also express. . . . What is there necessary for man to know which
the Psalms are not able to teach?   Heroical magnanimity'
exquisite justice, grave moderation, exact wisdom, repentance confessed, unwearied patience, the mysteries of God,
the sufferings of Christ, the terrors of wrath, the comforts
of grace, the works of Providence over this world, and the
promised joys of that world which is to come, all good
necessary to be either known, or done, or had, this one
celestial fountain yieldeth.   Let there be grief or disease
incident unto the soul of man, any wound or sickness
named, for which there is not in this treasure-house a
present comfortable remedy at all times ready to be found.'
To quote but one more eminent witness, Mr. Gladstone

[1] Many more instances might be quoted.   See Ker, *The Psalms in
History and Biography*, 1886.

says, 'All the wonders of Greek civilisation heaped together are less wonderful than is the simple book of Psalms—the history of the human soul in relation to its Maker.'

Yet priceless as is the value of the Psalms, they form but a small part of the Scriptures. The Old Testament abounds in inestimable spiritual lessons, and contains histories and prophecies which we could not lose without the world being left indefinitely the poorer. Yet not even the most precious portions of the Old Testament can be compared in worth with the knowledge which God has given us of that revelation of Himself in Christ which forms the one main subject of the New Testament. If we have but the grace to read that book aright we are

> As rich in having such a jewel
> As twenty seas, if all their sands were pearl,
> The water nectar, and the rocks pure gold.

And if any simple reader has been perplexed by questions on which the sacred interests of truth have here compelled us to touch, these few concluding words of the most eloquent of English divines will give him a safe and sufficient rule for his guidance: 'Do not hear or read the Scriptures for any other end but to become better in your daily walk, and to be instructed in every good work, and increase in the love and service of God.'[1]

[1] Jeremy Taylor, *Holy Living*, iv. 4.

INDEX